COREYOGRAPHY

COREY FELDMAN

COREYOGRAPHY

A MEMOIR

ST. MARTIN'S PRESS ≈ NEW YORK

The names of some persons described in this book have been changed.

COREYOGRAPHY. Copyright © 2013 by Corey Feldman.
All rights reserved. Printed in the United States of America. For information,
address St. Martin's Press, 175 Fifth Avenue, New York, N.Y. 10010.

www.stmartins.com

Design by Anna Gorovoy

Library of Congress Cataloging-in-Publication Data

Feldman, Corey.
    Coreyography : a memoir / Corey Feldman. — First edition
        pages cm
    ISBN 978-0-312-60933-7 (hardcover)
    ISBN 978-1-250-03878-4 (e-book)
  1. Feldman, Corey.   2. Motion picture actors and actresses—United States—
Biography.   I. Title.
    PN2287.F415A3 2013
    791.4302'8'092—dc23
    [B]
                                                                        2013020561

St. Martin's Press books may be purchased for educational,
business, or promotional use. For information on bulk purchases, please contact
Macmillan Corporate and Premium Sales Department at 1-800-221-7945,
extension 5442, or write specialmarkets@macmillan.com.

First Edition: October 2013

10 9 8 7 6 5 4 3 2 1

To the stars in my life that shone bright enough to illuminate my world: Jason Robards, Storm Thorgerson, Mary Goldstein, Bedford Goldstein, and my grandmother, Dena Goldstein, without whom I may never have survived my childhood.

And to the stars that faded much too soon: Corey Haim, River Phoenix, Michael Jackson, Sam Kinison, Marc Rocco, Jeff Conaway, Gary Coleman, and Harold "Pete" Pruett.

May God bless and keep you all.

He was supposed to be at the dentist.

"I've got a problem with this tooth," he'd said when we spoke on the phone that Monday afternoon. "It fell out again, man, but the soonest appointment I can get is a week and a half away."

He was plagued by problems with his teeth—decades of drug abuse had rendered some of them loose, or rotten and decayed. But he didn't have health insurance, which is why I had started sending him to my dentist. He was willing to work with him, let him pay when he was able to, in installments or whenever he got back on his feet.

In our business there are always ways to make money. Sign fifty autographs at twenty dollars apiece and you've got yourself an easy grand. Show up to a screening of *The Lost Boys* and you might make several times that. True, easy money used to be impossible for him to hold on to. He was impulsive and irresponsible, and—back when he

1

could still get steady work—would somehow manage to blow through thousands upon thousands of dollars in only a matter of days. But by 2009, shortly after his mother, Judy, was diagnosed with breast cancer, he was getting himself together. He moved her into his two-bedroom apartment in Burbank and started accompanying her to chemotherapy. He was doing his best to be a better man for his mom.

"I've actually got an appointment on Wednesday," I told him. "Why don't you take mine and I'll take yours next week?"

"Thanks, man, that would be great." He paused for a moment. I could hear him breathing on the other end of the line. "How am I supposed to get there?"

He didn't have a car, either. I told him that I would have my assistant Robin pick him up on Wednesday morning. She was on her way to his apartment when she turned on the radio and heard the news.

Someone was banging on the door to my bedroom.

"Corey? It's Eden. Get up, buddy. It's important."

"What?" I called out in the darkness. No response. Had I imagined the knocking? I wasn't fully awake yet, still halfway inside a dream.

"Corey? It's Mindy. You need to get dressed now and come downstairs."

I wiped the sleep from my eyes, reached for my cell phone, and pulled it off the charger: 8:45 in the morning, 135 new messages. That was unusual. I scrolled through the list until I found the first one, sent from Sean Astin at 5:32 A.M.: *I am so sorry, bro. If there's anything in the world I can do for you, please know that I am here.*

I sat up in bed with a start. *What in the hell is he talking about?* And then, slowly, I realized that if my brother and sister were here, in my house, waking me up this early in the morning, something had to be seriously wrong. Then came that banging on the door again.

"I'm coming!" I hollered, impatient now. I wrapped my bathrobe around me and began making my way down the stairs.

My living room was filled with people—Eden; Mindy; Robin; Dre, my head of security; and Scott, my manager, were all sitting around in a circle, maniacally working their cell phones, splayed out in front of the television. I padded across the carpet, tugged tighter on the belt of my bathrobe, and suddenly everything stopped. I looked at the television and realized that I was staring at myself, at clips from *The Lost Boys*, *License to Drive*, and *Dream a Little Dream*—all films we had worked on together—and then at more recent footage from *The Two Coreys*, the semi-scripted "reality" show we had shot for A&E. Every channel, every station, was reporting the exact same thing: Corey Haim had suffered a drug overdose.

That was it. I had gone to sleep, and when I woke up my best friend was dead.

"There's no way this is an overdose," I said to no one in particular. I didn't care what the news was reporting. I *knew* that he hadn't OD'ed.

When something goes down in Hollywood—when someone you're associated with gets arrested, or punches a member of the paparazzi, or runs off and gets married, or dies many, many years too soon—you *will* get a barrage of phone calls. My publicist, Stacy, was dialing me every two minutes now, trying to field requests from CBS Morning News, *Good Morning America*, the *Today* show, CNN, ABC, *E! News*, and Anderson Cooper. Every entertainment journalist, every talk show and news magazine producer, was hunting for a statement or an interview or something they could post on the Web. Everyone was pushing me to come up with some kind of media-friendly sound bite. Instead, I sat glued to the television and watched as helicopters hovered over the Oakwood apartments, where Haim had lived for the previous year.

"I know you're upset, Corey," I heard someone tell me, "but other people are already coming forward."

I looked up and there was Alyssa Milano, Corey's one-time teenage girlfriend. They had dated on-and-off throughout the final years of the 1980s, before any of us were old enough for a legal drink. Instead, we spent the weekends socializing with Drew Barrymore, Alfonso Ribeiro, Soleil Moon Frye, and other underage actors, loitering in expensive suites at the Hollywood Roosevelt Hotel or stumbling out of Ralph Kaufman's club, the private dance party for famous teens. Alyssa was one of the first to tweet her condolences, but then the names started to flash in quick succession across the screen: Dave Navarro, Melissa Gilbert, Ralph Macchio, Kevin Smith, Christina Applegate, Hoda Kotb, Khloe Kardashian, Lisa Ling. Everyone was buzzing about how much they already missed Haim, how sad they were to hear of his passing. Tamera Mowry called him her first crush. Ashton Kutcher said Haim was his childhood hero.

I felt like I was going to be sick.

I pulled out my laptop and tried to collect myself. If I could just write a two- or three-paragraph statement and post it on my Web site, I thought, then maybe these reporters could use excerpts and leave me to contend with my grief. But by nine o'clock, the press was starting to assemble. Local police had draped yellow tape at either end of the block, news trucks with their satellites cranked up were lining the street, and a group of reporters was milling around the base of my driveway. They were unruly and impatient, and some of them were starting to creep farther into my front yard. I was fiddling with the blog post, still trying to come up with something coherent and respectful to say, when Stacy burst through the front door and plopped down in the center of the room.

"Okay, what are we going to do?" she asked. "We've got to make an announcement."

I picked my head up from my hands and glared at her, but before I could say anything, I heard a reporter announce that I was preparing to give an impromptu press conference outside my Sherman Oaks home.

"Who in the hell said I was giving a press conference?" I shouted, standing up suddenly and throwing my cell phone directly at the television.

Stacy scooted over to me, trying to calm me down. "Look, we need something. Is there any way you can just get it together for two minutes and go out there and talk?"

"I'm not giving a fucking press conference!" I screamed. "I'm going to write this statement and take a shower and then I want to see Judy." I thought about Corey's mother, bald from the chemo, weak, and possibly all alone.

Stacy leaned in closer. "You've got to do one, Corey. You've got to do one interview and that'll be it, but you've got to give me one."

"Fine," I told her, disgusted. And then I chose Larry King.

The last time I had been a guest on *Larry King Live* was three years earlier—I had appeared, coincidentally, with Corey Haim to promote the upcoming premiere of *The Two Coreys,* our reality show on A&E.

Before I ever agreed to do the show, I had insisted that Corey get his act together. And for the most part, he was succeeding. He had lost a significant amount of weight—nearly a hundred pounds, down from a high of three hundred—and cut way back on the Valium, which he had been guzzling for years at a rate of forty-to-fifty *a day.* Midway through filming, though, he was suddenly backsliding: slurring his speech, or forgetting his lines, or delaying production for days on end. When we started the press tour that summer, I knew he was still reeling. I hadn't realized, however, just what kind of shape he was really in.

If you go back and watch it now, the *Larry King Live* episode plays out like a tennis match. What you see is the camera bouncing back and forth between me and Larry and Corey; rarely are we all on-screen at the same time. What you don't see is that Corey was nodding out while we sat there, literally fading in and out of consciousness in the middle of live television. The cameraman would cut away when he started to drift and suddenly you'd be watching clips from the films we had made together. Then he would cut back to Corey just as he opened his eyes.

At the commercial break, Larry leaned over and asked if Haim was going to be okay, but he never said anything like that when we were actually on air. I suppose that made me trust him; it's why I chose his show on the day Corey died.

When we pulled up outside Corey's apartment complex, I didn't see many reporters. That was good—I didn't want anyone harassing his mother. But as we walked across the parking lot, Dre pointed out a few photographers who had hidden themselves in the shrubs. I should have known. Corey's apartment complex is a hot spot for members of the Hollywood press.

The Oakwoods are affordable, prefurnished corporate apartments and temporary housing complexes. There are outposts all over the world, but the Burbank location is famous; it's situated just a few feet away from the front gates of Warner Brothers, across the street from Universal Studios, less than two miles away from Disney. Out-of-town actors who arrive to work in L.A. are often put up at the Oakwoods, and during casting for pilot season (January through early spring), the place fills up with legions of would-be stars. The first time I visited was back in the early '80s, when Kerri Green and Martha Plimpton were residents, but the list of famous people who have stayed there goes on and on and on.

Sometimes you'll hear the Oakwoods referred to as "cheap" or "cut-rate" housing—in reality, the apartments are quite comfortable and relatively spacious. Inside Corey's place, though, I felt claustrophobic. There was Judy, sitting on the sofa, surrounded by five or six of her so-called friends. Some of them I knew as legitimate and longtime supporters of the family, but others I recognized as neighbors, people that Corey and Judy had chatted with occasionally but hadn't known for much more than a year. Judy and I hugged for a long while, and cried, and she told me the details of Corey's sudden collapse, but I couldn't get over the feeling that we were being watched, that we were sitting in the middle of a room full of rubberneckers. When talk eventually turned to funeral arrangements, one of the neighbors slid right over.

"You know," he said, leaning closer, "my girlfriend is an incredible singer, and Corey was really supportive of her talent. I think he really would have wanted her to sing a song at his funeral."

I couldn't believe this guy had the balls to pitch me for a spot *in a funeral*. It was grotesque, and so incredibly surreal. And just when I thought things couldn't get any weirder, in walked Warren Boyd.

More than twenty years ago now, when I first decided to get sober, I enlisted the help of a man named Bob Timmins, a former addict-turned-addiction specialist, better known in Hollywood circles as "Dr. Detox." Timmins had become an expert at matching addicts with sponsors or "sober companions," often testified on behalf of his clients in courtrooms across L.A., and was constantly consulting on treatment plans for drug-addled (and usually famous) defendants. He had helped guys like Steven Tyler, Vince Neil and Nikki Sixx of Mötley Crüe, and Robert Downey, Jr. get themselves sober. If you were a celebrity with a spiraling drug problem, Bob Timmins was your man.

I always figured Warren Boyd had an eye on taking Timmins's place, but to me he seemed more interested in giving interviews and socializing with celebrities than keeping anyone's nose clean. Whenever Corey ran out of money, Boyd up and disappeared. The last I heard, he was buzzing around again when we began production on *The Two Coreys*, filling Haim's head with grand plans about coproducing additional shows. (Boyd had his own short-lived show called *The Cleaner*, a fictionalized portrayal of his life as an "extreme interventionalist," that aired on A&E.) That was more than two years ago. Now, with Corey dead and the press sniffing around, here was Warren Boyd again, right by Judy's side.

"We'll put together a memorial service," he was saying, "and I'll invite all my high-end clients. Whitney Houston, Mel Gibson, only the AA-list people. We'll do it in a studio backlot, so no one will have any access to it."

Why the hell would Whitney Houston come to Corey Haim's memorial service? I thought. *What the fuck is this guy talking about?*

"Corey didn't know any of those people," I told him. "I don't think that's what he would have wanted."

"Well, I'll tell you what," he said, pacing the length of the apartment. "Why don't you give me a list of people that you think should be there, and I'll have my list, and Judy will have her list, then we'll put it all together. When all is said and done, I'll try to take care of a few of your people."

My *people*? I couldn't believe this guy—I half-expected him to point two finger guns at me and suggest that we "do lunch."

"Lemme get this straight. You want to have a private memorial for two hundred to three hundred guests and you're going to fill a room full of famous people, none of whom actually knew him?"

"Or we could do a fund-raiser?" he continued blabbering.

I started gathering my things to leave. The guy was just on and on about this celebrity and that celebrity, the president of this studio and the president of that studio. I wasn't sure if he really knew any of these people, but I had had enough—and I was due to tape *Larry King*.

Larry wasted no time asking me if I thought drugs were to blame for Corey's death, and I wasted no time imploring people to stop rushing to judgment. "Until the coroner's report comes out, until we know exactly what the toxicology report says, nobody knows,"

I told him. I also talked about how—despite the recent outpouring of emotion—practically no one had been around for Corey when he was actually still alive. Five years earlier, he had no work visa, no work, no money, and almost no friends. His life was in the gutter, and nobody seemed to give a shit about him then.

When the cameras stopped rolling, Larry leaned forward to ask me one final question: "Do you really think the toxicology report is going to come back clean?"

"Yeah, I do," I said.

"What gives you that feeling?"

"I knew him better than anyone. Believe me, I would know."

"Would you be willing to come back on when the report comes out?" he asked. "Even if his death is classified as an overdose?"

I told him I would be happy to, and Larry called out to one of the producers to track the story, to be sure and rebook me when the official cause of death was revealed.

Corey Haim's official autopsy report was released on May 5, 2010—he died of pneumonia, with complications due to an enlarged heart. There were traces of eight drugs in his system, some prescription pills and some over-the-counter cold medicines, but none of them contributed to his passing.

Later that day I was booked to reappear on *Larry King Live,* but two hours before I was scheduled to arrive for taping, one of the producers called to cancel. We were bumped for coverage of the foiled Times Square terrorist bombing. Corey didn't stand a chance against Rudy Guiliani and John McCain.

People always ask me about life after childhood stardom. Do I have any advice for Lindsay Lohan? What would I say to parents of children in the industry? How can child stars avoid the pitfalls of fame?

My only advice, honestly, is to get these kids out of Hollywood and let them lead normal lives—which is exactly what I told the producers at ABC's *Nightline,* when they asked me to participate in an upcoming episode about the perils of underage fame. I usually don't give interviews unless I have a project to promote, but I had grown so tired of hearing how great it is to be famous. Plucking children out of school and exploiting them for profit isn't healthy; neither is turning your five-year-old into the family breadwinner, or living out dreams of celebrity vicariously through your kids. Is it really all that surprising that so many child actors have problems later in life? Since *Nightline* is a reputable program, I thought maybe I could do some good by throwing in my two cents. "If you're interested in hearing that perspective, then I'll agree to do the interview," I had told them. "But if you want to hear that Hollywood is a great place for children, you might want to talk to somebody else."

That was really all I was planning to say—that I think pushing kids into the spotlight is almost always a bad idea. But by the time I was sitting down in front of the cameras, weeks after I initially agreed to the interview, Corey had been bumped from the In Memoriam segment at the Oscars; it was the second awards show to snub him that season, and I guess I just sort of snapped. Despite the release of the autopsy report, people were still reporting that his death was the result of an overdose. I was fed up with people insisting—loudly, and in public—that Corey's tragic death was really his own damn fault.

"Well, whose fault is it?" the reporter asked me. "His parents? Who is really to blame?"

"I blame the entertainment industry," I said.

"How so?"

"Nobody talks about what the real problem is."

"What's the real problem?"

I could feel it coming, the words bubbling up in my throat. "The number-one problem in Hollywood," I said, "was, and is, and always will be pedophilia. That's the biggest problem in this industry, for children. It's the big secret. There's only one person to blame for the death of Corey Haim."

The *Nightline* episode aired in August 2011 and was instant national news. That part wasn't surprising. Neither were the accusations that I had done the interview to stay "relevant" or to try to advance my career—after nearly forty years in this business, I've come to expect that kind of cynicism, although it's still hurtful and difficult for me to hear. What I hadn't anticipated—and here you could make the argument that I was extremely naïve—was that trying to "guess the pedophile," trying to figure out who had molested and abused Corey Haim, would turn into a cheap parlor game. The comments sections of countless blogs, on YouTube, and even ABC's Web site turned into a veritable who's who of Hollywood. Suddenly, I was getting hundreds of phone calls and tweets and e-mails from people I had never even met—who, mind you, had absolutely no idea what they were talking about—saying that if I was *really* Corey's friend, I would stop "protecting" his abusers, if I *really* cared about Corey, I would publicly name names.

I can tell you that over the course of our more than twenty-year-long friendship, Corey and I often discussed going public with our respective stories. The closest he ever got, though, was in 2008, two years before he died. In a dingy diner in Studio City, during episode one of season two of *The Two Coreys*, Haim accused me of knowing that he had been molested at age fourteen and of having done nothing to stop it.

It's true that we were both molested by men in the industry, and that we knew each other's assailants. But the incident that we almost never discussed, the one that haunted Haim for the rest of his life, happened three years before we met.

Corey was raped at the age of eleven. And like many, many victims of sex abuse, drug use became an easy, if also tragic, way for him to escape the weight of that shame.

There is nothing I would rather do than publicly out the man who molested—and ultimately destroyed—my dearest friend. Unfortunately, that is not the way the world works. You can't go around publicly accusing industry titans without expecting to find yourself in the middle of a nasty lawsuit, to say nothing of the potential threat to my career, as well as to the personal safety of myself and my son. As for the idea of going to the police, it will perhaps surprise you to know that I have. Of course, I don't have any evidence, and Corey Haim is no longer alive to testify on his own behalf. As for opening cases against *my* abusers, there is a statute of limitations on sex crimes in California; and, apparently, I am too late. The only thing I know how to do, then, is to try and raise people's awareness, to somehow protect other children before the same thing happens to them.

In the fall of 2011, just a few months after the *Nightline* interview aired, a young boy and his parents came forward and pressed charges against Martin Weiss, a forty-seven-year-old Hollywood talent manager who specialized in representing underage actors. The news went viral instantly—Weiss had worked with hundreds of young stars since opening his talent agency in the early '90s; I've known him since I was twelve years old.

During the months leading up to Weiss's pretrial hearing, I spoke with the victim and his parents and discussed the case with the prosecutor. I offered whatever kind of help or guidance I possibly could. But, as is so often the case in these types of proceedings, Weiss was able to make a deal. He pleaded no contest to two counts of oral copulation with a minor. His one-year prison sentence was suspended in June 2012; he was released early for time served and "good behavior."

For a brief time after that, I lost faith in the system. Why should I put a target on my back or set myself up to become some kind of poster child for sex abuse if the courts can't protect abused children? But then I realized that something *was* happening—for the first time in years, people were starting to talk.

Weiss's arrest came just two weeks after arrests in two other high-profile Hollywood cases. In November 2011, an award-winning composer for *Sesame Street* was arraigned on charges of producing and distributing child pornography, as well as coercing a minor to "engage in sexually explicit conduct." One month later, news broke that Jason James Murphy, a registered sex offender and convicted kidnapper, had been working for years as a prominent casting director; he had placed underage performers in such high-profile films as *Super 8* and *School of Rock*. The following January, an article in the *Los Angeles Times* revealed details of more than one dozen arrests of various managers, casting agents, and production assistants on counts ranging from child porn to molestation, all in the last ten years.

How does this happen? How do so many innocent, talented, and even famous children wind up suffering in silence? The obvious answer is that pedophiles will flock to an industry where they can surround themselves with eager, ambitious children. But there's another answer, too: the bright lights of Hollywood are blinding, and the sanctity of childhood is easily trumped by the deafening drumbeat of fame.

In September 2012, a bill affording greater protection for underage actors was signed into California state law. For the first time, managers, publicists, and other Hollywood professionals who work with children will be required to submit to criminal background checks. The bill also prohibits registered sex offenders from representing minors in the entertainment industry. It's incredible that legislation like this has been such a long time coming, but it has a real chance of protecting children like my friend Corey—more real, I think, than just naming names.

———

I have always been a polarizing public figure; I know what gets written about me in the press. To the casual fan, I may come across as immature, or self-absorbed, or unsophisticated, or flat-out crazy, and—certainly—I've made my mistakes. Despite some of the more sensational headlines, though, I actually lead a relatively normal life. I've been sober for more than two decades. I make an average of one to three films a year. I'm a passionate environmentalist and an advocate for animal rights. I tour occasionally with my band Truth Movement and have a thriving solo music career. And I have a son, Zen, my most precious gift.

But in the three years since Corey died, I've spent less time thinking about where I am and more time wondering how I got here. I guess that's natural; thinking about the end of something—his life, our friendship—inevitably dredges up thoughts of the beginning. When I look back on my life, however, the memories that are the most vivid, the most complete and fully realized in my mind, are from times when I was on film sets and in television studios, from times when I was working. In fact, I've always marked the chronology of my life not by the year, but by the film, because so much of the rest of it I'd just as soon forget. There are entire chapters of my life that I don't want to remember, and some moments in time have been lost to me completely. But in the three years since Corey's death, I've been trying. In order to figure out how I got here, I have to go back to the start.

COREYOGRAPHY

CHAPTER 1

I am three years old, sitting at the small round breakfast table in our tiny kitchen, eyeing a half-open box of cereal. There's a toy surprise buried somewhere inside, and I'm itching for it. I bounce my feet impatiently atop the wooden rung of my chair, feel a cold dribble of milk slip across my lip and down my chin. As consumed as I am by that prize, however, I sense that there is something different, something even *more* exciting, about today. It's still early morning in the San Fernando Valley—the sun is streaming through the little stained glass window above the door frame, casting a rainbow of shadows across the linoleum floor of the foyer—but the whole house is already buzzing with energy.

"Boobie?" My childhood nickname for my mother's mother is a slightly more anatomical version of the term *bubbe,* the Yiddish word for *grandmother.* "What am I excited about?"

"Today is your first commercial."

"My first commer*smal*?" I ask between bites. "The things before cartoons on TV?"

"Yes. Now finish your breakfast, please. You don't want to be late on your first day."

I scoop up the last few spoonfuls of cereal, slide down my chair, and pad down the hallway to my bedroom, where my clothes have been carefully laid out for me. Even though I didn't know much about commercials (or *commersmals,* as I would call them for the next few years), I understood that this was serious business. I was a professional now.

At seven, my older sister Mindy was already a seasoned actress. She was the youngest cast member of the 1970s-era kids' show *The All-New Mickey Mouse Club* and often spent two-week-long stints at Disneyland in Anaheim, performing bad renditions of Beatles songs in bright satin jumpsuits and oversized mouse ears for throngs of screaming, preteen fans. As the family breadwinner, Mindy was granted a wide berth by my parents; she was enrolled in a fancy private school and, when she wasn't working, usually locked herself away in her room. I used to spend hours outside that door, straining to hear the music that sometimes rang out from her tiny record player (my favorite was the *Wizard of Oz* soundtrack). But when she was performing, I was generally allowed to wander through the theme park alongside her and her teenaged castmates. I watched, awestruck, as she navigated those early brushes with fame, signing autographs and posing for pictures, mobbed by her very own circle of groupies. I thought that being a Mouseketeer meant she had a perfect life. It made sense, then, that by following in her footsteps, my life was about to become special, too.

My first professional acting job was a minute-long spot for McDonald's gift certificates. The setup was fairly simple: I would wake up in the middle of the night on Christmas Eve, stumble downstairs in my blue-footed pajamas, and leave a fifty-cent gift certificate for Santa, right on top of his plate of cookies, next to his glass of milk. When my mother and I arrived on set, a rented two-story home in the Valley, the director, Rob Lieberman, came over to say hello. He had a warm smile and a hippie-ish, Cat Stevens–like beard, a popular style back in 1975.

"Today is a very big day, Corey," he said, kneeling down to speak to me at eye level. "Today, you're going to meet Santa Claus!"

"But it's the middle of summer!" I said, nonplussed. Rob patted my head and winked at my mom, and that was the end of that—off I went to be fitted in my pajamas.

As the day wore on, we shot take after take—I climbed in and out of bed, I teetered up and down the stairs—until, finally, it was time. Santa was going to reach his hand into the scene to collect his gift certificate and shout, "Ho, Ho, Ho!" while I looked on from between the wooden stair railings. I was crushed, however, when I realized that "Santa" was really just a regular-looking guy wearing a red coat sleeve with fluffy white trim.

"Where is the *real* Santa?" I asked. "Can I meet Santa Claus now?"

"The *real* Santa is going to come later," Rob said, no doubt aware that his three-year-old star was headed for a production-halting meltdown. "Right now we just have to pretend."

If shooting a Christmas commercial in July was my first clue that things in Hollywood are rarely as they seem, this sad excuse for a Santa was my second. And I never did get to meet the real Santa Claus that day. The McDonald's ad, though, would run for the next eight Christmases and win a prestigious Clio award, the Oscar of the advertising world.

When you ask most people to reflect on their very first memory, the recollections usually fall within a range of familiar vignettes— that first game of catch with Mom or Dad, playing with a beloved stuffed animal or favorite toy, or watching Saturday morning cartoons. My first memory is shooting that McDonald's commercial. I can't remember anything before the start of my career.

Until the age of five, I lived with my parents, Bob and Sheila Feldman, and my big sister, Mindy, in a modest three-bedroom California ranch in the once-sleepy community of Chatsworth, a district of Los Angeles situated in the northwest San Fernando Valley, bordered to the north by the Santa Susana Mountains. My father, a musician and producer, wasn't around much; most of his time was spent on the road, performing with his cover band, Scream, at Los Angeles–area theme parks, like Knott's Berry Farm and Magic Mountain. So most of my days were spent at home with my mom. Boobie might come over to babysit, or to take Mindy to rehearsals and act as her on-set guardian, on the days when my mother had a headache or was too sick to get out of bed.

If the door to her bedroom was open, I would grab my toys and set up camp in her king-size bed or lounge on the floor beneath the television for hours, staying up late into the night to watch *Saturday Night Live* with Dan Aykroyd and John Belushi or my mother's favorite show, the soap opera parody *Mary Hartman, Mary Hartman.* With the shades drawn, bathed in the blue light of the television screen, I would sit and study the hodgepodge of artifacts displayed around her room like talismans, the little ceramic frog statues that lined her windowsill (her favorite color was lime green), or the gilded frame that had sat on top of her nightstand for as long as I could remember. The pictorial had been torn from the pages of *Playboy*, and from it she smiled proudly, hand on hip. At five foot one she was the shortest among the waitresses at the Playboy Club in L.A. If I carefully picked up the frame to admire it, she might tell me stories about how she served drinks in a bunny uniform and did the famous bunny dip, bending at the knees instead of the waist so she wouldn't "fall out of her top."

"Hugh Hefner was a *gentleman*," she would say with a certain reverence, taking the frame from me and putting it carefully back into place. "And he always left big tips." I liked the way she winked when she said this, and I pictured Mr. Hefner as some sort of benevolent father figure, merrily dolling out "big tips" to other working women like my mom.

When she finished describing her days as a bunny, she might tell me about the wild parties she used to attend at Spahn Ranch, the sprawling five-hundred-acre stretch of land in the mountains above Chatsworth, once the backdrop for spaghetti Westerns and episodes of *Bonanza* and *The Lone Ranger* before Charles Manson and his "family" moved in, rent-free, around the time of the Tate-LaBianca murders in the summer of '69. It was strange to think of my mother that way, as a single, carefree woman in the days before she had children. She was beautiful but, as I sensed even then, somehow dangerous.

On the good days, we'd pile in the car and drive the hills and troughs of the Valley, searching for strays or wounded animals in need of a "good home," even though we already had a vicious black lab called Shadow, plus an Irish Setter and a little cream-colored Chihuahua, Twinkie, multiple cats, several ducks, a smattering of chickens, and two horses, a black-and-white gelding called Flash, and Wildfire, a brown mare.

More often, though, she was down, relegated to the confines of her bedroom, suffering from a mysterious range of maladies. In those days, I was too young to anticipate the high-highs and low-lows of someone with a depressive disorder, or to successfully navigate the unpredictable, violent swings that are borne of substance abuse. I just thought she needed my help.

"Corey?" she would call out, no matter where I was in the house.

"Come in here and rub my feet." I would trudge into the darkness and take her foot in my hands while she lay in bed, her forearm thrown over her face to shield her eyes from the light, her naked leg sticking out from deep beneath the blankets. She would cry and fidget and whine, and sometimes scream and curse and kick, even when I was brushing her hair or bringing her food or running her a bath. Those were the worst days—when her moods became like black holes, sucking the life from every corner of the house into that cold, dark room.

Sometimes her door would stay closed all day. If I had an audition, she might call my grandmother and demand that Boobie ferry me around town. If I wasn't working, or if my grandmother was busy with Mindy, I would make my breakfast, feed the horses out back on the farm, and then retreat to my room, locked away for hours with my action figures, acting out elaborate fantasies, playing heroes and villains or cops and robbers or pulling them apart at the joints to inspect the elaborate system of hooks and rubber bands that held them together. I wasn't allowed to have friends over, and I wasn't allowed to leave the house. So, sometimes I just zipped myself in the giant gray suitcase, warm and dank, smelling of sweat and leather and the sea. In those early days in the Chatsworth house, I learned to entertain myself.

"You were supposed to be a blond."

My mother is alternately scrubbing my scalp with her fingers and shoving my face under the faucet of the bathroom sink. The peroxide burns, and the smell is making me nauseous but, apparently, I was supposed to have been a blond-haired, blue-eyed child. Instead, she got stuck with me. With my head still wedged under the faucet, water rushing into my nose and mouth, she pauses long enough to wipe the sweat from her forehead with the back of her hand. "This is who you were *supposed* to be," she keeps telling me, though it's difficult to make out what she's saying with so much water in my ears.

The McDonald's commercial has energized her, and she is full of ideas, plans, and strategies—besides just changing my hair color—to help me with my new career. For example, if I can learn a repertoire of folky songs, like "Raindrops Keep Fallin' on My Head" and Jim Croce's "Junk Food Junkie," I will almost certainly book more jobs.

"You're going to sing a song and they're going to go, isn't he cute?" she tells me, before locking me in my room with Mindy's record player and instructions not to come out until I have learned every word.

Learning the words, however, is not the hard part—I have no trouble memorizing dialogue, even though I am only four. The problem is that I can't carry a tune to save my life. My voice squeaks and strains. I can't match the notes that I hear in the recordings.

When I emerge from my room to perform for her approval, she sighs. "You're not much of a singer, are you?" It's clear that she enjoys making fun of me. It's obvious that she finds pleasure in making me feel inadequate. She points her finger toward the narrow hallway and sends me back to practice more—however long it takes, she says—until I get it right.

I can't get it right, but I quickly learn how to stick my hands in the pockets of my Osh Kosh overalls at the end of an audition, don a sort of aw-shucks pose, and say, "Hey, do you mind if I sing a song for you?" Then I belt out some horrifically off-key, awkward version of "Put on a Happy Face" for a panel of casting directors. It works like gangbusters. I shoot ads for Apple Jacks, Colgate, Hawaiian Punch, Pan Am, Dole Pineapple, and Wyler's Grape drink mix, one right after the other. By the age of ten, I will have filmed more than one hundred.

Mindy and I are generally responsible for making our own breakfasts—my mother, after all, isn't a "morning person." But the sugary cereals I love, the cookies and crackers and snacks, have started to disappear, hidden on a shelf high in the kitchen that I have to crawl on top of a counter to reach. One morning, my sister and I take our seats at the small round table and Mindy pours herself a bowl of Alpha Bits. I love Alpha Bits. I can spell all kinds of words in my spoon. I reach to pour myself a bowl when my mother, appearing out of nowhere, suddenly yanks the box from my hand.

"You can't eat that," she says. "It's fattening."

"Why does Mindy get to eat it?"

She turns and glares at me. "Because *Mindy* isn't *fat*."

Whenever we happen to walk past an overweight person while we're out looking for strays, my mother physically recoils. "Fat pig," she whispers under her breath. Her secret nickname for my father's mother, admittedly a rather large woman, is Piggy Feldman. So I know that being fat is the worst thing you can possibly be. I do have round, chubby, cherubic cheeks, but I always thought that I would grow into them. Now she tells me that if I'm not careful, I'll grow up to be a fat, disgusting pig, too. She lifts my shirt and pinches a fold of my skin between her fingers. "See?" she says. "That's more than an inch." (My mother is obsessed with the new "pinch more than an inch" Special K campaign; she'll continue pinching me like this for years.)

Soon there is a new rule: No eating—at all—until she wakes up. This is especially challenging, because sometimes she stays in bed until two or three in the afternoon. I distract myself with my toys, or put on my grandmother's Rubbermaid dishwashing gloves and tie a blue hand towel around my neck, zooming around the living room like a superhero, flying off furniture, trying to ignore the low, gurgling sound of the rumble in my tummy. And then I decide, after a while, that no one will actually notice if I quietly make myself a snack.

"Corey, get in here." She's in her room again, the door barely cracked ajar.

"Yes?" I retrace my steps down the hallway until I'm standing outside her door. She's lying on her bed, half-dressed, watching a haze of gray static glowing from the television.

"Did you eat the cookies in the cabinet?"

I feel a knot forming in the pit of my stomach. "No," I say, in a voice no bigger than a whisper.

"*No?* Why are there crumbs in your bed?"

"I don't know."

"Well, perhaps you'd like to explain. Did the *dog* eat the cookies, Corey? Did Shadow climb up into the cupboard?"

"Maybe . . . ?" I venture, hoping she'll let my thievery go.

"Don't lie to me, Corey. You're lying. Did you eat the cookies?"

"Well, maybe I ate one."

"Maybe you ate one?"

"Or two."

"Which is it? One or two?"

I swallow, hard. "I ate two."

She sits up a little at my admission. "Well, then, you're grounded. Those cookies are not for you and you know it. So now I want you to come in here and stare at the wall for one hour. And you're not going to have anything else to eat for the rest of the day."

I walk slowly into her room and take my place in the corner. I look at my feet, at the wall, at anything but her. She drones on and on until I suddenly realize that I am afraid of her, that I hate her. Still, I want nothing more than to crawl into her big bed and watch *Mary Hartman, Mary Hartman,* or listen to her stories about bunnies and parties and what her life was like before me.

"You have no right to disrespect me like this." She's in a rage now, huffing and puffing. "You ungrateful shit. How dare you look at me like that?"

"I'm not looking at you," I say.

"Well then turn around and look at me when I'm talking to you! Do you have any idea how lucky you are? Do you realize that most women would *die* to look like this after two kids? Look at these tits," she says, cupping her breasts in her hands. But I don't want to look at her. I just want something to eat.

I thought back to the Baskin-Robbins commercial I had filmed just a few weeks before, to the mountains of pumpkin ice cream that had stretched before me, to the way the assistant director had smiled when he handed me a spoon. Actors are generally encouraged not to swallow on shoots like these; ingesting bite after bite, shooting take after take, would be enough to make most people sick. But I had learned a clever trick. I would only *pretend* to spit out my food in a napkin. That's how I went through one-and-a-half gallons, secretly savoring every bite.

I knew my mother was getting worse, her behavior more erratic. I couldn't, however, understand why. From my perspective, nothing much had changed, except that I was working more, booking more jobs, going on more auditions. And yet, she still knew how to turn on the charm, how to perform for people's approval. She might have spent the entire morning in bed, calling me "fatso" and "piggy" and ordering me around the house, but then we'd drive to an audition and she would immediately switch gears. As soon as we stepped onto the parking lot pavement, she'd jerk my arm and say, "That's enough now. Wipe off the tears." Then we'd breeze through the door of the casting office and she'd be bright and buoyant, a giant smile plastered across her face. If someone inquired about my red eyes and blotchy cheeks, she'd simply shrug.

"I don't know what he's so upset about," she would say. "He's such a good actor, this kid. He's *so* dramatic. Always acting. That's what he does best."

CHAPTER 2

People have always noticed my voice.

It's low and raspy; even as a child I was often mistaken for someone much older than my actual age. By my mid-teens, once I had become well known within the industry, directors would know I was on set just by the sound of my gravelly voice echoing down the hallway. But years before that, on a spring day when I was still just five years old, my mother schlepped me to Disney headquarters in Burbank because my sister, the Mouseketeer, had to work. As I entertained

27

myself in Mindy's dressing room, playing imaginary games with my superheroes, a casting director happened to walk by. Expecting to find an elderly woman with a smoking problem, she was shocked when she turned the corner—it was just little old me.

What I didn't know at the time was that the studio had just finished a major casting call and had all but given up trying to find a child who could emulate the voice of a young hound dog for their next animated feature. After several weeks of debate and a series of callbacks, the decision was made. Walt Disney Productions had found their Copper.

The Fox and the Hound would become the final "classic" of Disney's early animation era, and it marked my transition to working on the big screen (though it would be another few years before I'd make it back). When I got the part, I was taken on a tour of the animation building and shown artwork for my character, a droopy-eyed, long-eared pup, and his unlikely friend. "I want to meet the kid who plays the fox!" I said. I recognized Keith Coogan from auditions (he was the grandson of screen legend Jackie Coogan and would later star in *Don't Tell Mom the Babysitter's Dead*).

"You won't be meeting him," the casting director told me. "Voice-over work is done separately." Any visions I had had of Keith and I bringing our characters to life, side-by-side, were dashed, and I was reminded again of the strangeness of Hollywood. This time, I wouldn't so much as meet my costar.

A few weeks later, Mindy and I were playing together, huddled in front of the television in the den. I was sitting mere inches from the twelve-inch black-and-white set, turning the old-fashioned dial to change the channel, searching for one of the life-size puppet programs I loved so much, like *Kukla, Fran and Ollie; H.R. Pufnstuf;* or *Sigmund and the Sea Monsters,* when suddenly I noticed the faintest hint of a strange smell. Within seconds, a wall of smoke was charging at us, enveloping the house like a blanket.

"We have to get out!" My mother, who had been out back feeding the horses, was practically throwing us out the door by our shirt collars. "Get out! *GET OUT!* The house is on fire!" We ran to the neighbor's house, and from the safety of her yard watched as fire trucks barreled down the street and our home was engulfed in flames. We were lucky to have made it out in time.

The official story, at least according to the fire department, was that a burning candle had somehow been knocked over, igniting a nearby curtain. But there were murmurings within the family, hushed voices whispering in dark corners, suggesting that my mother had burned down the house to collect the insurance money. We moved into an extended-stay motel for a few weeks before ultimately settling in with my grandparents.

Woodland Hills, situated just a few miles south of our old home in Chatsworth, became like a refuge for me, a safe (if also temporary) haven from the volatility of my mother's mood swings. Which is ironic, because my grandfather, Bedford Goldstein, might be the most terrifying man I have ever met. By the time my family and I moved in, he was in his sixties, balding—the few white hairs he had left somehow stood straight up when he was angry, which was very nearly all the time—and his right arm shook constantly, a side effect of advancing Parkinson's. But when he spoke—in a booming roar, his stories dripping with profanity—you'd have thought he was a much younger man. Grandpa was a highly decorated WWII vet as well as a former boxer, so he often regaled me with sordid tales of either killing Nazi soldiers "with his bare hands," or slugging some man half his age who made the unfortunate mistake of cutting him off in traffic. (As it happens, beating up strangers on the 405 was a frequent occurrence, and continued well into his eighties.) Stories of his abuse were legendary, and I often wondered if the day would come when he'd chase *me* around the house with a baseball bat, just as he'd done to my uncles Mervyn and Murray when they were kids. In fact, all of the men from my mother's side of the family had hair-trigger tempers, an ample amount of barely contained rage rumbling just below the surface.

Despite the fear of impending violence, I felt free—for the first time in my life—during those months at my grandparents' house. I could spend the afternoons outdoors, riding my bike along the winding streets of the neighborhood or playing with other kids who were actually my age. I even had a real, properly enforced bedtime (though I sometimes slipped out of bed after everyone else was asleep to watch *Star Trek* and, later, *Solid Gold*, with the volume turned practically down to mute). On rainy days, my grandmother taught me to make macaroni and cheese or fried matzah or let me roll out the dough for sugar cookies, or sometimes she'd just busy herself in the kitchen while I pulled out all of her pots and pans and converted them into a mini drum set. The most incredible part was that she didn't even mind.

There was also Michael, my only friend, Uncle Merv's youngest son. We both loved screwball sketch comedy, and we spent hours imitating the greats from *Saturday Night Live*, such as Steve Martin and Gilda Radner, using a little cassette recorder to document our impressions, then playing them back, over and over, so we could improve on our "act." I had never had a best friend before—in Chatsworth, I'd hardly been allowed out of the house, to say nothing of actually inviting anyone over—and I'd never been on a sleepover. So when the time came for that, too, I was practically manic with excitement, picturing Michael and I chattering late into the night, snuggled under piles of blankets on the matching twin beds in his room.

Bedtime, however, was awkward. Around nine, Uncle Merv and his wife, Mary, came into the bedroom. They kissed Michael's forehead, they pulled the blankets tight up to his chin, and then told him, in affectionate whispers, that they loved him. I had only ever seen that on television. That's when I realized that what Michael had was normal, and that what I had at home was not. I ached for Merv to come over and say those things to me, to gently rub my back until I drifted off to sleep. I loved staying over at Michael's house, but on those nights, when the lights were finally out, I often turned my back to him and quietly cried myself to sleep.

By the late 1970s, I had more or less graduated from shooting commercials to becoming a day player in a string of successful sitcoms. With the money, we moved to a home on Singing Hills Drive, near the golf course at Porter Valley Country Club in Northridge, a thriving community in the northwest corner of the Valley. Since we no longer had the acreage to keep horses, or to house the city's overpopulation of stray dogs and cats, my mother began collecting smaller, more "friendly" family pets, namely birds and hamsters. She went through a string of parakeets, one right after the other, because our cat Meow kept eating them.

Shadow, our family's black lab, was bad enough. He was a rescue, taken in by my mother after a lifetime of abuse and neglect and, apparently, ample training as a guard dog. He once took a bite out of a burglar who was prowling around our house and was rewarded with a medal of valor from the local police department. But he was also vicious and destructive. He tore up carpets, shoes, Persian rugs and, evidently, people. It wasn't until years later that I learned Shadow had already attacked seven different strangers before lunging at my friend Eric, and that my parents had somehow managed to escape the city's orders to have him put to sleep.

We did have a routine in those days: before bringing anyone into the house, you were supposed to locate Shadow, drag him to the pantry, and lock him in. But that afternoon, walking home from the bus stop with Eric, I was so excited at the prospect of actually having a friend come over that I rushed inside and left the front door wide open. Shadow had Eric in his jaws before he had even crossed the threshold. Eric, wide-eyed in fear, stood stock still for a moment before bolting down the street. (My father, who certainly would have heard the screaming, came flying down the stairs, took one look at the carnage, and smacked me so hard across the head that blood came shooting out of my nose, staining the front of my shirt.)

Shadow was bad. But walking through the front door to find a dusting of yellow, bloodied bird feathers scattered all over the floor was truly terrifying.

For the first time in a long time—perhaps ever—my family was in a comfortable financial situation. As for me, I was growing to really love my work. Not only did it give me an excuse to get out of the house, an especially good thing, now that I was back in the care of my mother, but I was suddenly working alongside the actors I had grown up watching late into the night in the darkness of my mother's room. In quick succession, I was booked on *Eight Is Enough, Angie,* and *Alice*—I had gone from crying myself to sleep at night to sitting in Mel's Diner with Mel, Alice, and Flo. I adored Dick Van Patten, and was mesmerized by Charo, better known to me at the time as the "coochie coochie" girl. I even got to play the son of the great comedy duo Stiller and Meara on an episode of *The Love Boat.* But with my father in and out of the house, and my mother descending deeper into madness, there remained the issue of who would ferry me to and from set, who would act as my guardian during my eight- to twelve-hour long days. With increasing frequency, that responsibility fell to one of my grandparents. This also meant, mercifully, that I was still spending a lot of time at their house, even if I was technically no longer living there.

It was during the days at my grandparents' that I remember discovering music for the first time, on my own, when it wasn't being shoved down my throat, when I wasn't being made to memorize every schmaltzy lyric to "Raindrops Keep Fallin' on My Head." Boobie had an antique upright piano, which had once belonged to her mother, and which I now own and treasure. Sometimes, when my great aunt was visiting from Ohio, they would teach me how to play "Chopsticks," or show me the basics of playing scales. I had already discovered my grandmother's Bill Haley and the Comets album—the fact that she actually owned a record by the guys who sang the theme song to *Happy Days* was a revelation. Not long after that, I found Shaun Cassidy.

There was something about that album cover, the way his hair sparkled in the light, the way his eyes twinkled. I stared at that album cover for hours until, one day, I turned it over. On the back was a picture of Shaun at age two or three, standing in front of what I figured must have been his grandmother's piano. I was so impressed by that, the idea that music had been in his life practically since birth. I decided that I wanted to be like that, too. I wanted to have a music career, and to be able to look back and say, remember when I was standing in front of Boobie's piano, learning how to play "Chopsticks"? I decided that, next time my dad was home, I would tell him about my newfound idol.

My father always had dreams of becoming a rock star. A couple of times, he came pretty close. He played bass for Strawberry Alarm Clock, the psychedelic rock band that topped the charts with their hit single "Incense and Peppermints." That was years before my father joined, however, after the band had already broken up twice and reformed a third time with a smattering of new members. Sometime later he formed Scream with a few of his buddies, and they somehow managed to accumulate a loyal following of several hundred women who would travel from amusement park to amusement park, mad for my father in his vintage plaid shirt, which he wore unbuttoned practically down to his navel, exposing a forest of curly black chest hair.

When he wasn't busy performing, he sometimes took me with him to one of several rehearsal rooms he frequented; very often, these turned out to be someone's dank and dirty garage, lit up with black lights and lava lamps and reeking of dope. Sometimes the drummer might pull me onto his lap during a song and I would feel the pulse of the bass drum reverberate through my body, the nearness of the cymbal crash both exciting and terrifying. If I was lucky, one or two of my dad's bandmates would bring along their kids and we'd play on the floor of the rehearsal room, the feedback from old '67 Fender amps ringing in our ears.

Finally, after what felt like a year of waiting, I woke up one morning and realized that my father was home—I had smelled the familiar musty, skunky smell of smoke wafting beneath the door of my parents' bedroom. When I peered around the edge of the door frame, there he was, lounging in his bell-bottom jeans and the thick black dress socks he always wore stretched halfway up his shins, watching football. I hadn't had so much as a game of catch with my dad, and I wasn't an innately athletic child; I much preferred the sketch comedy and variety shows that Mindy and I watched with my mom. I hovered near the door to the bedroom until, eventually, I summoned the courage to tell him my news. He seemed impressed.

"You like Shaun Cassidy, huh? You want to see him in concert?"

"That would be fun!" I told him.

"Well then I'll find out when he's coming to town and I'll take you."

For weeks, I fantasized about what it might be like to attend my first real concert, what it might be like to see Shaun Cassidy, the teen dream, in person, close enough to reach out and touch. Of course, my dad never got the tickets. He left again, and I didn't see him for nearly a month.

During the two or three years I spent guest-starring on popular '70s sitcoms, Paramount Pictures, a sprawling sixty-five-acre complex on Melrose Avenue in Hollywood, became like a home away from home. I knew that the huge blue wall painted to look like the sky, which had been sitting idly in the middle of a parking lot for weeks, was actually the backdrop for *Gilligan's Island*. During breaks in filming, on the rare occasion that I didn't have to hightail it back to the school trailer, I loved wandering through the backlots meant to sub for the gritty streets of New York City, and I learned to recognize stars like Tony Danza and Robin Williams when they walked by (though in Robin's case, he was usually pedaling past on a bike). I spent so much time on the lot, in fact, that I developed a natural, easy rapport with the head of television casting, a sweet little old man whom I will call Bill Kaufman. I knew that if Bill was casting a show, I had a good shot at getting a part. So when he announced that he was casting a new series called *The Bad News Bears*, based on the movie starring Walter Matthau as the little league coach to a team of preteen misfits, I figured I had a chance, even if most of the actors were between the ages of ten and fifteen, while I was still only seven. Bill held cattle call–style auditions across the country, but I won the role of Regi Tower, a one-in-a-million gig.

None of the Bears were supposed to be particularly gifted ball players, but Regi was especially awful. He was angry and uncoordinated and constantly getting pummeled in the head by the ball. This, of course, was fitting. I had no innate athletic talent, and essentially no athletic experience. I'd certainly never been on a real Little League team before; I had always been too busy working. But the more the producers realized that I actually *was* inept, the more they played up the fact that I couldn't catch. Whereas the first few weeks of filming had been filled with adventures—water balloon fights, carnival rides, and go-karting—it suddenly started to feel as though the bulk of my time on set was being spent watching some young production assistant drag a bag of baseballs to a spot just off-camera, where he'd prepare to launch them at me, one by one. The entire *Bears* cast, including Jack Warden in the role of Coach Morris Buttermaker, had already become like a surrogate family to me, and though I had never been to summer camp, running around the Paramount lot with nine or ten other kids my age, I imagined this must be what it was like. But getting whacked in the head with a baseball, it turned out, was not near as much fun as launching water balloons at my costars, or learning to drive a go-kart. (Though it is perhaps misleading to say that I actually learned how to *drive*, because I burned out more than a few go-kart engines by slamming on the brakes and the gas at the same time. It's not like I had an idea what I was doing. I was seven. But it really pissed off the producers. Whether that added to the frequency with which Regi got smacked with an errant baseball, I can't be sure.)

The Bad News Bears was heavily promoted by CBS, and as the weeks wore on, my entire family grew more and more excited for the debut of my first "real" television show. I loved seeing myself in the commercials, and knowing that I would be on air every single week gave me something to look forward to on Saturday nights. But when the big day finally came and everyone gathered in my grandparents' den to watch the premiere, I suddenly felt sick to my stomach. In the original pilot, I only had one or two lines. "I'm not in it much," I began warning everyone around me. "You'll probably blink and miss me. It's probably the smallest thing I've done on television." I was terrified that my family would be disappointed when they realized how unimportant my role really was.

As we settled in to watch the show, however, it became clear that the editors had recut the pilot, using additional scenes from episodes we shot after the program had been picked up by the network.

"What are you talking about?" my grandpa barked, slapping my back for emphasis. "This is your show, kid!'

It was official—I had usurped Mindy's role as the star of the family. By the tender age of ten, her career was already on the decline.

Being a naturally clumsy, awkward kid apparently made for good television, but my dad—no doubt inspired by the size of my new paycheck—soon decided that he needed to teach me the finer points of baseball "for the job." I couldn't tell you why he was suddenly spending more time at home but, at first, I reveled in the attention. Other than the times he carted me with him to band rehearsal, we had never spent much one-on-one time together, just as father and son. Obviously, the Shaun Cassidy concert had been a bust. When it became clear that teaching me how to play baseball had quickly become the driving force in his life, however, I started to rethink things. Every evening, after a long day on set, I'd watch the minutes on the clock tick by until seven, when he would show up with a glove, a bat, and a ball and beckon me to the backyard. I reluctantly trudged behind him, dragging my feet the whole way.

"You have to focus on it, Corey. Keep your eye on the ball," he said, his eyes narrowed and his forehead crinkled in concentration. Then he hurled the ball across the yard.

I was terrible. It didn't matter where he aimed or how fast he threw it, the ball sailed over my head, or smacked me in the chest, or—on the rare occasions I actually managed a catch—stung my tiny hand. Once my father was sufficiently disgusted with me, I'd retreat to my room and the pursuits I was actually good at, such as the *Star Wars* spoof I was writing, based on an article I'd found in *Mad* magazine.

It was around this time that my father suddenly volunteered to become my primary on-set guardian. It was an unexpected development, and I had assumed it was because he wanted to keep a close eye on my progress as a burgeoning baseball star. I soon figured out the real reason: he had an excuse to spend the entire day away from my mother, whooping it up with the other *Bears* dads in the Paramount Studios parking lot. Within weeks he had become such good friends with the other parents that he announced we were taking a trip to Knott's Scary Farm, a seasonal Halloween event where all of Knott's

Berry Farm is turned into a series of haunted houses filled with monsters and mazes. We piled into the back of someone's rusted-out Chevelle wagon. In the middle of I-5, somewhere south of Bell Gardens, somebody sparked a joint.

I turned to Kristoff St. John, my closest friend in the cast. (He would later star as Neil Winters on *The Young and the Restless*, a role he has played for more than twenty years.) "What's that smell?" I asked him.

"It's weed," he said casually.

"What's weed?"

"It's stuff parents do," Meeno chimed in. Meeno Peluce was Soleil Moon Frye's half brother. Their mother looked—and sounded— exactly like Janice, the hippie guitarist on *The Muppet Show*.

I recognized the smell, of course. It was the same smell that wafted from my mother's bedroom whenever my father was home, the same smell that sometimes greeted me when I climbed into his car after I'd wrapped on the set of the *Bears*. I knew instinctively that "weed" probably wasn't something he should be enjoying with me in the car, but I was still only seven. I didn't know anything about drugs, and my parents weren't exactly the type to sit me down and talk about the dangers of them.

With our family finances on the rise, we moved to a beautiful new home at the top of a colossal hill in Tarzana, complete with huge Corinthian columns, a sweeping marble entryway, and a swirling spiral staircase. My dad traded in his old beater for a Mercedes, and my mother bought herself a Cadillac. We also hired a full-time maid.

Technically, I was not allowed to ride my bike anywhere around my new neighborhood. The hills, my mother explained to me, were far too steep and a scrape or a scratch might jeopardize my job. "You have responsibilities now," she told me, shoving my bike into the far corner of our two-car garage.

But one particular morning, when my mother was still asleep, I decided to take it out anyway. Clear blue, cloudless skies stretched for miles. I let go of the handlebars and leaned my head back, closing my eyes, feeling the sunlight warm on my face until, suddenly, I was going too fast. I felt my foot slip from the pedal, the front tire shake from left to right, and then I went careening over the handlebars, tumbling end over end down the street. When I recovered, the skin was gone from my elbow, I had scrapes all over my hands and face, and there was a pool of blood on the sidewalk.

"Goddamnit, Corey," my mother said when she saw me, crying, covered in blood and gravel and snot. "You're going to fuck everything up. I swear to God, if that director sends you home tomorrow, I'll make you *wish* you were still tumbling down that hill—that'll feel like nothing compared to what I'm gonna do to you."

The next day I slid from my father's car and scampered over to the makeup lady's chair, set up just to the left of third base underneath an enormous yellow umbrella.

"Please fix it," I told her, trembling. "My parents are going to kill me if I can't work."

California law dictates that child actors can work a maximum of eight hours a day, three of which must be devoted solely to education. For the bulk of the last two years, I'd been given a lesson plan from the public school where I was still technically enrolled and studied on set with a private tutor. Lessons are conducted in a designated "school trailer" or, if there aren't any other kid actors on set, in the privacy (and cramped quarters) of my dressing room. The mandated three hours, however, almost never comes in one uninterrupted block of time; it's broken up into chunks, no fewer than twenty minutes, squeezed into natural gaps in the shooting schedule, in between camera setups or while other actors are at work on a scene.

Occasionally, a really well-organized producer will arrange for my day to be "shot out early," meaning that all of my scenes will be shot one right after the other so I can be dismissed from set with a full three hours (or more) still left in the day. More often, though, we would wrap a scene and the assistant director would call out, "Okay, Corey goes to school." Then I'd stroll over to my dressing room, transitioning from a foul-mouthed little leaguer to an ordinary second-grader, cramming for a quiz on consonants and vowels or learning the fundamentals of fractions.

Working with child actors is, frankly, a giant pain in the ass. They bring with them a cadre of on-set guardians and labor workers, private tutors and chaperones (all of which are expensive), but if a production is running behind schedule, "school time" is the first thing that gets cut. Producers get around the legal implications of that through a system called "banking." On a day when you're not much needed, you might go to school for, say, five hours rather than the mandated three. Those two extra hours can then be rolled over, applied to a day when there isn't time for school at all. This jiggering of schedules makes learning difficult, to say the least.

Midway through shooting season two of the *Bears,* the producers call a cast-wide meeting on the set of our little league locker room. We shoot on the soundstage where *The Brady Bunch* was filmed, but it's now clear that *The Bad News Bears* will not have that kind of longevity: we've been cancelled.

Looking back, I can't believe this came as that much of a shock; our show aired at eight-thirty on Saturday night, and our lead-in was a new sitcom called *Working Stiffs* with Jim Belushi and Michael Keaton. It was a tough time slot for a kids' show. But everyone, from the cast to the crew to the production team, seems completely and utterly crushed. (At the wrap party, someone from the cinematography department got drunk and sobbed on my shirt collar.)

The cancellation, aside from throwing my family's finances into sudden disarray, comes at an awkward time for me personally: I'll be sent back to public school, just as my classmates are making the transition from simple mathematics to the single most baffling concept I had ever encountered in my life: multiplication.

I had always excelled in my other classes, subjects like spelling and reading and social studies, and have a near photographic memory—hand me a script and I can remember every single word on the page—but multiplication, for some reason, just does not compute. Both my parents and teachers begin referring to this as a "mental block." I spend most afternoons doing my times tables over and over and over, picturing an errant LEGO or a Lincoln Log floating in the middle of my brain.

As one would perhaps expect, child actors are required to maintain a decent grade point average. Anything less than As and Bs (or the occasional C) would be an indication that my "career" was taking a toll on my education, and I would have been refused a work permit. So, I probably shouldn't have been surprised that my parents chose this particular moment to start caring about my academic standing. Bad grades equaled no income.

Shortly after returning to public school, my mother started sending a daily report card along with me, little pink slips that my teacher was supposed to fill out at the end of the day with little boxes she could check to indicate whether my performance had been satisfactory or unsatisfactory, whether my behavior in class had been excellent, good, fair, or poor. It was usually my father who reviewed them and, based on my daily "grades," administered what was quickly becoming a regular punishment.

"Go upstairs and wait for me," he said on a day when I brought home a particularly ominous combination of letters, a bright red P and an unforgiving U. I marched upstairs and lowered my pants down around my ankles, until my father sauntered in and grabbed one of his leather belts. I was crying, counting off the spanks in my head when, midway through swat number four, the leather belt broke clean in half. For a brief moment, I closed my eyes and sent up a silent prayer, thanking God that it was over. My father, however, simply retrieved a fresh belt from his closet.

He turned and looked at me on his way out the door. "You know I don't want to do this, Corey. But I have to. It's the only way you'll learn what's right."

I wanted to believe him. But later—when I was squirming my way out of yet another spanking—he tied my hands to the bedpost to ensure that I stayed put. He swung the belt wildly, and the buckle caught me in the eye. It bruised and swelled immediately, and I thought, surely there's a better way to teach your kid about right and wrong than this.

CHAPTER 3

A blanket of early-morning dew had set-tled across the front yard and tiny blades of grass were sticking to my ankles and the tops of my bare feet. I trudged through the fog, along the winding walkway and out into the street. The windows of my father's car were all steamed up from the inside. I pulled the sleeve of my shirt over my hand and used it to wipe away the condensation, cupped my hands together, and peered inside.

"Dad?" I called out. "Are you coming in the house now?"

Shortly after my brother Eden was born, in the fall of 1979, my father moved out of the room he shared with my mother and started sleeping on the couch. This did nothing to allay their constant fighting, however, which was intensifying and—with increasing frequency—dragging on late into the night. They covered a revolving door of subjects, from the (apparently untenable) fact that my mother was spending all day, every day, at home, alone, caring for *us*, while he was out carousing, and the fact that she was pretty sure he was stepping out on her with a sea of different women, including my pretty blond teacher Mrs. Hart. After several months on the sofa, my father began sleeping in the car, curled up on top of piles of clothes and shoes and a couple of worn-out old amplifiers. How my parents managed to conceive yet *another* child amid this chaos is one of the great mysteries of my young life, but by the time Devin came into the world, in January 1981, my father was gone for good. He didn't even show up at the hospital.

The divorce threw our family finances into sharp relief. I had been working steadily for more than five years, but my parents had no idea how to manage their money. After befriending a real estate agent, they snapped up properties with abandon, then ended up taking out a second and, later, a third mortgage on our home in Tarzana before eventually losing the house to the bank. My mother, my sister, my new little brothers, and I piled into her car and moved to a one-story rental in Canoga Park. There was nothing left to show for my success; just like that, we were back to being broke.

"You need an operation."

My mother was coming at me with scissors and a syringe, which she had no doubt pilfered from Actors and Others for Animals, the nonprofit where she occasionally volunteered. She had recruited Mindy to help hold me down and suddenly I was on my back on the floor. My wrists were pinned and my mother was straddling me, one knee on either side of my stomach. "Your nose just keeps growing," she said, doing her best impression of a surgeon, cupping my chin in her hand and angling my face from side to side. "Yep, you definitely need a nose job." She started lowering the syringe down closer to my face. Mindy howled with laughter—she still thought it was a game.

I squirmed and bucked, desperately trying to wriggle out from underneath my mom. My legs were flailing, I was trying to backpedal my way across the carpet, but it was no use. When the tears started, Mindy let go of my arms.

"Mom, it's not funny now. Come on, stop it," she said. But my mother didn't stop. Mindy clearly didn't know what to do, so she got up and walked out of the room, leaving us all alone.

"You need an injection to sedate you for the operation." She took the scissors and pressed them against my throat, poking but not quite piercing the skin. I screamed for her to stop, squeezed my eyes shut and craned my neck as far away from her as I could. My chest heaved with deep, guttural sobs. Finally, she got up and went to her bedroom, cackling the whole way down the hall.

My mother was unraveling. She was either glassy-eyed and listless and starting to slur her words, or she was manic, barreling through the house like a freight train, trying on hot pants and see-through tops and chattering on about how she was going to find us a new father, one who actually "gave a shit" about the family. One evening, when I poked my head into her bathroom and asked what time she might be home, she ripped the toilet seat from the hinges and threatened to bash my face in. Her newest trick, which was especially terrifying, was to sneak-attack my sister and I in the middle of the night, seizing on a shirt left on the floor of my bedroom or a pair of pants casually tossed on a chair. "What the fuck is this?" she would yell, waking me up from a dead sleep, holding up the offending pair of pants in her hand. Before I even had a chance to respond, she would yank clothes from the hangers, pull them from the drawers, and toss them around the room. It looked like the aftermath of a category 5 tornado.

"Clean your fucking room, you slob," she told me. It was four in the morning. I had to be up for school in three hours. I learned that the only time I was really safe was when she was asleep.

Though I can't pinpoint the reasons why, my mother suddenly announces that she wants to live more "independently." Instead of relying on my aging grandparents, she hires my first set-sitter, someone to drive me to and from jobs and, essentially, to babysit me while I'm at work. Her name is Sheri. She's a sweet woman with bright red hair, but her sneezes—and there are a lot of them—smell terrible. This is my first sneeze-odor experience. I'm not sure what to make of it.

I get hired to film an episode of *Mork & Mindy*. I'm one of several children—the show is in decline and the writers are trying all kinds of new subplots to boost the ratings, so Mork is now running a daycare—and I only have three or four lines, but Robin Williams and I get along famously, even though he insists on calling me Damien, because he thinks I look like the kid from *The Omen*. Every time he sees me, he starts whistling the movie's haunting theme song, and shouting, "Daaaamien . . . *DAMIEN*!" The producers like me, too, so I'm quickly written in to another episode, and there's talk of bringing me back later on in the season, perhaps as a regular guest star.

By the second episode, though, things at home are starting to take their toll. I am desperate for some kind of positive attention, but I have no idea how to get it. So, I whine. I complain. I act out. I ask repeatedly when we're going to wrap, when I might have a break, when is it going to be lunchtime. The word *obnoxious* is thrown around a lot, and my chance to become a series regular is quickly scrapped.

I get rebooked on another episode of *The Love Boat*, but things aren't any better over there. I am inconsistent and bratty. I am nominated for a Young Artist's Award for Best Young Actor, Guest on a Series, but there are a lot of calls to the agent. Then comes strike number three.

All the Way Home, a Pulitzer Prize–winning play by Tad Mosel, was nominated for a Tony award when it debuted on Broadway in 1960. Now it's going to be adapted for television, but the producers want to broadcast it live on NBC. It's an ambitious project with an impressive cast. Sally Field, fresh off an Oscar win for *Norma Rae*, will star in the role of Mary Follett, a newly widowed woman in 1915-era Tennessee. William Hurt will play her dead husband. I assume that I will be cast as their son, Rufus, but the role goes instead to a boy named Jeremy Licht. He seems like a nice enough kid; I've palled around with him at auditions, but he doesn't have much of a résumé. (Eventually, he will play one of the Hogan boys on the 1980s sitcom *Valerie* alongside Jason Bateman.) I am cast in some tertiary supporting role, way, *way* down in the billing. I have one, maybe two, whole lines.

Rehearsals for the play, which are scheduled to last for a couple of months, start out well, though I have such a small part that the majority of my time at work is spent at "school" (which, for this production, is a room in the basement), banking hours. Some days I don't even get called to the set at all. Jeremy, however, quickly proves to be a bit of a prankster. He starts out innocently enough, flicking my ear or tugging on my hair or tripping me on the way to lunch, but he is a master at making *me* out to be the troublemaker. As soon as I react, he raises his voice just loud enough for the nearest adult to hear. "Hey, why are you fighting with me?" he says. "I'm here to work. I'm trying to do my *job*." You have to hand it to him, actually. He really is one hell of an actor. And I am an easy target.

I sink deeper and deeper into despair. My parents are divorced, I have virtually no relationship with my father, my first real television show has been cancelled, and now here I am doing this tiny part in this stupid play and taking crap from Jeremy Licht. The more he teases me, the angrier and angrier I get. And then finally I decide I can't take it anymore. Instead of being a punching bag, I hit him back.

For the first time in my life, I get fired.

"Please, please, please don't tell my mom." Sheri is driving me home and I am begging her—pleading with her—not to break the news to my mother. The closer we get to the house, the more desperate my begging becomes.

"I have to tell her, Corey," she says. "There's really no way around it."

"But she's going to kill me."

"She's not going to kill you. You're overreacting. Your mother seems like a lovely woman. I'm sure everything will be fine."

Everything will certainly not be fine, I know, and I'm convinced that Sheri must be some kind of a moron. I glare at her. How does nobody else see it? That my mother has gone completely and utterly insane? I make one final plea as she steers the car into the mouth of the driveway, then follow her slowly to the front porch, my chin tucked tightly to my chest, cowering behind her as she rings the doorbell.

The next few moments play out in slow motion. My mother comes to the door, looking slightly dazed, and Sheri begins explaining the situation. I can hear their voices, but they sound distant and far away, like the "wa wa wawa wa" of the adults in the *Peanuts* cartoons, like I have water in my ears. When I hear Sheri use the word *dismissed*, though, everything comes back into focus, the truth of the thing rushing at me all at once. My mother snaps her neck and glares at me.

"You got *fired*?"

We stare at each other for a few awkward moments.

"Go inside and wait for me," she says. She closes the door behind her, and they talk for a while on the porch. When I hear Sheri's engine rumble to life in the driveway, I freeze. It's going to be bad. I know it.

"*Corey!*" My mother slams the door behind her. It rattles in the frame. "Get your ass in that room. Right now."

It's my brother's room. His crib is in the corner. I don't know where Devin is. I think my mother and I are the only two people in the house. "Take off your clothes," she hisses. I do as I'm told while she bolts to the other end of the room and starts pulling at the window. It dawns on me what she's reaching for—the long wooden dowel resting in the sash, acting as a window stop. It's at least an inch in diameter, solid oak, heavy. For a fleeting moment, I feel like laughing. Surely this must be another of her games. Surely, she must be joking.

The first blow stings, but it's more of a shock than anything else. It's when she raises the dowel high over her head, again, that the pain starts to register, searing the top of my back and my shoulders, and I start running in circles around the room.

"How could you fucking do this to me?" she screams. She is out of control, wild-eyed, like an animal. Her face is bright red and blotchy, her cheeks are streaked with mascara. "You know I need this fucking money. I will kill you. I will fucking *kill you*, you worthless piece of shit."

I drop down on all fours and scurry underneath Devin's crib, wedging myself as far back as I can, my spine stretched out flush against the wall. I can see her feet, the chipped toenail polish, and then the sawed-off end of the stick as it comes charging toward me. She's bent at the waist, ramming the pole under the cotton eyelet dust ruffle, jabbing at my ribs, my arms, my face. My skin is raw and bleeding. I think that, maybe, she is serious. She really does want to kill me. Then everything goes black. No matter how hard I try, I can't remember what happened after that.

The next morning I fed and changed Eden and Devin, crept out into the living room, and turned on the television. I was scrolling through the channels, looking for something to watch, when—all of a sudden—I couldn't breathe. The wind had been knocked out of me with a swift swat to my back, the remote ripped from my fingers, flung across the room to the couch.

"You think you're going to watch TV? You're not watching TV, pal. You're fucking grounded."

It was Tom, my mom's new boyfriend.

Ironically, things with Tom had started out pretty well. I liked him better than Max, the first in a steady stream of men who filed in and out of our house in the months following the divorce, the guy who drove a Harley and wore a leather motorcycle jacket and more or less left me alone. Tom, unlike those other men, had actually taken an interest in me. He would rattle up to the house in his rusted out pickup and take me for long hikes in Chatsworth Park. I loved climbing the switchbacks, scrambling to the top of a boulder outcrop and looking south over the sprawling suburbs of L.A. But then Tom started inviting some of his buddies along on our regular hikes, and someone would inevitably show up with a six-pack. Tom, it turned out, was very different when he drank. By the time I realized that, he had more or less moved in.

At first, the worst part about having Tom around was that he would emerge from my mother's room and stumble down the hallway to the bathroom, stark naked. I had never seen a grown man naked before. It made me feel strange and uncomfortable. But then one night he came home drunk, reeking of booze. He punched his hand clear through the front door, leaving sharp shards of wood and glass, as well as smears and drips of blood, in the foyer. This was *after* he ripped the screens from the windows and left them in twisted heaps and piles around the lawn, and screamed—demanded—to be let in. Finally, Mindy called the police. My mother swore that we'd never have to see Tom again, but a month later he was back.

"You're spoiled and you're lazy and now you got yourself fired. The least you can do is clean your mother's fucking house," Tom is saying to me now, towering over me, a towel wrapped around his waist. "I'm going to teach you what *real* work is. You're going to learn some fucking responsibility. Get the broom."

My mother has stumbled out of the bedroom. She's half-dressed and her makeup is smeared across her face. She slumps down in the couch cushions. I look at her, but she shrugs.

"Didn't anybody teach you how to fucking sweep?" he asks after I've pulled the broom from the pantry and started dragging it across the floor, pushing mounds of dog hair into tidy little piles.

"We always had a maid," I say.

"Well, no more maids when you lose your job. That's what happens when you're broke."

"I'm going to kill you."

My mother delivers this line in a sing-song cadence, like she's just suggested we go on a picnic, or make balloon animals, or fly a kite in Chatsworth Park. I haven't seen her fully lucid in weeks. "On Saturday," she says, with a wink.

All week long she taunts me, ticking down the days until my eventual demise. Years ago—no, *weeks* ago—I would have thought she was kidding, that this is just her macabre sense of humor talking, but after the beating under the crib, I can't be so sure. I need help. Real help. And then it occurs to me where I might get it.

On Saturday morning, I make my escape. After scribbling a quick good-bye note and packing a small bag of clothes, I sneak out the back of our house, scale the privacy fence, tear through the neighbor's yard and down the hill, and for another mile or two, all the way to the local police station. I push open the giant glass doors and walk right up to the first man I see in uniform. I try to explain to him that my mother is torturing me, that I'm lonely and abused and afraid for my life. That I think, next time, she really will kill me, but the words are coming out in a jumbled heap.

"Please don't make me go back there," I finish, out of breath. "I'll go anywhere but back there with her."

He peers down at me from behind a clipboard. He seems annoyed. He sighs. "Is your father around?"

I think about how to answer that, how to explain that my father isn't much of a father, that he left home because at least *he* knows that my mother is crazy, but he didn't take me with him. But I soon realize none of that matters anyway, because I can't remember his new phone number. When the officer dials the number I've given him, instead of my father answering, it's my agent on the other end of the line.

CHAPTER 4

By early 1982, I've gotten my career back on track. I'm in the pilot for *Gloria*, a spin-off of *All in the Family* starring Sally Struthers. I work with Gary Coleman on a made-for-television movie called *The Kid with the Broken Halo*. I snag the role of Corey "Kip" Cleaver in *Still the Beaver*, a two-hour "reunion" movie on CBS. And then I get a call from my agent about an upcoming film. It's big, she tells me. Very hush-hush. They want me to come in and read for a part.

"Great," I tell her. "What's the movie?"

"It's called *E.T. the Extra-Terrestrial.* Steven Spielberg is directing."

Nine years earlier, in the summer of 1973, a virtually unknown director was hired to make a film abut a maniacal great white shark terrorizing a tiny New England town. Despite a ballooning budget, massive production days, and a finicky animatronic title character, he created an Academy Award–winning masterpiece, spawning "Jawsmania," inventing the "summer blockbuster," and grossing nearly half a *billion* dollars in the process. The twenty-nine-year-old then rebuffed offers to direct *Jaws 2,* as well as a smattering of superhero movies, opting instead to write and direct a strange little film about UFOs. *Close Encounters of the Third Kind* earned nine Oscar nominations, including one for Best Director. By the time I show up at the MGM lot in Culver City, *Raiders of the Lost Ark* has just hit theaters. Steven Spielberg has been anointed. He is the Next Big Thing.

I'm reading for the part of Elliott's best friend. It's a pivotal role and I'm nervous. But Steven, who at thirty-six looks to me like a young Chevy Chase, is nothing like what I expected. He is free-spirited and funny; we hit it off right away. These days it's a bit of a cliché to talk about how nice Steven Spielberg is, but it's true—he really is one of the kindest men in the business.

"That was great. Really great," he tells me when I've finished with my audition. "You've got the part." Then he drapes his arm across my shoulders and gives me a squeeze. "Why don't I show you how things work around here?"

Steven is busy producing (and according to murmurings within the industry, unofficially directing) a new horror film, so he takes me on a tour of the various soundstages until we reach a giant set, which will be at the center of a terrifying scene: the actress JoBeth Williams and her on-screen children will appear to be flying through the air, grabbing onto headboards and doorjambs to avoid being sucked out a window in their California home by a strange demonic force called The Beast. Steven shows me how the actors will dangle from harnesses, how their hair and clothes will be blown back by the strength of several industrial fans, while the interior of the room—a huge motorized set piece—will rotate completely upside down. Effects-wise, this is groundbreaking stuff. The film, he tells me, is called *Poltergeist*.

E.T. still had a solid six months left of preproduction, so I knew it would be awhile before things got rolling. In the interim, I auditioned for a show called *Madame's Place*, a sitcom featuring the bawdy, double-entendre-laced comedy of "Madame," a lifelike puppet.

Madame's Place was unusual in that it was a first-run syndication show, meaning that it was scheduled to air on a lot of different channels (rather than owned—and aired—by only one network), five days a week. The first order was, therefore, enormous, somewhere between fifty and a hundred episodes, way more than the standard thirteen. This would guarantee a steady income, and my family needed the money. But I was worried that I'd be tied down to a silly television show when the call for *E.T.* eventually came. "Go in on everything," my mother told me. "Better to get the offer and turn it down than to not get the offer at all."

I did get an offer, though it was for less money than I had been making. My mother made me take the part anyway. So, I became Buzzy, Madame's nosy next-door neighbor.

Working with Madame—to my surprise and utter delight—was a lot like working with a major Hollywood movie star. Her personality was so big; I could be doing a scene and completely forget that I was talking to a puppet, that she wasn't actually real. Her puppeteer, Wayland Flowers (who was already famous for his appearances alongside Madame on *Hollywood Squares, Laugh-In,* and *Solid Gold*), made her seem larger than life. And Wayland, I quickly realized, was one of the sweetest men I had ever met. On breaks during filming he would invite me back to his dressing room and show me how he operated the sticks to move Madame's hands and head, how he transformed his own voice to create something entirely new. At home I had a little stuffed monkey with Velcro hands and feet. It reminded me of Madame, so one day I decided to bring it in to show off to my new friend.

"Can I borrow that?" he asked me.

A few days later, he brought it back to set, completely restyled to look like one of his puppets, complete with the little sticks to move the monkey's hands and feet.

"I gave him an upgrade," Wayland said when he showed me. "Now he works just like Madame."

I was elated. The great Wayland Flowers had *made* me a puppet. But when I showed it to my mother, she harrumphed.

"Wayland Flowers is gay," she told me.

I didn't know what that meant, of course, but it wouldn't really have mattered if I did. Practically no one in the entertainment industry was "out" back in the early '80s.

"How do you know he's *gay*?" I asked.

"*Trust me*," she said. "I just know."

Wayland was the first in a series of older men in the industry to take me under his wing. The second was an actor named Joe Penny, who guest-starred with me in an episode of *Lottery!*, a short-lived show about two guys who travel the country presenting lottery winnings to strangers and watching how the money changes their lives. I played a troubled kid (a role I was starting to get cast in a lot), and I remember that at the end of filming, Joe Penny gave me his phone number. "Call me anytime," he told me, "if you ever want to catch a ball game."

Joe and I spoke on the phone several times over the next few months. He gave me career advice. We talked about what kinds of roles I might take. He was someone I could actually trust. I didn't have many people like that in my life.

My grandparents, however, were not impressed.

"Why is this grown man giving you his number?" my grandmother asked me, when she caught me up late, talking on the phone. "It's not normal, Corey. It doesn't make any sense."

"Joe just wants to be my friend," I told her. "This is how Hollywood works. The older guys reach out to the kids." That was how I saw it and, eventually, that's how my family saw it, too. The more adult males I befriended, the less strange it started to seem.

As production on *Madame's Place* dragged on, I started to become more and more concerned about *E.T.* I hadn't heard a peep in months—not from my agent, not from the casting director, not from MGM, not from anyone. *Nada.* And then finally, on a rainy, otherwise uneventful afternoon, Steven called me at home.

"Hey, Corey," he said. "How ya doin'?"

"When are we getting started?" I blurted out. "I've been waiting and waiting!"

I could hear Steven breathing on the other end of the line and, immediately, my heart sank. I could already tell, this was not going to be the call I had been hoping for.

"Unfortunately," he continued, "I have some sad news. As you know, we've been working on rewrites, and the last one we did was major. It was an overhaul. Bottom line: your character has been cut down to nothing. If you want one of the small parts, one of the friends, you're welcome to it. But I think you're a leading role kind of guy. My advice to you is to wait for the next one."

"What's the next one?" I asked.

"Well, I don't know yet. But I give you my word, Corey. Whatever it is, you'll be in it."

Losing *E.T.* was agony. When it opened, in the summer of 1982, it became another instant record-smashing blockbuster as well as a critical darling, and—by the following year—the highest grossing film of all time. Billboards lined the boulevards of southern L.A., urging you to become "part of the experience." Reese's Pieces was everyone's new favorite snack (and in fact, sales of the candies *tripled* within two weeks of the film's debut). When my mother and I finally managed to snag tickets to a showing at the Cinerama Dome in Hollywood— nearly a month after *E.T.* premiered—there was still a line of people snaked around the building.

I was old enough by then to understand the movie business, that things changed and it wasn't anyone's fault, that Steven hadn't cut the character because he didn't like me, that he certainly didn't have to break the news by calling me at home. But I was still crushed. It didn't help that—while driving back and forth to auditions—my mother felt the need to point out every single billboard along Sunset Boulevard, as well as the prostitutes loitering below. My mother thought it was cute for her eleven-year-old son to stick his head out the window and yell, "How much?" as we drove by.

Like any true Southern California kid, I have never seen snow. So I know the first day of filming is going to be magical. We're shooting in Courthouse Square, a backlot at Universal Studios, the same set that would become Hill Valley's quaint town square in *Back to the Future*. Today, it's been transformed into the fictional setting of Kingston Falls—and it's beautiful, a perfect representation of small town suburbia, an idyllic depiction of Anywhere, U.S.A., at Christmastime, awash in a sea of twinkling lights. As soon as I step foot on set, however, I realize that the "snow" is nothing more than acrylic paint chips mixed with bits of Styrofoam.

"Where's the real stuff?" I ask a grip, kicking the fake snow with the toe of my shoe.

"This is how we do it in movie world," he tells me.

But I know that can't be right. I quickly rattle off a list of movies in which the main characters go sledding, or make snowmen, or throw snowballs at one another—there's no way anybody can make a snowball out of this stuff.

"Sometimes we use Styrofoam," he says. "Sometimes we use salt. If we're shooting on a closed set, we might be able to make it. And if we're filming on location, we might even use the real thing. But when you're shooting outside in L.A. in the middle of summer, kid, this is how it works."

I felt like I was three years old again, discovering that Santa was just a guy in a glove.

True to his word, Steven does cast me in the next one, which turns out to be a film called *Gremlins*. Joe Dante, an up-and-coming science fiction director, will helm the project; Spielberg will executive produce. The film—about a strange creature called *mogwai*, and the evil, destructive little monsters it eventually spawns—will become the first to feature the official logo of Amblin Entertainment, a silhouette of Elliott's bike flying across the face of the moon.

"How ya doin, Corey?" Joe Dante said, hustling over to me just moments after I had discovered the fake, movie-set snow. "You're gonna be great! Now, we just have to get you in this Christmas tree."

"*What?*" I choked out, probably a little too loudly. I had read the scene, of course—it's the first of the movie, it comes immediately after the opening credits—but I always imagined that I'd be standing *behind* the tree. I didn't think I'd actually be in one.

"Oh, no," he explained. "We built this costume for you. You're going to be wearing it."

He seemed way too excited about this, in my opinion, because that costume was itchy, scratchy, and weighed a ton. Actually, it sort of sucked.

The scene is a small one, but it takes nearly two full days to shoot. Sheriff Frank saunters up to the town Christmas tree tent—as "Christmas tree Pete," I have apparently donned the tree costume as some sort of sales tactic—and accidentally ruffles my branches, not realizing that I'm inside.

"What the hell is this?" he says, confused. "Pete? What are you doin' in there?"

"Don't ask," I say, pulling the branches apart to reveal a tiny sliver of my face, before running off to deliver a different tree to Mr. Anderson's truck.

When filming finally wraps, Joe Dante calls out to me, "See you next month!"

"Uh, don't I have a pretty big role?" I asked him. "What do you mean, 'see you next month'?"

"This is a six-month shooting schedule," he explained. And so began what was, for me, a very unusual acting experience—I'd shoot a few days out of every month and then return to my regular life.

By the time *Gremlins* began filming, in the summer of 1983, I was back to living at my grandparents' house more or less full-time. Mindy stayed behind in Canoga Park, effectively raising my two little brothers. Tom, my mother's boyfriend, was thankfully gone, but my mother was back to going out every night. Sometimes she didn't come home until morning. Sometimes she'd up and disappear for a week or more at a time. Since she didn't want—or couldn't handle—the responsibility of delivering me to set on time, she agreed that moving out for a spell would be for the best. Of course, she had no trouble cashing my paychecks.

Though it is the first time in my life that I am living almost fully outside of my mother's grasp, it is not the first time the subject has been broached. When I was eight, around the time of my parents' divorce, my uncle Merv—bless that man—pulled me aside one afternoon and locked me in my grandmother's bathroom.

"Listen, Corey," he said, more serious than I had ever seen him. "You need to understand something. You are a very bright young man. You have magic in you. I see it. I don't want you to listen to the negative things people put in your head."

I stared at him, wide-eyed. No one had ever said anything like that to me before.

"Mary and I have been discussing the possibility of bringing you to live with us," he continued. "What would you think of that?"

I was instantly flooded with images of what my new life at Uncle Merv's house might look like: home-cooked meals, everyone eating around the table. Being tucked in to bed every night. Being hugged. Being told that I was special. I could have kissed him. Instead, I threw my arms around his neck.

"Thank you, thank you, thank you," I told him, my shrieks reverberating against the tiles of the tiny bathroom. Merv promised that he would speak with my mother and find a way to make it all work. But then his wife, Mary, was diagnosed with cancer and the issue of me coming to live with them was put on hold indefinitely.

When Mary died, little more than a year later, something in Merv broke. We sat *shiva*, the Jewish tradition of mourning a loved one for one whole week. He strung her wedding ring on a chain and wore it around his neck. He wore black. But he never recovered. He became further and further disconnected from the family, recluse-like, and I knew that I would never be invited to stay.

There was talk, briefly, about going to live with my uncle Murray after that. Of all the Goldstein children, Murray was the most financially successful; he lived in a sprawling home in Encino, complete with an in-ground pool. But Murray was strict and severe—more strict, even, than my grandfather. I wasn't convinced that living with

Uncle Murray would be any better than staying with my mother. So, I settled in with my grandparents and enrolled in a school near their home.

Public school, to put it mildly, was awkward. I had been in and out my entire life, so maintaining normal friendships with kids my age was virtually impossible. I was small and scrawny and, as my experience on *The Bad News Bears* could attest, decidedly not an athlete. Add to this the fact that I was an *actor*—something that, even this close to Hollywood, was met with suspicion, a raised eyebrow, and quite a bit of teasing—and it's no wonder that by age twelve, I had officially and irreconcilably been labeled an outcast. I did not fit in with the effortlessly cool surfers and stoners, the Valley preppies, or the Mexican and black students, who were bused in from east L.A. Girls were a complete mystery. Though I had started to notice them, they were definitely not interested in me.

I confided in my cousin Michael. While I had been busy acting alongside a life-size puppet on *Madame's Place*, he had somehow managed to get himself an actual, honest-to-God girlfriend. They had even made out. I was astounded at his prowess. "How'd you do it?" I asked him. I could barely get a girl to look at me, let alone agree to lock lips.

"The best way is to make a game out of it."

"What do you mean, a game?"

"You know, like 'spin the bottle' or 'seven minutes in heaven.'"

I did not know, but I was excited to find out. "Let's do it!" Within minutes, Michael had arranged for two girls from school to come over and "hang out." Both Amanda and Leighann, he informed me, were excellent kissers.

Before the girls arrived, Michael and I decided to play a quick game of "rock, paper, scissors" to determine who would go with who. I was desperate to be with Amanda—the doe-eyed brunette with a face full of freckles—but Michael's paper covered my rock. Amanda would go with Michael, while I would be stuck with Leighann. She was a sweet girl, and we did share one passionless peck, but most of that afternoon we spent just talking. When we finally went looking for Michael and Amanda, however, they were full-on making out in the closet.

Back at school, still reeling from the fact that Amanda was clearly more into my cousin than me, I decided to rethink things with Leighann. I wasn't even sure if I liked her, but I felt like a shoo-in. Better to start off with a sure thing, I thought, and then graduate to a girl like Amanda once I had some experience under my belt. That day in class, I wrote Leighann a little note: "Will you go out with me?" She wrote back quickly, a simple one-word response.

"No?" I shouted—*out loud*—as soon as I read it. Then I cowered in my seat while everyone turned around to stare. I spent most of the rest of that day in a haze, completely and totally crushed, until after the last bell rang and Leighann asked me to go for a walk.

"As you know," she stated, oddly professorial about the whole thing, "you don't have a very good reputation around here. You're not really one of the 'cool kids.'"

I stared at her.

"But I like you. I wouldn't mind being your girlfriend. . . . We just can't tell anybody. As long as it stays our secret—and you don't tell anybody, *ever*—then I'll go with you."

That was good enough for me.

I'm more comfortable, more at home, back on the set of *Gremlins*. Joe Dante, who has a reputation for working with the same actors on project after project, has managed to create a little family out of the cast. Zach Galligan, who plays the lead role of Billy Peltzer, and I play arcade games like Food Fight and Paperboy during breaks in filming. (In fact, Zach likes Food Fight so much that he asks Steven

Spielberg to relocate the game from the offices of Amblin Entertainment right to the *Gremlins* set. Amblin Entertainment, it turns out, is filled with arcade games; Steven is also a fan of them.) And Joe becomes another in a long list of substitute fathers. He is something of a cinefile, a huge fan of the classics. Sometimes, on days off, he invites me along for private screenings of old prints he had pulled from the WB vault, like 1953's *The War of the Worlds*. It marks the beginning of a long and treasured friendship and the first of several projects we will work on together.

I am also captivated by Gizmo, who seems even more real to me than Madame. *Gremlins* employs a lot of sleight-of-hand tricks to make Gizmo and the other Mogwai believable on screen. When Billy first meets Gizmo, for example, the puppet he pulls from the gift box is an inanimate, stuffed puppet. The Gizmo he cradles in his arms is a moving, mechanical device. And the Gizmo that pops out of the gift box is a different animal all together (if you'll excuse the pun). All of this means we're often working with multiple puppets at once, as many as three or four different Gizmos for one, seemingly simple scene.

I quickly befriend the men of the special-effects crew—the inner-workings of the mogwai remind me of the days when I would pull apart my superhero action figures—and they patiently explain to me how everything works. Some Gizmos are mechanical, their heads, eyes, and arms animated by remote control. Some are hydraulic, fixed to the surface on which they appear (a counter, a desk, etc.), but open at the bottom; a jumble of cords passes beneath the stage to a crew of four or five different men, all lying on their stomachs, staring at a tiny monitor, controlling Gizmo's movements.

One day I strolled over to the special effects area. There were five or six different puppets strewn across the table—a stuffed puppet, a mechanical puppet, several versions of Stripe and the green monsters—and, suddenly, I had an idea.

"Can I take one home with me?"

The special-effects guys looked at one another, before one of them decided to speak. "Yeah, that's not gonna happen."

"How about just a piece of the fur?" There were yards and yards of the stuff lying around. I figured that if I could just have a piece to carry in my pocket, I'd have something that no one else in the whole world had. I would be ahead of the curve. And if I could take it to school and show it off, maybe I would—finally—be cool.

Things at school, however, did not go as planned.

"What the hell is *mogwai* fur?" someone yelled out. The kids in the back of the class—the cool kids—erupted in a fit of guffaws and snickers.

"Mogwai are part of a movie that Steven Spielberg is making called *Gremlins*," I said, completely undeterred. "Trust me when I tell you, this movie is going to be *huge*."

"Who the hell is Steven Spielberg?" A spitball flew through the air, landing on the floor near my shoe. Needless to say, my mogwai show-and-tell did nothing to help my reputation.

CHAPTER 5

I ran out of the school trailer as soon as I heard the commotion. Joseph Zito, the director, was pacing along the lakeshore, alternately mumbling to himself and screaming at the producers. Several members of the crew had donned wetsuits and were now bobbing up and down in the water. "What's going on?" I asked, running up alongside Joe, my feet sinking into the muddy shore.

"It's Crispin," he said, visibly distressed. "He was out in the lake, playing with his submarine. I guess it went down too far and didn't come back." He put his hands on his hips and gazed at his men in the water. "*Fuck*," he spat. "It's gonna be awhile."

Camp Crystal Lake, the fictional stomping grounds of the serial killer Jason Voorhees, has been created and re-created in small towns in New Jersey, Connecticut, and California for each of the three Friday the 13th films. To make *Friday the 13th: The Final Chapter,* the fourth movie in the franchise and my follow-up to *Gremlins,* we're shooting near the tiny town of Buellton, two hours north of L.A. It was my first road trip—Grandpa sat up front with a teamster; he'll be my on-set guardian for the duration of the shoot. And though I am by far the youngest member of the cast, Crispin Glover is easily my favorite. He reminds me of a young James Dean, a shadowy figure, good-looking but in an off kind of way, always dressed in a long trench coat pulled tight at the base of his throat. While the other young actors spend their free time drinking and flirting and socializing, Crispin can usually be found down by the lake, alone, staring out at the water, into nothing.

A few days earlier, most of the cast had driven into the neighboring town of Solvang, a village of half-timbered houses with thatched roofs and four different windmills, all done in the Danish provincial style, in search of a bar. But Crispin had wandered into an antique store and come out with a thousand dollars' worth of toys. His favorite was a novelty yellow submarine. I remembered hearing the story— the way he had whined and complained until the other actors reluctantly squeezed themselves into the already overpacked van in order to make room for his purchases—but that still didn't explain why production had been delayed. By the time I popped up alongside Joe, we'd been shut down for nearly two hours.

"I don't get it," I said. "What's the problem?"

"He won't come back to set until we find it."

I looked over at Crispin, who was now in the middle of a full-on star fit, huffing and puffing and stomping on the ground, and laughed out loud. I couldn't help it—this was hilarious. I was also totally impressed. Here was a fully grown man (at twenty, he seemed fully grown to me), throwing a childlike tantrum—and it was working! I thought that's what it meant to be famous. And being famous, to me, meant that you were loved. It would be many, many years before I learned the difference.

Nobody seemed to think it was strange that, immediately after wrapping a PG-rated family film for Amblin, I would be starring in an R-rated slasher flick. In fact, the greater concern among the casting directors had been whether or not I was big enough and strong enough to properly wield a machete. In the final scene, it would be my character, twelve-year-old Tommy Jarvis, who violently hacks a deranged serial killer into pieces.

"They think the machete is almost as big as you are. They're worried you won't be able to pick it up and swing it," my agent explained.

Pretending to be a serial killer, however, was not my particular concern. I was much more worried about a scene several pages earlier, when my character was supposed to shave his head.

"There is no way in hell I'm having my kid out of operation for three months because he shaved his head for a movie," my mother yelled into the phone. For once, I actually agreed with her. I ended up wearing a bald cap for the final scenes of the movie (and though I was able to master the machete, I had blood-soaked, gory nightmares for months).

Friday the 13th: The Final Chapter and *Gremlins* both hit theaters in the spring of 1984; their premiere dates were less than two months apart. I had actually gone to the movies with Mindy and a few of her friends to see *Friday the 13th* when I noticed a poster for

Gremlins hanging up in the lobby. "This is my movie!" I shouted. I couldn't wait for it to come out.

When I saw that poster, I could sense that something was starting to happen. I felt like I was on the cusp of something. Not really stardom, which seemed unthinkable, too outrageous then to be true. It was more like a promise, the hope that good things were on the horizon. The idea that if I could just hold out a little bit longer, I might find a way out of my shitty life. It was around that time that I started "running away" from home, usually to Mann Valley West, a giant movie theater on Ventura that has long since closed. Saturday matinees ran for three dollars; I would usually pilfer enough money from my grandmother's purse to get in, then sneak from theater to theater, watching as many movies as possible until nightfall, when I was typically ready to return home.

Later, after *Gremlins* debuted at number-two (right behind the original *Ghostbusters*), and raked in nearly $150 million, it occurred to me that I should probably be getting in to see movies for free. I caught a bus from Northridge to Woodland Hills, where I transferred and took a second bus to Tarzana, walked right up to the box office and pointed to a nearby poster.

"You see that movie? *Gremlins*?" I said to a bored-looking teenager, chomping on a piece of gum, seated behind the glass. "I'm in it."

"Really?"

"Yeah. Can you let me in?"

I spent most of that afternoon bouncing in and out of screening rooms, watching all the movies I wanted, including my very own. By the end of my second viewing, though, people had started to recognize me.

I had been recognized in public before, of course, as far back as my time on *The Bad News Bears*. Between that show and *The Shining*, actually, I got recognized—or mistakenly recognized—quite a lot. I *did* look an awful lot like Danny Lloyd (mostly due to our matching bowl haircuts), the kid who had become famous for the creepy way he said "red rum" in Stanley Kubrick's classic thriller. People sometimes asked me for my autograph even after I explained that I was Corey Feldman. But I had movies in theaters now. Things were different.

A lot of people dream about getting famous. And I would be a liar if I said it didn't have its perks. But that day in the theater, I was just a sullen twelve-year-old, sneaking in and out of movies and hiding from my mom. I was contemplating the strangeness of that while waiting in line for some popcorn, when a young girl approached me. "Can I take a picture with you?"

She was just shy of fourteen, nearly two years older than me, and pretty. She told me her name was Laura.

"So, what are you doing here?" she asked.

"I ran away from home."

"Oh. I'm here with my family." She gestured to some adults milling about behind her. Later, I would find out that she was Laura Mc-Anally. Her father, John, was a horse trainer, famous for his work with John Henry, one of the most successful thoroughbreds in racing history. "So, you're a tough runaway kid, huh?"

I smiled. She had managed to see through my tough-guy exterior.

We exchanged numbers, and then I watched her disappear into the darkness, ambling slowly behind her parents, peeking over her shoulder at me the whole way. I watched as the heavy metal door to the screening room swung shut behind her. Laura would eventually become my second "girlfriend," though I think we only went out on one official date, to a horse race with her parents.

I stood in the lobby for a while, half hoping Laura would reappear, before finally scrounging up some change and dialing my grandmother's house from a nearby payphone.

"Where have you been?" Boobie answered. "We were so worried about you!"

"I ran away."

"Oh, Corey. We love you. Come on, now. It's time to come home."

It was dusk. The streetlights along the boulevard were blinking to life. It was quiet, and I was alone. Also, I had run out of money.

"Okay. Have Grandpa pick me up on the corner by the theater." I felt a gurgling in my stomach. I was hungry. "And maybe we can stop by Burger King on the way home."

CHAPTER 6

My hand was trembling as I opened the en-
velope and pulled out the pages. It was another Spielberg project, which
meant that—like so many of his films—it was completely and utterly
top-secret; you had to sign a nondisclosure agreement as soon as you
pulled out the script. I thumbed through quickly. Every single page, all
120-plus of them, had a giant red stamp on it, proof that what you had
in your hands was an authentic original copy. Scripts with black stamps,
sure signs they had been (illegally) run through a machine, were strictly

verboten. I let the pages flutter through my fingers until I was staring at the big bold letters printed across the cover. There were the words I had been waiting more than six whole months to read:

Amblin Entertainment and
Warner Bros. Pictures
present
The Goonies

The ceiling in my grandparents' kitchen was rather low; it couldn't have been much higher than seven feet, but I jumped up and down, higher and higher, high enough to brush the exposed beams with my fingertips. High enough to reach the roof.

"I just got the *Goonies!*" I yelled. "I'm a Goonie! I'm a Goonie! *Whahoooo!*"

My grandfather, halfway through his evening shot of whiskey and a cigarette, looked up from his black-and-white television.

"What's all this racket?" he grumbled. "And what the *hell* is a Goonie?"

Almost a year earlier, not long after finishing up on the set of *Gremlins,* I had gotten another call—again, at home—from the offices of Amblin Entertainment. Steven was requesting to meet with me the following Saturday. I had never heard of taking a meeting on the weekend, so I figured it had to be important. It had to be something unique.

When I got to Amblin, it was just Steven and Kathleen Kennedy, Steven's coproducer, waiting for me in the boardroom.

"I've got this idea for a kids' action-adventure movie," he said. "Think *Indiana Jones,* but with kids. We're thinking it would be you, and maybe Ke Huy Quan—Short Round from the *Temple of Doom*— and a bunch of other young actors. What do you think?"

"That sounds like a great idea!" I said. "I'd love to see the script."

Steven chuckled. "Yeah, well, we'd all love to see the script. But we're a ways off on that. I just wanted to get a general meeting to gauge your excitement level."

"Well, of course I'm excited," I said. In fact, I was ready to go right then. "Sign me up!"

I didn't hear another word about it for about six months.

Making movies is a slow, arduous process. Even after a project has cleared the two biggest hurdles—securing funding and getting a green light from the suits upstairs—there are still a million potential pitfalls in the preproduction process, from script approval and rewrites, to finding an appropriate-sized hole in everyone's schedule (when you're Steven Spielberg, you tend to get a little busy), to location scouting and procuring filming permits, to culling together the perfect cast and negotiating everyone's salaries. Some movies can get bogged down in this process, stalled for months or even years. Some films never wind up getting made at all. Deep down, somewhere in my subconscious, I knew that. But it was still tough to wait.

Eventually, I got another call from Amblin. This time, though, they were requesting that I come in and audition. That was odd. I had been under the impression that I was one of the *chosen ones*, one of the kids Steven wanted to, essentially, build the movie around. I consoled myself with the idea that, maybe, he just wanted to get all of us together, see what our chemistry might be like.

It wasn't until I arrived that I realized I was walking into a massive cattle call. There were easily a hundred kids there, milling around the lobby and the waiting rooms of Universal Studios, where the Amblin offices are housed. I quickly scanned the room, looking for familiar faces. Any kid who's ever been in this business can write you a term paper on those rooms; you might find yourself there for three, maybe four hours, waiting and waiting and waiting, depending on the size and scale of the project, and you never knew who might show up.

(Back in the late '70s I was more than a little starstruck when Danny Bonaduce breezed through the doors, igniting a firestorm of whispers and murmuring in the process.) I scanned the room until my eyes rested on an unknown actor, also reading for the part of Clark "Mouth" Devereaux, the wise-cracking smart alec of the group. It would be several years before I learned that this had been a young Corey Haim.

The audition—pretty much old hat by then—had gone smoothly. "You're great, you're great. You know I love you for this. We just have to go through the protocol," Steven said. And then another two months went by and I still didn't have an offer on the table.

Forget what I said about the movie-making process being slow and arduous. This was ridiculous. I thought I was a shoo-in, then I was made to come in and read for the part, and I still hadn't gotten a callback. What was going on here? I called my agent at the time, Iris Burton. She was a legend, and also something of a crazy lady. (She once told *People* magazine: "I hate to say it, but kids are pieces of meat. I've never had anything but filet mignon. I've never had a hamburger. My kids are the choice meat." Though she did have a point: at various points in their careers, she represented virtually all the Phoenix kids—River, Joaquin, Rain, and Summer—as well as Henry Thomas; Fred Savage; Kirk and Candace Cameron; Mary Kate and Ashley Olsen; and Kirsten Dunst, to name but a few.) She gave me a slew of assurances—"They definitely want you"; "You're definitely in"; "Everything is going to be fine"—and then two more months went by without another word.

Finally, I got another call from Iris. "There's been a little hiccup," she said. "Steven is no longer directing the film."

My heart sank. This is what I was afraid of. I could practically feel the job slipping through my fingers.

"The new director is open to you," she continued. "But you're going to have to go in and reprove yourself to him. And from what I hear"—she lowered her voice a bit, a sure sign that she was about to dish some insider dirt—"he's tough, kid. Don't be intimidated."

I wasn't intimidated. I was terrified.

The first thing I noticed about Richard Donner was his size. He's only actually about six foot two but to me he seemed like a damn giant, just a towering hulk of a guy with a big, booming voice—he was usually, *always,* yelling. The second thing I noticed were the toys. There were models and toys and trinkets on every available surface. I remember, vividly, the skeleton from *Tales from the Crypt* propped up on a chair in the corner (but that must have come later; the show, of which he was an executive producer, didn't premiere until 1989). And everywhere—stashed on tables and bookcases and sofas and on the desk in the center of his office—were mementos from *Superman,* the film that launched the career of Christopher Reeve.

"You directed *Superman?*" I blurted out. My whole life, up to that point, had been about dressing up in superhero costumes. The fact that Richard Donner had directed what was easily one of my favorite films made him, officially, one of the coolest men I'd ever met. Suddenly, he didn't seem all that scary. I immediately relaxed.

"I just have one simple question," he said, reclining a little in his chair. "Tell me why you should play Mouth."

I took a deep breath. I exhaled. And then I launched into a twenty-minute dissertation, just an absolute onslaught, an avalanche of words. He kept trying to interrupt, trying to get a word in, and I absolutely would not let him. I was like a little used-car salesman. "Whaddaya want? You want character voices? I can do character voices." Then I'd run through my whole carefully rehearsed repertoire, all those voices and sketches and improv routines I'd honed with my cousin Michael and a tiny cassette recorder. "You want a cool guy? I can be a cool guy." Then I'd pop the collar on my jacket, pretend to slick back my hair, and do my best impression of The Fonz, the coolest guy I knew. When I finished my sermon and finally shut my mouth, Donner leaned forward a little in his chair.

"Well, I'm not going to argue with you," he said. "You definitely seem like Mouth to me."

The Goonies was the first job that I really, really wanted. I wanted to perform. To deliver. I wanted to redeem myself from that earlier streak of being an obnoxious brat on the set. Plus, I knew that if Steven was producing it, it would be a great movie. And if Richard Donner, the director of *Superman,* was doing it, it would definitely be a great movie. Now I just had to wait around and see if they would give me a chance.

I will never forget the day that script arrived. I had been sitting in my grandparents' kitchen when Iris called to tell me I got the job, that they were messengering the pages right over. Not only did this mean I had done it, it meant at least three months of freedom, of shooting on location. It meant being around other kids my age. It meant three months of a normal life. Ironic, considering that I was signing on to make an epic adventure movie, for three months of intense work, for more professional pressure than I had ever before experienced. But all of that sounded like a field trip. And I needed one. Because only weeks before that initial call from Amblin, I had swallowed a bottle of aspirin. That was the first time I tried to kill myself.

It was all over a spelling test.

I was living with my grandparents, which was certainly better than living with my mother. My grandmother, after all, was a saint. And my grandfather, though still a terrifying figure, had never chased me around, naked, with a window stopper, had never actually beaten me bloody. In fact, the angriest I had ever seen him was a summer earlier, when he came to pick me up at Uncle Merv's after my cousin Michael and I had engaged in an epic water fight. "What the hell? Why are you all wet?" he said as soon as I climbed in the car. Then he reached his hand behind my neck and slammed my forehead against the dashboard. It hurt, sure, but I had definitely been through worse.

Even though I wasn't technically living with my mother, I was still being closely monitored, still being sent to school with those daily report cards. I knew that if I talked out of turn in class, if I laughed, if I so much as burped, or if I came home with a U or an F, I was going to see some trouble.

I no longer remember if my grades had dipped, or if I had brought home a string of poor progress reports, but the pressure to do better had been mounting, and it culminated with my performance on this test. Every night my grandfather was in my ear. "You've been screwing around too much lately," he bellowed. "*This* is why your mother's always so upset. If you want to keep treating her like this, I'm not going to let you stay in this house. So you had better take your schoolwork seriously. If you don't get this right, I'm going to beat the living hell out of you."

I didn't know what "beat the hell out of me" might look like, but I was picturing something biblical. I had to pass that test. The ridiculous part is that I was usually great at spelling. But I was so nervous, so completely consumed with dread, I couldn't focus. I could barely even sleep.

I had tried praying, down on my knees with my hands clasped firmly under my chin but, according to my grandfather, that was the wrong way to do it. "Jews don't get down on our knees!" he hollered. "That's for *goyim*. That's what the *schvartzes* do!"

I hated that. I was fairly certain that I could have my God any way I wanted Him. And then, finally, I just gave up. *This is ridiculous,* I thought. *I can't live in fear like this! I'm just going to kill myself.*

I went rooting around my grandmother's medicine cabinet. I found a giant bottle of Bayer aspirin, one of those vintage brown bottles with the 1950s-style label and—for some reason—decided to *chew* them, the entire bottle of pills. And then I went to bed.

Two hours later, I was sicker than I had ever been in my life. I woke up vomiting, violently, over and over again. I could tell that my breathing was slow and shallow. When my grandmother found me, pale and sweating and puking, she immediately started poking around on my stomach. Like any respectable Jewish grandmother, Boobie was something of a hypochondriac. All the Goldsteins are, really. Everyone in that family was usually suffering from some kind of mysterious ailment or trying to diagnose one another. The scary part is that they were usually right.

Boobie, however, was especially obsessed with the appendix. For some reason, when she was a younger woman, everyone around her started dropping like flies, all victims of a sudden, unexplained rupture. So whenever I had a stomachache she feared it was my appendix. If I fell and bumped by *head*, she still had to check my appendix. So there I was, lying on the floor of her bathroom, probably dying, while she frantically jabbed her fingers in my abdomen. "Does this hurt?" she yelled, as if my hearing had been afflicted. "How about this? What about now?"

I didn't want to tell her that I had swallowed a bottle of pills. But, by then, I had also decided that I definitely did not want to die. The thing about killing yourself is, in that moment of incomprehensible, utter despair, it seems like a good idea. Once you've done it, though, once you've actually made the decision to go through with it, you immediately start to wish that you hadn't. It is a natural instinct to save your own life. Lying on the floor of that bathroom, I started to panic. I didn't want to die. So, when she pushed on my stomach again and asked me if it hurt, this time I said yes.

"It does?"

I nodded.

"Well, if it's right here, then it's your appendix. Is this worse?" She pushed into my stomach again.

"Yes, Boobie. It's worse," I groaned. "It's definitely my appendix." I would gladly have told her that I was suffering from an acute case of smallpox if that's what she needed to hear. I just wanted to get to a damn emergency room.

But I didn't tell anyone at the hospital what I had done, either. I was too ashamed. I figured all the doctors and nurses fluttering around me were brilliant, surely they would be able to figure out what was wrong. I remember a doctor coming in and asking where it hurt. I just repeated everything I had already told my grandmother.

"Do you *feel* like it's your appendix?" he asked.

"Oh, yeah, it's my appendix all right."

"Well then," he said, "I guess we better get that taken out."

So, that's exactly what they did. I had my appendix removed, unnecessarily, by the good doctors at Tarzana Medical Center. But my five-day stay in the hospital proved to be a relaxing kind of vacation—three meals a day, unlimited ice cream, and all the movies I could watch on my very own television.

I knew that *The Goonies* would change my life. I had envisioned it. I believe, very heartily, in the power of positive thinking. Call it The Secret if you want, or the law of attraction, but I believed in putting good things out into the universe and getting good things back, despite what the bulk of my life had looked like up until that point. Maybe that's how I survived it all.

Plus, I had read the script. Whenever you read something—a novel, a play—you naturally start to envision the characters in your head, you see them in your minds' eye. When I read movie scripts, I do that, too, except I don't just envision the characters, I mentally cast all the roles. (I've actually been right on quite a few occasions—the very actors I had envisioned wound up playing those same parts.) But when I read *The Goonies* script, the entire world opened up to me. I could picture us riding our bikes along the foggy coastline of Oregon. I imagined us traversing the dank and crumbling caves underneath the abandoned restaurant where the Fratellis were hiding out. I could *see* One-Eyed Willie's pirate ship. I knew, even before that first day of filming, that this would be something special. And *The Goonies* couldn't have come at a more appropriate time; in real life I felt like a reject; now I was making a movie about a group of awkward kids who didn't fit in.

I immediately fell in love with the coastal town of Astoria, Oregon, an antithesis of sorts to the hustle and bustle of L.A. Astoria is perennially muggy and rainy and overcast, and very much a "fish town" (which is what, in those days, I called it). Fishing communities have their own distinct rhythm; they tend to be insular and isolated, outsiders are often met with wariness and suspicion. Once you're "in," however, these are some of the warmest, most generous people on the planet.

Getting "in" in Astoria can be attributed to the brilliance of the *Goonies* production team, who had intuited that an uninvited Hollywood film crew, descending on a tiny town for four long weeks (by the time we were done, it ended up being closer to nine), might not be something about which the locals were excited. So, they printed buttons and T-shirts and ball caps with the words "I'm a Goonie" or "I [heart] Goonies" and stocked them in the town gift shops, a sort of subliminal way of ingratiating ourselves, of subtly rooting ourselves in their culture. And in a lot of ways, that town, to all of us, became like home. For nearly three months, we walked their streets, watched movies in their theater, ate in their restaurants, and shopped in their stores. We rode our bikes down Main Street, past the pizza parlor where we sometimes ate as a cast (where John Matuszak, who played Sloth, once got so drunk that he peed in the bathroom sink), or played games in and around the Walsh house, which was an actual home in Astoria, as opposed to a façade or a set. In fact, the only place we *weren't* welcome was inside Richard Donner's trailer.

On a kid-centered movie like *The Goonies*, it's common for the director to become your personal hero, a sort of father figure. Which is exactly how we had all grown to feel about Dick. He never had children; I've often felt as though the kids he worked with became like kids of his own. And despite his penchant for yelling, he was really just a big softie. So it was natural that we all wanted to spend time with him. But we were not allowed—under any circumstances—to bother him when he was in that trailer. It was a monstrous box of a thing with heavily tinted windows; he usually kept it parked at the bottom of a giant hill just below the Walsh home. (There's a scene in the beginning of the movie, a panoramic shot of Mikey staring out at the Goon Docks from the rickety front porch. If you pay attention, you can see Dick's Winnebago, tucked behind the bushes in the corner of your screen.) It's precisely because we weren't allowed in Dick's Winnebago that it became a wonderful mystery. What did they do in there? What was so private and secret that we couldn't be a part of? But we were forbidden even from hanging around outside. We were to leave the trailer alone. Whenever Dick was in the trailer, we were supposed to disappear. So we did.

Part of the magic of *The Goonies*, for me, was spending so much time among kids my own age. (Though, at sixteen, Josh Brolin was a few years older than the rest of the cast; most of his time off-screen was spent with Kerri Green, and most of Kerri Green's downtime was spent with Josh Brolin. And Martha Plimpton, the quintessential New York actress—both a graduate of the Professional Children's School in Manhattan and the daughter of two well-known stars—was full of East Coast bravado; we famously didn't get along, and she spent a lot of time in her own world, with her mother. So that left me, Sean Astin, Jeff Cohen, and Ke Huy Quan, a sort of rag-tag Four Musketeers.)

One thing about Sean Astin, which has never changed, he's a

mile-a-minute kind of guy. He's laser-focused, and once he gets an idea in his head, it's nearly impossible to convince him otherwise. He'd be motor-mouthing on set about something—*Guys! You have to listen to me! This is the way it's supposed to be! Trustme! Doitlikethis!*—and I would look at him and say, "You *definitely* should have been Mouth." The kid's a closer. If the acting thing hadn't worked out, he would have made an excellent defense attorney. I say that with great respect; out of the entire cast, we're the only ones who have remained great friends. As I write this, we're actually at work on a new project. I believe it's the first time that any two *Goonies* alums have collaborated in more than twenty-five years.

Meanwhile, Jeff Cohen, otherwise known as Chunk, quickly became known for his hat collection. Every day he wore a different outrageous hat to set. He had one with a giant moose head, another with a giant pair of hands poking out of the top; when you pulled the strings, the hands would clap. It was a gimmick a day with that kid. But I liked him, which made the fact that my job was to *bully* him, to poke fun at his weight, to goad him into the "truffle shuffle," one of the most awkward and uncomfortable parts of filming.

In many ways, Mouth was just the first in a series of roles in which I played, well, a bit of an asshole. Here's this loudmouth, smart alec, joke-cracking, wise-ass kid; he certainly wasn't what you would call *nice*. I followed that up by playing a bitter, abused boy in *Stand by Me*. In *The Lost Boys*, I became a sort of rambunctious Rambo, and in *License to Drive* I am, again, the wise-cracking loudmouth. It would be years before I realized that people were starting to perceive *me* that way, like so many of the characters I once played.

CHAPTER 7

What a lot of people don't realize about
The Goonies is that Richard Donner picked Steven Spielberg as his
second unit director shortly after filming began in Oregon in the fall
of 1984. A second unit director is typically responsible for shooting
"pickups" (panoramic views, background shots, or "establishing" shots
of the film's setting and location), as well as special effects and action
sequences, which might be filmed on a closed soundstage, rather than
on location, or with stuntmen instead of the principal cast. But when

you're making a movie as sweeping and epic as *The Goonies*—with 1984 technology, no less—second unit directing becomes a fairly massive job. That probably wasn't such a bad thing, because even after wrapping in Oregon (roughly six weeks or so behind schedule), we still had a *ton* of work to do.

We reconvened at Warner Brothers in Burbank to shoot the remainder of the film—the underground sequences, the pirate ship reveal, and the battle with the evil Fratellis—on a closed soundstage; four of them, actually. Two of those four, stages 15 and 16, are the biggest soundstages on the entire Warner Brothers lot. Generally speaking, Steven would utilize two of the four, working on stunts and inserts and pickups, while Dick was running the others. This meant they were directing concurrently; Dick might be shooting with me on stage 16 at the exact time that Steven was working with my stunt double over on 12. So there were often three or four different versions of Mouth (and all the other principle characters) running around on set—the real me; the stunt version of me, same height, same build, same clothes; and the stand-in version of me. It was all very *Invasion of the Body Snatchers.*

It wasn't until we started shooting in Los Angeles that the sheer size of this film began to sink in. For one thing, what was supposed to have been a three-month shooting schedule had ballooned to nearly six months. For another, everybody who was anybody was stopping by to check out the set—that's when you know you're involved in a giant project. Harrison Ford, fresh off the massive success of *Indiana Jones*, was one of the first. We lead him through the caves under the Fratellis' restaurant, over the log bridge and past the waterfall, and I just kept thinking, this is absolutely unreal. We were taking Indiana Jones—*Indiana Jones!*—on a tour of what was, essentially, a kid-friendly version of his blockbuster film. After that came a string of random celebrity appearances. Dan Aykroyd stopped by and so did

Cyndi Lauper; she wound up performing "The Goonies 'R' Good Enough," the title song on the *Goonies* soundtrack.

The Goonies was filmed at a time when music videos were not only a new and exciting medium for the music industry, but also an excellent new way to market a movie. (Pair some young, good-looking actors with a pop star or two, shoot a video and—*boom!*—smash success.) That was virtually unheard of before MTV debuted in the summer of 1981; very few television programs dedicated to music even existed. Casey Kasem's *America's Top 10*, a spin-off of his popular radio show *American Top 40*, comes to mind. So does *Solid Gold*. Once MTV launched, however, there was suddenly an entire channel dedicated completely and solely to music. Yet, in the early days of the network, there weren't nearly enough music videos in existence to fill up twenty-four-hours of airtime, so they pretty much played the same songs over and over and over—like "Video Killed the Radio Star," Billy Idol's "White Wedding," and "Thriller" by Michael Jackson.

Of course, I knew who Michael Jackson was even before the launch of MTV. *Sort of.* I had heard "Rock with You" and "Don't Stop 'Til You Get Enough," though at the time I hadn't realized they were by the same person. Actually, I hadn't even realized they were by a *man*. The Michael Jackson of the late 1970s, I didn't really get. But the Michael Jackson I watched—mouth agape, standing stock-still in the middle of my grandparents' living room—in May 1983, *that* was a guy I wanted to know more about.

Motown 25: Yesterday, Today, and Forever, the concert at which Jackson debuted his now legendary dance moves, is one of those iconic moments in history, like the moon landing or the day President Kennedy was shot; everyone knows exactly where they were when it happened. It is etched in my memory, indelibly printed on the film reel of my mind. That jheri curl! The glittery glove! The moonwalk! I had never seen anything like it. Even my grandfather, admittedly something of a racist (throughout my entire childhood, he referred to black people as *schvartzes*), was impressed. And that performance marked the birth of an infatuation for me just as it did for so many others. I immediately went out and bought the album; it was the first LP I purchased with my own money. Not long after that came the debut of "Thriller," the greatest music video of all time. Fourteen minutes of pure magic directed by none other than the great John Landis.

The "Thriller" campaign, of course, was monstrous, and a then-burgeoning MTV was playing it round the clock. So every hour—on the hour—I would drop what I was doing and jump in front of the television. I studied that video until I had learned every beat, every breath, every bit of dialogue and, of course, every single second of that dance.

My mother had enrolled me in a dance class, briefly, back when I was seven. It was a tap class, a lot of "shuffle, heel" and "kick, ball, change." I spent the majority of the time staring at the wall or looking at my feet. When I emerged, my mother took one look at me and shook her head. "God, you must be the most uncoordinated kid in the world," she said. It was just like being made to sing "Raindrops Keep Fallin' on My Head" during all those auditions—I couldn't carry a tune. Clearly, I wasn't much of a dancer, either.

But there was something about watching Michael, the way he moved, so smooth, so fluid, as if sliding across the ice; I guess I sort of got the fever. Because suddenly, I could dance. Just like Michael Jackson. Not that I was prepared to show anybody (not yet at least). But locked in my room, practicing the moonwalk in front of the mirror, I felt good about myself. I had this newfound self-confidence. That's part of the magic of Michael. Somehow, just by striking a pose, just hearing that opening drumbeat of "Billie Jean," he made you feel better about yourself.

By the time I was finishing up *Gremlins,* in the winter of 1984, my love of Michael Jackson had turned into a full-blown obsession.

Someone, I no longer remember who, bought me one of those glittery Michael Jackson gloves, a cheap little thing, a crappy little glove dipped in glue and covered in glitter. In the mid-eighties, they were *everywhere*, but I adored it. I used mine as a sort of change purse, twisting the top and sticking it through my belt, like an extra-sparkly version of a fanny pack. I bought all the fan magazines, spent hours staring at pictures of him performing, and decided—improbably— that we were destined to meet. I can't really explain that. But I was eleven, and more than a little incorrigible.

One day I was working with Joe Dante, wrapping up a few days of ADR (also known as "automated dialogue replacement," the process by which actors re-record bits of dialogue in order to improve sound quality, clarity, or, sometimes, to make minor alterations to the script). During every break in the recording session, I went on and on about Michael Jackson. I couldn't shut up about him. Until Joe, exasperated, turned to me and said, "You know he came to the set one day?"

I stopped dead in my tracks. "What?"

"Yeah, yeah, he came and visited us."

"He *did*?"

"Yeah, well, you know, he's a friend of Steven's, so he came down to check out the set. Spent the whole day with us. He came to my house, actually. Steven brought him over."

"Did you get to *see him DANCE*?" I asked.

"Yeah, yeah, he moonwalked for us."

I imagine Joe told me all this to, once and for all, shut me up. It had the opposite effect.

By the time I began work on *The Goonies*, about a year later, it was widely known that Steven Spielberg and Michael Jackson really were friends. (Jackson even performed the theme song for *E.T.*, called "Someone in the Dark.") I started to put two and two together: if Michael Jackson had visited the *Gremlins* set, why wouldn't he come to see the *Goonies*? All I had to do was ask Steven. So I did. Every day. About 150 bagillion times. I pestered him for the entire three months we spent in Oregon, and every day we continued to shoot in L.A. I couldn't help it. I was going to meet Michael Jackson if it killed me.

In the meantime, I was hard at work on the set. One day in particular, I was headed back from Richard Donner's office toward the end of our one-hour lunch break. Dick's office was tucked all the way in the back of the lot, past the commissary, at the end of Avenue D. We usually rode from soundstage to soundstage on our bikes, but on that day I was walking.

As I passed the commissary, I noticed a man—slight build, with a full beard and thick-rimmed glasses—sitting outside on a bench. He seemed at once familiar and yet, somehow, sort of strange. Creepy, almost. I couldn't quite put my finger on it. And then suddenly, he waved his hand in my direction. I turned and doubled back.

"I'm Paul," he said when I approached him. "What's your name?"

"I'm Corey."

"Nice to meet you, Corey. Listen, I'm here working on a movie and I think you've got a really great look. Have I seen you in something? You're an actor, right?"

"Yes," I answered tentatively.

"How long have you been acting?"

"I guess about ten years now."

He seemed impressed. "Well, as I said, I'm doing this movie, and I think there may be a part for you in it. Basically, the main character's bike gets stolen by this kid. I think you might be perfect for that role, playing the kid who steals the bike." He paused to adjust the glasses riding down the bridge of his nose. "Have you heard of Pee-wee Herman?"

Had I heard of Pee-wee Herman? Of course I had heard of Pee-wee Herman! "I love Pee-wee Herman!" I told him.

"Oh, well, great. That's great. Actually . . . it's me."

I raised an eyebrow. This guy looked nothing like Pee-wee Herman, which is exactly what I told him.

He laughed. "It's me. I just shave the beard and put on some makeup and the suit." I hadn't realized that the man sitting in front of me was actually Paul Reubens.

We chatted for a while, about *The Pee-wee Herman Show* and his upcoming film, which would be shooting directly across the lot from stage 16, where the *Goonies* pirate ship was being built. Tim Burton, at the time a virtual unknown, would be directing. "So, are you going to be available, you think? What are you working on?" he asked me.

"I'm doing *The Goonies*."

"*The Goonies* . . . I've heard of that. What is that?"

"It's the new Steven Spielberg movie."

"Oh, I'm so sorry." He suddenly seemed flustered. "I didn't realize. I'm so sorry. I really didn't mean to insult you."

"Insult me? What are you talking about?" I asked, genuinely confused.

"*The Goonies* is the biggest movie Warner Brothers has going, it's way bigger than my movie. We're practically an independent. I'm sure you wouldn't want to waste your time."

I was stunned. Pee-wee Herman didn't want *me* to waste *my* time. This was truly incredible.

As it turned out, I couldn't do the film; I was way too busy with *The Goonies*. But I did go over and visit his set on several occasions, which I loved; it was like one big life-sized cartoon. *Pee-wee's Big Adventure* went on to become a beloved cult classic, paving the way for his Emmy-winning kids show. Of course, at the time, nobody knew—could have known—that it would be that big. But I did. Pee-wee Herman, as silly as it sounds, felt like my own private discovery. I was only twelve, but I knew Pee-wee Herman was going to be huge.

Not long after my run-in with Paul Reubens, I was in the school trailer, working away with the other *Goonies* cast members, when we were interrupted by a sharp rap on the door. We had a delivery, a giant cardboard box addressed to all the kids in the cast. Inside were seven satin jackets, emblazoned with the words "The Jacksons Victory Tour." I realized, right then, that my dreams were about to come true.

The Victory Tour was, not surprisingly, the biggest thing happening in music. I had been hounding Steven for tickets, as well as calling in to KIIS-FM hoping to win one of their daily giveaways, but a box of tour jackets from Michael Jackson was beyond even my wildest dreams. The tickets came soon after that, along with an invitation to meet Michael after the show. I believe there were sixteen passes in total; enough for the principle cast and one of each cast members' parents, our two on-set tutors, and Mark Marshall, Steven's assistant at the time. Mark was used to wrangling child actors, so it seemed only natural that he would lead us all on the trek to Dodger Stadium. It would be one of the last times all six Jackson brothers performed together; it was December 1984, the final stop of the six-month tour.

At that point, the only concert I had ever been to was to see Styx at the Forum, around the time "Mr. Roboto" started climbing the charts. The Victory Tour was something else entirely. You could feel the energy of the crowd pulse through you in waves—even from our seats all the way at the back of the stadium. We were in the nosebleed section, so high up that the Jacksons looked like ants on the stage. But it didn't matter. I had dreamed of this moment. Then, as I sat there in a sea of more than fifty thousand fans, waiting anxiously for the lights to go down, I felt a tap on my shoulder. I turned around. Two rows back was Ricky Schroder.

At the time—just a few years after his star-making turn in Franco

Zeffirelli's 1979 remake of *The Champ*—Ricky Schroder was, arguably, the biggest kid actor in the business. I had actually been up for the role of TJ, the son of ex-champion boxer Billy Flynn (played by Jon Voight), and had spent a ton of time preparing. My mother desperately wanted that role for me, but I wound up losing out. For months I wanted to know, who's the kid that got that part? When the film premiered (and Ricky Schroder won a Golden Globe, at age ten, for New Star of the Year in a Motion Picture, an award that is no longer given out), I sat in the theater thinking, man, this kid is amazing. What a brilliant performance. The scene at the end? All that crying? I was totally impressed.

As an actor, crying on cue was easily my biggest fear. I felt as though I had managed to fool everyone around me, to make them think that I was good at my job—at least up until that point. But after watching that performance, I knew there was no way I could have done anything so intense and meaningful as *The Champ*. In fact, I couldn't believe that *any* kid my age had managed to pull that off. I figured he was probably one of those kids who went to acting class every day, probably a graduate of Stella Adler—hell, he was probably *method*—but I still had oodles of respect for him. So when I turned around in my seat at the back of Dodger Stadium, I had to laugh. At least we had better seats than Ricky Schroder.

The rest of the concert is mostly a blur to me now; what I remember most was how desperately I wanted it to be over. That's when it would happen—that's when I would meet Michael. But as the lights came on and the stadium started to empty out, there was a sudden change of plans: Michael would go back to his hotel. It was suggested that we would meet him there. As we filed back on the bus, however, word came that we were going home. This was not the plan. We were supposed to go to the show, then Michael and I would meet, and then we would become friends. What in the hell had happened?

Back at Warner Brothers on Monday morning, I wasted no time finding out. Who knew what Michael would be up to next? Maybe he would go off to tour another part of the world. Maybe he would go into seclusion to work on his next album. I was not going to let this chance slip through my fingers, so as soon as I got to set, I ran right up to Steven Spielberg.

"What happened? We didn't get to meet Michael!"

"Yeah, I know. Sorry about that."

"What? Why are *you* sorry?"

"Well, I didn't think it was appropriate. Michael wanted to invite everyone back to his hotel room, but I told him no."

I stared at him.

"I thought it would be a little overwhelming," Steven continued. "All sixteen of you, stuffed into his hotel. He's just finished a pretty major tour, you know. He's probably pretty tired."

I scoffed. Michael Jackson—I ridiculously assumed—did not get tired.

"Corey?" Steven said, obviously sensing my frustration. "I do have some good news." He waited a moment, until I had picked my head up and looked him in the eye. "He's going to come to set."

"When?"

"Not sure yet. We're looking at a day two weeks from now, but it's not a hundred percent. Check back with me next week."

I did check back with him the following week, and every day after that. But every time I asked, something unexpected had "come up" or Michael's schedule had changed. I was afraid I had been duped, that maybe the meeting would never happen. I was constantly in a state of agitation, the excitement and anticipation rumbling below the surface, but I was afraid to get my hopes up. I had been disappointed so many times before.

———

Like most days on set, I had been running back and forth between Dick's and Steven's soundstages. Over on 12, Steven was working on second-unit shots in the caves under the Fratelli's restaurant, while Dick was busy preparing for the reveal of One-Eyed Willie's pirate ship back on stage 16, a massive (and expensive) undertaking.

The pirate ship was an actual full-scale working set. There was the main deck, with the plank and the sails, and below, an empty hall filled with canons and skeletons as well as the captain's quarters, where the remains of One-Eyed Willie sat amid mountains of treasure. We weren't supposed to see the ship, however, until that exact moment in the film—after we slide down the water chutes and land in the middle of a lagoon. In order to ensure the most authentic reactions from a cast full of kids, the production designers built an entire lagoon right inside stage 16, erected huge walls around it, and strung a sort of clothing line along the top, up by the rafters, from which they hung a giant black nylon curtain. Outside the curtain was stationed a security guard, who granted access to set only after checking your very official photo ID.

Later they would fill the lagoon with water, adding in some sort of chemical dye to turn it royal blue. I don't know what the hell was in that stuff; you didn't even have to be *in* the water, just spending a day on the set was enough to turn your boogers blue. Same goes for the pirate treasure. All of those glittering jewels and coins were dusted with some sort of fake gold plating; but the plating would sweat and then turn black. After a full day shooting on that stage, you'd have black stuff coming out your nose. Basically, we wound up with different colored snot depending on where we'd spent the day shooting. I don't know where they found that dye, but it was probably not the healthiest stuff.

I was just finishing up another mandated twenty minutes in the school trailer when a production assistant showed up, summoning me to Steven's set. We were working on the scene where the Goonies start yanking on the town water pipes until I yell out, "Reverse pressure!" Then, the blast from an exploding water main blows open a secret passageway, leading us to the remains of Chester Copperpot. In terms of plot, this marks the true beginning of our journey; it's the halfway point between the "real world" and total fantasy. In particular, Steven was ready to work on the delivery of my line; the camera would slowly pan toward my face, then speed up, ending on a tight close-up. This is a signature Spielberg move; he's utilized it in most of his movies.

Steven took his seat behind the camera, which was rigged to a dolly track, and I took my place on top of an apple box so I could pretend that I was actually hanging from the elevated pipes. We did a few takes—I swung from the pipes, the camera zoomed in on my face, I yelled my line, "Reeevvveerrseee preeessssuuuuree!"—but Steven just wasn't getting the reaction from me that he wanted. Finally, he brought production to a grinding halt.

"Listen," he said, once he'd left the comfort of his chair and come to speak to me privately, "I need a certain look from you, a certain expression on your face. So here's what we're gonna do. I have something to tell you. And as soon as I tell you, I'm going to say 'action,' and we're going to zoom in tight on your face."

He returned to his spot behind the camera. "You ready?"

"I'm ready," I said.

"Okay. Today's the day, Corey. Michael Jackson is coming to set." As promised, he immediately followed this up with "Action!" And it worked—that's the very take they ended up using.

Waiting for Michael to arrive was agony. I have no idea what I was supposed to have been studying in school that day; I certainly couldn't concentrate. Mostly I just prayed that his schedule wouldn't change again, that he wouldn't back out at the last minute.

Whenever I had a break, I would run across the lot to Steven's set, because it seemed like the most likely place for Michael to show up. I watched as Sean, Ke, Jeff, and Steven worked on a scene in one of the caves, positioned all the way at the back of stage 15. I was standing near the mouth of the cave, letting my imagination wander, when I suddenly felt a chill. My skin broke out in goose bumps. It was him. I could *feel* it. I turned around slowly and there, all the way at the other end of the stage, was Michael Jackson, walking directly toward me with his longtime head of security, Bill Bray.

It was like he had stepped right out of a music video—he had the black military jacket with the giant gold buttons, the glittery belt buckle, the penny loafers, and the exposed white socks. (Later, I would realize that I had also noticed his smell. Michael always doused himself in cologne; in those days it was Giorgio Beverly Hills. I hounded my grandmother until she took me to a fragrance store and I was able to take home a free sample.) I took off at a full sprint from my spot outside the cave—halfway there I managed to get my composure; I didn't want his bodyguard to think I was about to bum rush him— until I was standing right at his feet. That's when I realized I had no idea what to say. I was standing there, right under his nose, right in front of his face, and then I stuttered. "Um . . . excuse me? Are you Michael Jackson?"

He looked down at me from behind those giant Ray Ban aviators, tinted so dark you couldn't see his eyeballs at all, and said, very quietly, in that famous falsetto, "Yeah, who are you?"

"I'm Corey Feldman," I said. "I'm a Goonie."

"Oh, hi, Corey. How ya doing?"

I felt a smile creep across my face, squeaked out another "Hi," and then sort of scampered off so I could watch him more comfortably from afar. I had made the introduction, we had finally, officially, met, but I was too nervous to say much else. I hovered close, and watched as Michael said hello to Steven, as they gave each other a hug, as a production assistant sidled over and offered to get him something to drink.

"Apple juice," he said. "I'd love some Apple juice, please."

Huh. He didn't ask for a Coke, or a water, or anything I would have considered a remotely adult sort of beverage. That's interesting, I thought. He seemed—I don't know—relatable.

All that afternoon, I was back and forth between stages, in and out of the school trailer. I couldn't just follow Michael around; I still had responsibilities on set. Finally, I was summoned back to Steven's stage, this time to film the scene where we match the skull key to a set of "triple stones" on the wall of the cave.

Someone had set up a director's chair for Michael. After we finished blocking the scene, Steven went over and sat down next to him. As I stood in the cave, idly chatting with Sean and Jeff, I noticed that Steven and Michael were laughing, joking, and whispering to each other. Then, Michael was pointing directly at me. Suddenly, Steven was ushering me over.

"Did you have a different haircut in *Gremlins*?" he asked.

"Yeah?"

Steven turned to Michael. "Well, there you go. You were right."

"I knew it!" Michael laughed. And then something incredible happened—Michael turned and spoke to me. "Corey, you were so great in that movie."

"You saw it?"

"Oh, yeah. My brothers and I used to get out early from rehearsals for the Victory Tour so we could watch it over and over. We used to sneak in and sit in the back of the theater. That was my favorite movie that whole summer."

"Are you serious?"

"Yeah! You were so good. I think you're one of the best kid actors in the world. I think you're the next Marlon Brando."

The greatest entertainer in the world had just told me he thought I was good. I almost fainted.

Moments later I found myself posing for a picture—someone had arranged for the cast to take a group shot with Michael—and then I reluctantly went back to the school trailer. When I later returned to the set, he was gone.

CHAPTER 8

The phone was ringing.

I had already brushed my teeth, put on my pajamas, and slid between the sheets on my bed when I heard it. I wondered if it could be him. Then I laughed. That was ridiculous. I lay down, tucked my arm behind my head, beneath the pillow, and closed my eyes. Then Boobie opened the door to my bedroom, throwing a wedge of light across the carpet. "Corey?" she whispered. "Michael Jackson is on the phone for you."

I sat up. *Oh my god, it was happening.* I threw off my blankets and scrambled out of bed, down the hallway, past the kitchen, where my grandfather was finishing his cigarette, smoking it down to the filter. He flashed me a look. I knew this look. This look said, "You've got five minutes, kid." I knew, too, that I had already broken the rules, stayed up way past my bedtime waiting for the phone to ring. I wouldn't be able to get away with that forever, but there was no way this was going to be a five-minute phone call.

I never got to say good-bye that day, now more than one month earlier, when Michael visited the *Goonies* set. I felt like I didn't have closure. Everyone around me, including Steven, was placating me, saying things like, "Don't worry, he'll be back," or "I'm sure you'll have another chance." But I couldn't understand why everyone was so cavalier. Did nobody realize this was, for most people, a once-in-a-lifetime opportunity? It's not like every day you walk down the street and bump into Michael Jackson. How, in their estimation, was this going to turn out fine? How was I supposed to "not worry?" It was terrible advice to give to a twelve-year-old.

I desperately wanted to see him again but, on some level, I had assumed that that was it. I *had* been given the chance to meet him, after all, to take a picture with him, to exchange a few words, to say hello. I did fulfill that goal. So I did the only thing there was to do. I went on with my life. We had recently transitioned from a five- to a six-day workweek. It was a hectic schedule for a kid. I was able to lose myself in the work.

One day I was finishing up lunch in the Warner Brothers commissary, which is divided into two distinct sections: the main, public room, where the food is served cafeteria-style, and the VIP dining room, which has reserved seating, a waitstaff, and a smartly dressed maître d'. Of course, we never ate on that side. That side was for the suits.

When I finished, I began making my way back to stage 16.

Suddenly, I noticed a huge swirl of people milling around outside. Someone was standing, alone, in the middle. As I walked closer, I could just see the corner—the sleeve—of a white leather jacket, the coils of someone's curly black hair. This, I immediately realized, was not just any hair, however. This was *Jackson hair*. That's when I realized the person I was staring at was actually Michael's big sister. I ran up alongside Mark Marshall, also making his way back from lunch.

"Is that La Toya?" I asked.

"Yeah. Didn't I mention they were coming by today?"

"*They?*"

"She's here with Michael."

"He came back? What for?"

He looked down at me, a sly smile tugging at the corner of his lip. "Why, to see you, of course." (This is just one example of the epic kindness of Mark Marshall; he was not above telling little white lies if it meant making a young kid's day.)

"Nobody told me they were coming!" I called out, already running off, pushing my way through throngs of people until I had made my way to the middle. There was La Toya, and Michael, and Steven. Steven, with a wave of his hand, said, "Come on. Let's show you guys some stuff."

We had been working on the scene in the organ chamber, when Andy (Kerri Green) must play a series of chords to unlock a secret door. If she played a chord incorrectly, however, the floor beneath us would crumble, leaving us dangling in the air, holding on for dear life and, perhaps, plummeting to an untimely end. When you looked at the set from the outside it resembled a sort of funnel; wooden boards formed the cone, and the entire structure stood high above the ground.

Shooting this scene became the height of our do-your-own-stunts experience. Steven had been positioned below us, his camera angled straight up, while we stood on a ledge above him, tethered to the organ by heavy cables and a harness fastened underneath our clothes.

When the floor fell out, we were supposed to cling to the walls of the cave and try not to fall into the abyss. This was actually sort of terrifying. If you looked down, you could see Steven, his crew, and a sea of expensive lighting equipment. Not exactly a soft landing if one of those cables were to snap.

This was all terribly fascinating to Michael, who started asking if he could walk up the exterior stairs and stand inside the moveable set. The special effects team sort of stared at each other—this was not exactly something the production was insured for. What would happen if Michael Jackson fell and seriously injured himself? The kids, however, immediately started begging, and eventually Steven decided it would be fine.

I positioned myself right next to Michael, told him I'd help him navigate through safely, that he just had to "follow me." Once I saw that it was working, that he was comfortable chatting, I realized now was the time. I summoned every bit of strength in my preteen body, took a breath, and said, "You know, I was really sad last time you left. I thought I would never see you again."

"You should have known I was going to come back," he said. "Of course I would come back and visit you guys."

"Well, right . . . but . . ." I thought of all those pictures I had seen of Michael with kids like Emmanuel Lewis. I wanted to be one of those kids. "I don't know why," I said, "but I feel like we're supposed to be friends. I know you're friends with kids . . . Do you think that, if I gave you my phone number, maybe you could call me sometime?"

"Sure."

Well, that was easy. "Really?" I asked, making sure I'd heard him right.

"Sure, yeah. No problem."

I was emboldened. "So, if I give you my number, you *promise* you'll call me?"

"I promise."

"When?" I asked.

"I'll call you tonight."

By the time I got back to my grandparents' house, I was wired, bouncing around the house, drunk with anticipation. But when I told my grandmother that Michael Jackson was going to call me, she gave me a quizzical look.

"Don't you think he has better things to do with his time?"

She had a point. Still, I sat by that phone for hours. I refused to come to the dinner table. I refused to move out of the living room. I was going to wait all night for that phone to ring, or at least until 11:00 P.M., when my grandparents finally forced me to go to bed. As I trudged down the hallway to my room, my grandmother laid her hand on my shoulder. "He's a very busy man, Corey. You can't expect him to just drop everything, you know."

I did know. Which is why, when he finally called, I nearly passed out.

We talked for two-and-a-half hours, until a little after one in the morning. What I remember most is that it was like talking to another kid. He did speak a little about Paul McCartney, and though I loved "Say, Say, Say," that was really the extent of my Beatles knowledge. Then he told me that McCartney had written another song for him, back in the late 1970s.

"It's called 'Girlfriend,'" he said. "Do you know it?"

"Uh, I'm not sure." I didn't know it, but I wasn't about to tell him that. "How does it go?"

Then he sang the hook for me. My God, I thought, Michael Jackson is singing to me on the phone.

When the conversation ended, around the time I could no longer hold my eyes open, I asked him if we would stay friends.

"Of course we're going to stay friends," he said.

"Are you sure?"

"Yes."

"How do you know?"

"Because I have your phone number now. I just added you to my little black book."

That's something that sticks out in my mind, too.

Befriending an already legendary entertainer was improbable enough. Staying in contact with him was a whole other matter. These were the days before cell phones and the Internet, after all, and Michael was a person who traveled the world, lived in a sort of self-imposed (if also necessary) bubble, and was something of a paranoid. He had his phone number changed every few months.

The first time I figured this out was when I called him and got an automated recording telling me the number I had dialed had been disconnected. *That's it!* I thought. *We're never going to talk again!* Eventually he explained this was just a matter of course.

"No, silly. I'm not changing my number because of *you*," he said. But I soon learned that when Michael changed his number, he changed *all of his numbers.*

At the time he was living at Hayvenhurst, the Jackson family compound in Encino, which by then had been outfitted with a recording studio, production facilities, and multiple offices, including space for his personal assistant. All of these "departments" had their own private telephone lines, but the numbers themselves were sequential. So, if Michael's private number was, say, 788-8234, it stood to reason that the other numbers—to the main house, to the recording studio, to his production offices, and to the security gate—would be 788-8235; 8236; 8237; and so on. If I hadn't yet been given his new private line, I could usually figure it out. I'd just punch the numbers on the keypad—each time someone would answer "MJJ Productions" or sometimes just "MJJ"—until I found the one that rang in his bedroom.

The thing about Michael is that, once you were *in,* he was just like anyone else. He didn't have his personal assistant answer his private line. He didn't have some sort of elaborate screening process. What he had was a great sense of humor.

Michael had many voices. One of his favorites was an imitation of what sounded like an uptight, conservative Caucasian; not unlike the way comedian Dave Chappelle sounds when, during some of stand-up routines, he pretends to be white. Sometimes Michael answered the phone that way. If you didn't know this game and you asked to speak to Michael, he might say, "There's no Michael Jackson here. I don't know what you're talking about, mister." But for those on the inside, you'd recognize this voice and introduce yourself accordingly. Then he would immediately switch back into that familiar, high-pitched falsetto. "Oh, hi, Corey," he'd croon. "How are you?" I figured it was a clever way to avoid talking to people he didn't want to.

Sometimes he would answer the phone but he wouldn't say anything at all. You could hear the receiver pick up, and you'd call out, "Hello? Hello, Michael? Are you there?" but there would be no one at the other end of the line. This used to drive me nuts. Usually, after quite a long pause, he would eventually start talking. But sometimes that silence would drag on for, literally, ten or fifteen straight minutes. Most people, of course, would have hung up the phone. Not a tenacious twelve-year-old.

Occasionally, I would hear this strange tapping, as though someone were banging the receiver against some hard surface. When I finally asked him about it, he told me it was probably Bubbles. "If he gets out of his cage, he sometimes tries to answer the phone." This, however, didn't sit right with me. I felt like he was toying with me, and I didn't appreciate it. It made me wonder who the *real* Michael might be, behind those dark glasses and all the glitter.

By the time production of *The Goonies* was drawing to a close, Michael and I were speaking regularly, about once every two weeks.

Around that time, I decided that I wanted to invite him back to the set, this time as my personal guest. "There's so much more for you to see," I told him. "You still haven't been through the full adventure."

"What do you mean?"

"I want to take you on a private tour. Show you inside the pirate ship, all of the secret places. I want to show you how everything works." I also wanted to show him my dressing room. I guess, when you're a kid and you have a friend over, you can't wait to show him or her your room. My dressing room at Warner Brothers was a close second to that.

There was a long silence. I started to get nervous. Had I overstepped? Had I said something I shouldn't have? Finally, he spoke.

"What should I wear?"

It would be years before I realized that part of Michael's magic, part of the reason he was such a genius performer, was that he was always, always *on*. Between the glasses and the costumes and the sparkles, even the way he smelled, he was completely devoted to his craft. He was never out of character. He was never not "Michael Jackson." It wasn't until later that I started really paying attention to those details. It's sort of natural to want to emulate your idol. Everything he did would become a mold for me to try and fit into. But back then, I just didn't get it. I thought it would be cool to see him in normal clothes.

"Don't you have just jeans and a T-shirt?" I asked him.

"Oh, sure, I've got that," he said.

The plan was for him to visit on a Saturday, when things on a Hollywood lot aren't quite so hectic as usual. I took it upon myself to make all the arrangements; I informed Steven's office at Amblin of Michael's impending visit. I spoke with Richard Donner. I made sure there was a drive-on pass waiting for him at the main Warner Brothers gate. But when he showed up, in a black Mercedes with heavily tinted windows, he had on the whole getup—the black penny loafers, white socks, black pants, and some ridiculous jacket with all the rhinestones and sparkle. His hair was perfectly curled, his sunglasses were in place.

"What happened to the jeans?" I asked him.

He looked down at his pants. "These *are* jeans."

"Oh," I said, skeptical. "Is it okay if they get dirty?"

"Sure!"

That's around the time I noticed he had brought along Emmanuel Lewis. Everything seemed to be working just as I had planned—I was being introduced to his other underage friends. I was becoming, finally, a part of Michael Jackson's inner circle.

In the final weeks of filming, Jeff Cohen showed up to set in this ridiculous ensemble; a Hawaiian shirt and that hat with the giant clapping hands, inside of which was a little piece of paper. On it was written: "Maui or Bust."

Everybody knew that Richard Donner had a vacation home in Hawaii. Everyone also knew that he was positively desperate to be in it. Dick was a kind, sweet, and caring man. He loved us like his own. But after nearly six months of filming with a cast of rambunctious kids, we were starting to drive him a little nuts. For much of those final weeks, he stomped around set, exhausted, repeating the same refrain: "Oh, God, I can't wait for this to be over. I can't wait to get away from these brats. I just want to get to Maui. I can't wait until I never have to see these kids again!" Of course, we all knew that Dick was only joking. Sort of.

When Spielberg saw Jeff's little note, however, he got a great idea for a practical joke. What if, after finally escaping all these kids and boarding a plane bound for Maui, Dick walked through the doors to his vacation home to find the entire *Goonies* cast waiting patiently in the middle of his living room? A memo was quickly circulated (to everyone, of course, except Dick), outlining plans for what would become one of the most talked-about wrap parties in Hollywood, as well as one of the most elaborate jokes in the history of filmmaking. Each of us was given two tickets; enough for ourselves and a guest.

Boobie was the one who stayed with me in Astoria (she's actually in the final sequence of the film, when the Goonies wash up on the beaches of Oregon), and my grandfather usually drove me to set during the time we spent filming in L.A. My mother, however, was not about to let one of them wind up with a free vacation. My grandparents had done all the work, but my mother wanted the reward. She was supposed to swing by and pick me up on the morning of the flight. She was supposed to be there by 7:30.

She wasn't. This wasn't exactly surprising. She was always late; I was generally the last one picked up at school, used to being stranded there, in fact, for hours. But this was different. We could not miss that plane.

At 8:00 A.M., I begged my grandparents to go inside and call her. It was another thirty minutes before I caught sight of her BMW careening around the corner, kicking up a cloud of dust before screeching to a halt at the curb. Our plane was scheduled to take off in less than an hour.

"Get in the car, Corey." I opened the passenger door, but what I saw stopped me cold. She was pale as a ghost. Mascara was tracked down her cheeks. Her eyes were only half open. I had never seen her like this.

"Mom, we're not going to make it. We're going to miss the plane."

"It's fine! Just get in the fucking car!"

I got in, slumped in my seat, and crossed my arms against my chest. "You didn't even have to come," I said under my breath. "This was supposed to be for *me*."

She slammed on the gas and we jerked forward. "Stop being so fucking dramatic."

How we made it to the airport in one piece I do not know.

When we got to the airport, I left my mom at the curb. She hollered after me to "hold the plane," but as I ran through the main terminal, I realized I had only flown on small commuter planes; I had never been to an airport the size of LAX. I had no idea how to read the giant board—arriving flights, departing flights, boarding times, and tickets and gates. That's when I realized they were paging me over the loudspeaker: "Corey Feldman, please report to gate 23. Your party is waiting."

Someone must have pointed me toward the gate, but I made it just in time to watch the plane pull back from the jet bridge. It was like a scene from a bad Lifetime movie; I pressed my face against the glass, tears streaming down my cheeks, and watched that plane take off with all the Goonies on board. Everyone except me.

There is video footage somewhere out there (which I would actually love to see), of Richard Donner walking in his home and being bombarded by the kids in the cast. He was, of course, a good sport about the whole thing. But, after threatening to kill Steven Spielberg, he had looked around and said, "Wait a minute. Where's that Mouth kid?"

We did, eventually, make it to Maui. I had called Steven's office, explained that my mom had been late picking me up and that we had missed the plane. The folks at Amblin were wonderful; they managed to get us on a later flight. But we had missed the big surprise. I never forgave her for that.

CHAPTER 9

The first cut of *The Goonies* was consider-
ably longer than the standard two hours. That was only part of the
problem. Immediately after Dick screened it, he realized he was going
to have to re-record almost every line of dialogue in the movie. With
seven kids running through every scene, yelling, ad libbing, and hamming it up for the camera, the soundtrack sounded like a muddy,
slow-moving wall of sound. It was a tedious process, having each of us

come in and create an individual audio track, and it lasted for something like seven weeks, an unheard of amount of time for ADR.

It was during those weeks in Studio City, sometime in the winter of 1984, that I got a call to audition for a new film based on a novella by Stephen King. *The Body* was a coming-of-age story about four young boys who, in the summer of 1959, set out from their hometown of Castle Rock to locate the body of a local boy who'd gone missing that spring. I was reading for the role of Teddy Duchamp.

I walked into a giant casting call—there must have been hundreds upon hundreds of kids there—but Rob Reiner would later tell a reporter from the *Daily Telegraph* that I was the only one who could make Teddy's pain seem believable. Rob Reiner saw the pain in my eyes. I got the job.

So, I was back in Oregon.

This time we were filming in the tiny town of Brownsville, about thirty miles north of Eugene, in order to take advantage of the rainy, overcast climate of the Pacific Northwest; the producers had envisioned making a dark and grainy film. What they got were three-straight months of blistering sun and cloudless skies. We touched down in Oregon in the middle of a record-breaking heat wave. (Several weeks into filming, all four of us started suffering from blistering sunburns, especially on the backs of our bare necks; we had all cropped our hair in short styles reminiscent of the 1950s. Every five minutes or so, members of the crew would douse us in washcloths soaked in Sea Breeze; it's an astringent, but it's known for its cooling effect.) It was a long, hot summer, but it would be one of the best of my life.

I no longer remember, however, why my mother volunteered to act as my on-set guardian. It was a ridiculous arrangement; she certainly wasn't mentally or physically up for it. Which is probably why, three or four days into rehearsals, she left without any real explanation. In her place she hired another set-sitter, but this time she chose a local woman, someone neither she nor I had ever laid eyes on, let alone worked with before. Lucky for me, Kathy was lovely. She had a son, Pete, who was about my age, busy working on a play for a local theater. I imagine that's why Kathy took the job at all; in order to learn about the industry from the inside out.

None of us could have known that the picture we were making would become an instant classic, a model from which many other coming-of-age films were made. At the time, Rob Reiner was still an up-and-coming director—he'd only made two movies, *This is Spinal Tap* and *The Sure Thing*—and this was a small, independent production. We didn't even know if anyone would actually see it. (Which turned out to be a well-founded concern: halfway through filming, the studio found itself on the verge of folding. Short on cash and in danger of having to shut down his entire production, Rob threw together a rough-cut and shipped it off to Columbia Pictures. Columbia came on board and bankrolled the rest of the film, but only after Rob agreed to change the title. That's when *The Body* became, instead, *Stand by Me*.)

The first few weeks in Oregon were devoted to a series of acting exercises. One was called "Mirror," where two actors sit directly across from each other and attempt to mimic their partner's movements, expressions, and gestures. Another was an exercise in escalating volume; one actor would say some bit of dialogue, the other would repeat that a little louder; the first would say it again a little louder than that, and so on. These are all traditional games employed in acting workshops across the country; graduates of professional schools, the Stella Adlers of the world, would have recognized them at once. For me, they were totally alien. I had met with acting coaches from time to time, mostly to help prepare readings, but I had never been to a proper class. I would have been intimidated, but with my mother out of the picture, feeling weightless and free, I was perfectly happy to go along with whatever Rob wanted. I would have happily stood on my head had he asked.

The goal of these games, of course, is to create a kind of camaraderie among the actors. We were, after all, pretending to be four boys who had grown up together in a small town; it was important that we knew one another's characters inside and out, so that if someone came up with a bit of dialogue or some gesture on the fly, the rest of us would intuitively know the correct way to respond. By the time we began shooting, we felt secure with one another, if not entirely sure of ourselves.

I always thought I was given the easiest role in *Stand by Me*. I was, of course, playing an abused child who, at twelve or thirteen, had already had one hell of a life. Teddy's father, in fact, had once held Teddy's ear to the stove, practically burning it off, leaving him physically deformed. That actually sounded like something that could have happened in my house, so it didn't seem like it would be much of a stretch. It was cathartic, too, to portray some of the insanity I had lived through. During those initial weeks of filming, Rob and I had long talks about Teddy's nature, about all the reasons he was so angry. "You've got to realize," he once told me, "Teddy's not a bad kid. It's not his fault his dad is crazy, but he is. So Teddy is bitter. He's hurt. All of that has to come across in your character." I'd like to think that it did.

The campfire scene is probably one of the most famous in the entire movie, even if it wasn't filmed at a campfire at all (but rather a fake campfire, constructed on a soundstage). It is, however, the scene in which Jerry O'Connell's character utters the famous line: "If I could only have one food for the rest of my life? That's easy: Pez. Cherry-flavored Pez. No question about it." Most of that now iconic dialogue—the debate about whether Goofy was, in fact, a dog; the obsession with the rapidly increasing size of Annette Funicello's breasts—was not actually in the original script. Rob and Bruce, one of the screenwriters, thought the most authentic way to reference 1950s zeitgeist would be to incorporate it all in casual conversation. Those lines were written in at the very last minute, and we had to learn it all pretty much on the spot.

Immediately following that sequence—after we've decided to take turns standing guard against coyotes or wild dogs or, *maybe,* the ghost of Ray Brower—comes Wil Wheaton and River Phoenix's big emotional scene: River confesses that he did, in fact, steal the milk money, that he wishes he could "go somewhere" where no one knows who he is. I remember sitting back and watching them run through their lines. It would become River's breakout moment, but he was nervous. We all felt the pressure to perform, to deliver for Rob and the good of the film; but to do that, River was going to have to cry.

The first run-through was sort of stale. Rob spoke to Wil and River privately for a bit; they tried again, but it still wasn't there. They ran through that scene three, four, maybe five times, and it just wasn't clicking. Rob decided to close down the set. "Everybody out," he said. "I want to talk to the actors alone."

I don't know what Rob said to River. I'm not in this particular scene—Jerry and I are supposed to be sleeping by the fire—but I cracked an eye open to watch.

River nailed it. I got choked up just watching him. At the same time, I couldn't help feeling a bit jealous. Because *my* chance to knock everyone's socks off had come a few weeks earlier, and I was pretty sure I had blown it.

My big scene—there are two of them really—happens in the junkyard, when Milo Pressman chases us out and starts calling my dad a "loonie."

"Now, when this guy starts talking about your dad," Rob explained, "it's *really* got to piss you off."

I couldn't connect with that at all. In the movie, my dad's an asshole. He abused me. He burned my ear off, for Christ's sake. "Why would I care so much if the junkyard guy calls him a 'loonie'?" I asked.

"That's true," Rob said. "Your dad's an asshole. But he's also your father, and you love him. It's just the way it is. He may be the worst father in the world, but he still puts food on the table. Maybe it's the only way he knows to show you love, but at least you know he loves you, even in some kind of fucked-up, dysfunctional way. So when this guy starts trash-talking your dad, you have to go through the roof. I don't care what you say. I don't care if you come up with your own line. But I need to see that rage."

I had never really experienced rage before. Fear, yes. Pain, certainly. Anger, even, but not rage. My emotions were mostly rumbling under the surface, sort of a steady simmer; I had never really allowed myself to explode. I didn't know what rage was supposed to look like. So, I did the only thing I knew to do. I borrowed a line. My first official contribution to a screenplay—"I'm gonna rip your head off and shit down your neck"—was cribbed from a movie called *Doctor Detroit,* in which Dan Aykroyd plays a college professor posing as a pimp.

Immediately after the confrontation with Pressman comes my big emotional breakdown. I remember thinking, *This is it! This is my moment! I've really got to deliver.* I was going to have to cry on cue. I thought of every bad thing that had ever happened to me, all the times my mother had told me she hated me or that she wanted me dead, but I still had to wet my eyes with a little spit. I still had to let someone on the production team blow menthol vapor in my eyes until I could produce my own tears. So in the end, it looked like I was crying, but I wasn't.

Weeks later, as I sat there watching River crying by the campfire, tears and snot streaming down his face, I realized just how much I had dropped the ball. River had really pulled it out and I hadn't. I was so disappointed in myself.

People don't often realize just how difficult it is, especially for a child, to dredge up all those emotions. Because when the scene is over, they don't just go away. There are plenty of people who've spent a hell of a lot of time and money in psychotherapy, learning how to move beyond old injuries or resentments. As an actor, though, you're trying to mine your past for memories, to bring all those old fears and hurts to the surface and use them in a scene. But when it's over, you don't know what to do with all those feelings, so you end up stuffing them down even further and walking around feeling pretty miserable for the next day or two.

I was miserable for weeks. I was completely convinced that everyone's work far surpassed mine. I was just shattered that River had managed real tears. It wasn't until years later that I learned the truth.

"They blew that menthol stuff in my eyes, too, man," he once told me, when we got together for a meal in L.A.

"What?"

"Yeah, someone came over and blew in my eyes until I started to cry."

"But it looked so real. So believable." I was stunned.

"Well, the emotions were real," he said. "But I still needed some help with the tears."

Wil Wheaton once explained—in an interview with NPR—what he thought was the key to *Stand by Me*'s success:

Rob Reiner found four young boys who basically were the characters we played. I was awkward and nerdy and shy and uncomfortable in my own skin and really, really sensitive; River was cool and really smart and passionate and even at that age kind of like a father figure to some of us; Jerry was one of the funniest people I had ever seen in my life, either before or since; and Corey was unbelievably angry and in an incredible amount of pain and had an absolutely terrible relationship with his parents.

Wil was right. In a classic case of life imitating art, or of art imitating life, we were the characters we played during those sweltering three months in Oregon in the summer of 1985, the year that I turned fourteen. It was a summer of firsts for all of us—first kisses and first beers; back at the hotel, River and I smoked marijuana for the first time, and he lost his virginity that year—but all around us was the sense of an ending. Just as it did for Chris, Gordie, Vern, and Teddy, that summer marked the end of our innocence.

I had already known River Phoenix for a few years by the time we began filming together. Every kid in this business—any kid who's ever been through the riggers of the Hollywood audition process—remembers the hours upon hours spent in waiting rooms at studios and production offices all over town. As for the Phoenix clan—River, Rain, Joaquin, Liberty, and Summer—they always traveled together, packed inside a giant van. So whenever River and I showed up at the same cattle call, we'd usually wind up playing with his brother and sisters or tossing a football around in the parking lot. River was always positive, always up for fun. When we met up in Oregon to work on *Stand by Me*, we immediately went looking for trouble.

One day, River and I were hanging out with a member of the crew, an assistant to the sound engineer, when we spotted a bong perched high up on a shelf in the closet. River pointed, and we both giggled.

"What *is* that thing?" I whispered.

"It's for smoking weed."

"What does it . . . *do*?"

"I don't know," he said. "My parents smoke it all the time, but I've never tried it."

"Me either. Maybe we should try it together."

I still can't believe we managed to convince that guy from the sound department to let us smoke (though we did pester him, aggressively, with lots of promises and pledges not to "tell anyone"), but he did eventually pull down the bong, pack the bowl, and gave us each our first hit. We coughed like crazy, shouted, "Thanks, dude," and took off down the carpeted hallways of the hotel. We giggled and laughed, hamming it up for each other, acting as though we were high, until finally I turned to River. "I don't feel anything."

He blinked. "I don't, either."

"I thought that was the whole point?"

Of all the boys in the cast, River and I spent the most time together. Wil was a bit of a brainiac; he had something called a *computer*, a completely alien invention to us at the time. Jerry, meanwhile, was a full two years younger than the rest of us. That's a huge age gap among a group of fourteen- and fifteen-year-olds. He might as well have been an infant. (Though I do remember sneaking down with him to the indoor pool at the hotel one night and submerging all of the patio furniture. This, of course, was hilarious.)

Around that time, the parents among us—Wil's, Jerry's, and River's, that is; my mother was long gone by then—had had about enough of the mischief, the late nights trolling the hotel hallways, and my generally rowdy behavior. Suddenly, Jerry was spending nearly all of his time with his parents. Wil went back to his computer. And River's family rented an old farmhouse twenty miles outside of town. For much of the remainder of that summer, I would be left to my own devices.

By then, River and I had long since discovered a sort of nightclub on the outskirts of town, set up specifically for underage teens. It was located inside an old, abandoned warehouse; local kids would congregate along the cement ramp outside until the doors opened sometime around 8:00 P.M. It would still have been light outside at that hour, the sky just starting to swirl into the faintest hints of pink and violet and blue. I walked up to the kids on the ramp, alone, and said hello.

"We're drinking!" one of the local boys yelled, holding up a forty-ounce bottle of beer. "Come drink with us!"

I had never had a drink before; I'm not even entirely sure if River and I had yet had the experience with the sound assistant's bong. "That's okay," I said. "I don't drink. It's not really my thing."

Then I saw a girl, seated halfway down the ramp, swinging her feet beneath her. She was kind of a goth character, with jet-black hair, black lipstick, black fingernails, and a face full of stark white makeup. But underneath all of that, she was beautiful. I knew right then, I would do whatever she wanted.

"You should drink with us," she said.

I held up my hands, palms up, to show her that they were empty. "I don't have any beer."

Several of the kids then pointed down the road, in the direction of the local (unscrupulously run) liquor store, and explained how I might give some older patron some money and allow him to procure me a forty-ouncer. It was surprisingly simple. When I came back, I sat down next to the goth queen, twisted off the cap, and took a sip. It tasted terrible. I screwed up my face in disgust.

"Just rip it back," she said.

"What do you mean?"

She raised the bottle to her beautiful black lips and took several long, deep swallows.

Impressed, I brought the bottle to my mouth, and just kept swallowing until it was empty. That's pretty much all I remember.

What must have been hours later—I can only assume we went

to the club—I was walking back into town, alone, stumbling over myself, laughing, tip-toeing through the grass as if walking on clouds. Then I happened upon some train tracks and realized, suddenly, that I had absolutely no idea where I was. *Where am I? What town am I in?* I actually remember looking down at the tracks and thinking, *Huh, this is just like the movie I'm in. I guess I'll just lie down and see what happens.*

I lowered my body to the ground and positioned my hands beneath my head, resting, at an angle, on the galvanized steel of the track, and looked up at the stars. I had never seen stars like that in L.A. It was a warm, sticky night, and I had a warm, full belly. And I thought to myself, God, I love being drunk.

After wrapping in Brownsville, we relocated to Shasta, a tiny town in northern California, to film the sequence on the elevated train tracks. The trestle itself is real, it soars more than a hundred feet in the air, spanning the width of Lake Britton, but some of the shots of Wil and Jerry—their jump to safety; their narrow escape from the oncoming train—were re-created on a soundstage in L.A. with the use of a green screen and a fabricated bit of track. I was still in Shasta when I got a call from my dad.

For the first few years following the divorce, I had seen my father once every few months. He would show up to take my brothers and I to Chuck E. Cheese or to catch a movie. But by the time I got to work on *The Goonies*, I had hardly seen him at all. When he explained that he wanted to come visit me on the set of *Stand by Me*, I was happy. I missed him. I wanted my father in my life.

He showed up in Shasta with mountains of paperwork. "I know your mother lies to you, and fills your head with stuff that's not true. I know she tells you that I don't pay child support. But I have all these pay stubs and receipts," he said, rifling through the giant stack of papers.

"I know she tells you that I don't want to see you, that I don't love you, but I do."

The next day we took a paddleboat out on Lake Shasta. The water was calm, glassy, the only sounds were of our shoes squeaking against the paddle pedals, and a raven's call echoing through the valley. I closed my eyes, felt the rays of the sun warm my face. And then my dad said, "I was thinking about having you move back in with me. What do you think?"

"It would beat the hell out of living with Mom."

I was due back at my mother's in just a few weeks, as soon as *Stand by Me* finished filming. I imagine my mother was worried about losing her grip on me—and by that I mean my paycheck—completely; every few months she'd announce, "That's enough! I want him home." I was not at all looking forward to the reunion.

CHAPTER 10

Michael Jackson and I had been friends for nearly a year when he called me up, shortly after filming on *Stand by Me* wrapped, to invite me to a party at his home. I had never actually been to Hayvenhurst, the sprawling mock-Tudor mansion Joe Jackson purchased for his family in the early 1970s, but stories about the compound were already the stuff of legend: Michael bought his father out of the house in the early '80s, and immediately staged a two-year-long renovation, adding a thirty-two-seat theater, a Japanese koi pond, a zoo, a Disney-style candy shop, and—as reporters so often love to point out—a "six-foot-tall *Snow White and the Seven Dwarfs* diorama." (To my dismay, the Pirates of the Caribbean did not live in a subterranean lair beneath the backyard—that turned out to be just a rumor.) Still, Hayvenhurst was, in many ways, Michael's first attempt at creating his Neverland. But when he called to invite me to the party, I had yet to see the place with my own eyes.

The estate was crawling with kids—I believe Sean Astin and Ke Huy Quan were there (I may have even invited them)—as well as other random people in some way affiliated with the Jackson family. I was introduced to Dr. Steven Hoefflin, Michael's plastic surgeon, who was there moonlighting as a magician, and Steven's son, Jeff, who would one day become *my* plastic surgeon. (He had a cameo in the second season of *The Two Coreys,* when I had liposuction performed on my abdomen.) Elizabeth Taylor, however, turned out to be a no-show.

As for Michael, he was busy balancing atop a unicycle, dressed in some kind of antique vaudevillian ensemble.

Beyond the living room was a first-floor game room; there was a spiral staircase in the corner, and an exterior staircase that ascended to a balcony. It's the exterior staircase that Michael took on his way back down to the party, entering the game room from the backyard patio. (He was always appearing and disappearing, and he was always, perpetually late. He loved making an entrance. Sometimes one just wasn't enough.) I noticed then that his hair was longer than usual; he had already started experimenting with new looks for the *Bad* album.

"Corey!" he said when he saw me. "Have you met the magician?"

I started to indicate that I had, in fact, met the doctor, when I realized that Michael was gesturing now to someone else, apparently a second magician. Later, I would discover that there were actually three different magicians at the party.

"I'd like you to meet Majestik Magnificent Magician Extraordinaire," he said, holding a hand out to his friend. "Majestik, this is Corey Feldman. He's a Goonie."

Majestik chuckled.

In recent years, Majestik has spent a fair amount of time in the public eye, in particular after Michael's death in 2009 and during the subsequent trial of Dr. Conrad Murray. He often appears alongside Joe at events and interviews and sometimes even speaks on the family's behalf. The true nature of his relationship to the Jacksons, however, is something of a mystery. I've often wondered if he's actually a blood relative. All I know for sure is that he's been around for decades, intertwined among the Jacksons for as long as I can remember.

As the party dragged on, I was free to wander through a number of rooms on the ground floor. That's when I happened upon piles and piles of boxes, all labeled "Jackson Victory Tour," stacked up in a room down the hall. I couldn't help but look inside. I pulled out a rhinestone glove and put it on.

"You like it?" Michael asked as he came around a corner and walked farther into the room.

Michael had many, many different sequined gloves—he'd been wearing them for years. Some were blue, or red, or covered with rhinestone netting, but this one was a white glove emblazoned with tiny Swarovski crystals. I couldn't believe it—I was wearing a piece of history on my hand.

Michael, however, was disarmingly casual about the whole thing. To him, these items weren't historical artifacts, they were just pieces of his wardrobe. If you admired a pair of his famous Ray-Bans, he might pluck them from his head and give them to you, to *keep*. Or, if you asked about the letterman jacket he wore in "Thriller," next thing you know, you'd be trying it on. The jacket, after all, was just hanging there in his closet.

The Hayvenhurst party was the last time I saw Michael for a matter of months. In the meantime, I was back at home with my mother. My father's offer to live with him hadn't materialized, and I didn't bother to pursue it. Despite the massive success of *Gremlins* and *The Goonies*, work was slow. I filmed an episode of *Cheers*, an episode of *Family Ties*, but there weren't any film offers on the table. Those long, slow-moving months immediately following *Stand by Me* were the closest thing to a hiatus I've ever had in my life.

The dogs were older now; they'd relieve themselves in the house, leave fecal matter all over the floors. Of course, my mother wasn't home to clean it up. She'd be gone for the night as soon as Eden and Devin had been put to bed. Rarely did she make it home before morning. Mindy, just seventeen, had started drinking by then; her room was sometimes littered with empty beer bottles, and she spent most of her time locked away with her friends, which left me to clean up the mess. The only time *I* was allowed out, on my own, was to go jogging. My mother was still convinced I had a weight problem.

Having recently smoked marijuana and tried alcohol, though, on the set of *Stand by Me*, I was more curious than I once had been. So one night when I was home, alone, cleaning, when my mother was out and my brothers were asleep, I went rifling through her things, searching through her drawers. I guess I was looking for some sort of explanation, some reason for her behavior. At the very least, I thought I might find some weed. And that's when I came upon a little white cardboard box. Inside were twenty or thirty little glass vials filled with white powder. I had heard—somewhere—that cocaine makes your tongue numb. I had never actually seen cocaine before, but what else could this possibly be? I dipped my pinky in one of the vials and placed some powder on the tip of my tongue. It went numb almost instantly.

I took one of the vials back to my bedroom, poured out a thin line along the surface of my dresser—that's the way I'd seen it done in the movies—and snorted it. I don't remember much from the few hours that followed, other than feeling a surge of adrenaline, of zooming through the house, completely and utterly unable to sit still, but I do remember thinking: *This isn't half bad. Everybody talks about how drugs are dangerous and can kill you, but this is pretty fun.* I put the rest away, locked in a kid-size safe in my bedroom. At the time, I thought it might one day come in handy, as evidence to be used against my mother, or perhaps as a tool to get her some help.

That September, I enrolled in a new school, a private academy called Stoneridge Prep, located at the base of a canyon in the valley. I had hoped Stoneridge would prove to be a friendlier, more collegial environment, since the students had to pay to attend. Unfortunately, it was not.

The students at Stoneridge broke down into the same cliques, the same social hierarchy as every other school I had ever attended: the geeks, the yuppie preps, the jocks, and the heshers, which is what we called the stoners, the kids with long hair and AC/DC T-shirts and generally antisocial behavior. It was the heshers, especially Eric and two other remarkably aggressive boys, who gave me the most trouble; there was constant taunting and teasing, near daily threats of physical violence, and though I had not yet had to leave class early or take a long leave for a role, it was as if they were on the lookout for any signs that I might be getting special treatment. They were juniors, but for some reason we were all in the same classroom, even though I was only in the ninth grade. (It was a small school, maybe forty or fifty students total.) Of course, this meant that the taunting and teasing wasn't confined to brief moments in the hallway between classes, but rather lasted all day, every day.

At lunchtime, a little catering truck would pull up alongside the single L-shaped building that comprised the whole of campus, from which you could buy soda or snacks. Off to the side of the building was a chain-link fence. If you crawled through a hole in the bottom and walked fifty feet or so down the lane, you'd arrive at a little wooden gardener's shed. This is where the heshers would sneak off to smoke.

I started joining them in part because I liked the feeling of being high, and in part because I thought, by hanging out with the heshers, by proving I could be one of them, perhaps they would leave me alone. At first, my arrival was a funny thing, a novelty, the little actor kid coming to hang out in the shed. But I managed to ingratiate myself somewhat, at least until one of them agreed to sell me some weed for twenty bucks. I was way too young and naïve to realize I had massively overpaid.

Around this time my mother came up with a brilliant new way to get my weight under control. She ordered a load of diet pills, all sorts of different ones, five or six different jars' worth, and started doling them out every morning, placing two or three in my palm. "Take these and you won't even *be* hungry at lunch," she said.

I looked at her suspiciously, palm up, pills still resting in my hand.

"They're just caffeine pills," she told me, shaking her head.

I did as I was told, took the pills, but I didn't like the feeling: anxious, sweaty, empty, dizzy, hopped up on fake caffeine. It was different than being high on marijuana; I didn't feel relaxed or calm, just jittery and on edge, like my heart might beat out of my chest. Before long I stopped taking them altogether. Once I had amassed a little collection, maybe fifty or sixty pills, I had an idea, another strategy to keep the teasing at bay. *These guys sell me weed*, I thought, *so I'll sell them speed*. Which is how I became a small time "drug" peddler, selling off my mom's diet pills at a couple of bucks a pop.

I only lasted another month or two at my mother's. She was constantly hitting me (even if I hadn't done anything *specifically* wrong,

I'd still get a beating on what she called "general principles"; in her mind, there was nothing wrong with administering random beatings just to keep me in line), and had recently taken to smearing Clearasil on my face at night while I was asleep. During the day, Eden and Devin, each just a few years old at the time, would run into my room, bounce on my bed, and shout, "You're fat! Corey, you're ugly!" or launch toys at my head while I was busy with homework, before running out and hiding behind my mother, peaking out at me from behind and between her legs. It wasn't a mystery where this mischievousness was coming from.

Back at my grandparents' house, I soon made a discovery. In a chest of drawers in his bedroom, I found my grandfather's gun collection and a small box of bullets. I was mesmerized by it. I would sneak into his room every day, slide out the drawer, and stare at it, until one afternoon, when I put five or six of the bullets in my pocket, dug a small hole in the front yard, and buried them. I found this oddly comforting; the idea that, if I really needed them, I could come back and dig them up. A few weeks after that, I took the smallest gun and its holster from the drawer. Since he had quite a few different firearms, I figured he wouldn't notice if this one was missing.

It was a semiautomatic pistol with a removable magazine. I put the magazine in the grip, placed the gun underneath my bed, and fantasized about it more or less every day, over the course of the next six months. The worse things got at school, or at home, or in my life, the more I started to think, I'm gonna use that gun. I had already tried the aspirin. A gun was a much easier solution; all I had to do was pull that trigger.

One day, I was standing in the breezeway at school, making my way to my next class, when this girl I sort of liked, a little punk rocker with pink and purple highlighted hair, Jamie, approached me. She had a wide smile plastered on her face. She was holding a Styrofoam cup.

"Oh, Corey," she cooed. "I have a present for you."

"For me?" I must have stopped in my tracks. Jamie and I had barely spoken during the two or three months I'd been at Stoneridge. A present—out of the blue like this—seemed a little too good to be true.

"Yep, just for you," she said. "Do you like surprises?"

"I love surprises."

"Okay, close your eyes."

I hesitated. "Are you sure?"

"Yeah, yeah, just close your eyes."

I closed my eyes, and she inverted the cup, spilling the contents— spit, from ten or fifteen different kids—over my head. Someone in her class had actually passed the cup around so that every single student could hawk up a giant loogie and spit it into the cup. I was standing there frozen, covered in spit and snot; I could feel it oozing down my face, could smell it even, but it was the sound of her laugh, the way she turned on her heel and sauntered over to her friends that stuck with me. That's what hurt the most.

At home that afternoon, I pulled the gun from beneath my bed, sat on the floor of my room, cocked the hammer, and pointed the muzzle at my temple.

Pull the trigger. Pull the trigger, you pussy. Just pull the fucking trigger. I held the gun so tightly that my whole hand started to shake. I asked God to give me the strength to pull the trigger. *Please let me die.* I begged.

But no matter how hard I tried, I just couldn't do it.

CHAPTER 11

"I'm directing another movie about kids.
It's gonna be like *The Goonies,* but with vampires. What do you
think?"

Richard Donner and I were sitting in his office at Warner Brothers, and I was excited. I needed this film—I needed the time away
from home, an escape from the torments of school, a chance to be
around other like-minded kids my age, another excuse to get away from
my mother. I would soon come to realize, however, that this film, *The*

Lost Boys, really was going to be a lot like *The Goonies,* but not in the ways I had imagined.

Just like with *The Goonies,* no one was ready to actually start casting the film; this meeting with Dick had been called solely to "gauge my interest." A few months later, I'd find out that, just like on *The Goonies,* the director with whom I had a rapport would step down midway through preproduction, opting instead to executive produce. (Dick wanted to free himself up to make the first *Lethal Weapon.*) Just as I'd had to read for—and impress—a then-unknown Dick Donner to win the role of Mouth, I'd have to read for and impress a new director to secure my part in this film. To win the role of Edgar Frog, I'd have to get past Joel Schumacher.

I met Joel at the casting offices at Warner Brothers. He seemed sweet, if also a little flamboyant. He wore a neatly knotted scarf around his neck.

"Here's the deal, dude. This kid's gotta be a badass. He's gotta be tough," he said, once I'd finished my read.

"I can be tough."

"Yeah, well, you don't *look* tough. You look like a sweet little kid. So, here's what I want you to do: It's gonna take us a few months to develop this, so start growing your hair out. Don't cut it. And I want you to go home and watch the *Missing in Action* movies with Chuck Norris. Watch *Rambo.* Watch Arnold's movies. Then come back to me in three months."

So, that's exactly what I did. And while I was gobbling up every action movie I could get my hands on and waiting for my hair to grow out, someone—either my mother or my publicist—told me about a man whom I will call Ralph Kaufman, the son of Bill Kaufman, the great casting director at Paramount who had placed me in *The Bad News Bears.* Ralph was throwing a party—described to me as a sort of young Hollywood mixer, a way for all the rising stars in the business to meet and mingle with one another.

By 1985, Hollywood was populated with a lot of young rising stars: Henry Thomas and Drew Barrymore from *E.T.*, River Phoenix and Ethan Hawke from *Explorers*, the *Goonies* kids, Alyssa Milano, Scott Grimes, Andre Gower, Harold Pruett, who would later star in *The Outsiders* (the 1990 television series), as well as *Party of Five*, and Ricky Schroder and Alfonso Ribeiro, both from *Silver Spoons*. Many of them were at the party that night, held in the little house in Hollywood that Ralph shared with his father. I met some older actors, too, in particular Tony Burnham, an overweight character actor in his twenties, who I recognized immediately from *Friday the 13th: A New Beginning*, the fifth film in the Jason Voorhees franchise, in which I made a cameo appearance. I liked Ralph and Tony both; talking with them was easy, and they seemed to communicate on my level. The fact that Ralph was throwing parties for us only made him seem that much cooler. Every time Ralph hosted another party, I did my best to be there.

In the meantime, I was spending an increasing amount of time with another new friend, another man much older than me. In the spring of 1985, I was nominated for a Saturn Award—Best Performance by a Younger Actor—for my work in *Gremlins*. A man from the Academy of Science Fiction, Fantasy, and Horror Films, Marty Weiss, had called to give me the news. He introduced himself, invited me to a special screening, and mentioned that he'd recently struck up a friendship with my mother; I remember he emphasized that point.

I had expected him to be older; he was probably in his early twenties. But at the screening that evening, he went on and on about all the young actors he knew in Hollywood. He seemed like a good person to know. He stuck by me most of the night, and later, as I was preparing to leave the event, he asked if I might want to hang out.

"My mom doesn't really let me out much," I told him. "I'm not really allowed to go out with friends." (Encouraging me to attend industry parties was one thing; letting me out on a random afternoon just to have "fun" was not something my mother was going to agree to.)

"Hmm . . ." He thought for a moment, brought his hand to his chin. "Maybe we could have a *secret friendship*?"

That sounded like a great idea to me, but I still needed to manufacture an excuse to get out of the house. By then, my brothers needed constant supervision, and my sister had already begun slowly easing her way out the door. That left me as the sole "responsible party," the only one available to watch my brothers while my mother slept all day in her cave.

There was only one surefire way to get out: my mother was still obsessed with my weight, so she permitted me to leave to go jogging. I'd put on my sweats and run a few blocks, to a poured-cement stairway that descends a grassy hill, and wait for Marty to pick me up on the street, where he'd be out of view if my mother happened to look out the window. Marty would take me to the local mall or an arcade, for a half hour to an hour at a time. If, upon returning, my mother seemed at all suspicious, I'd just explain to her that it was "a long run."

Within weeks, Marty had introduced me to Jason Presson, the third star of Joe Dante's follow up to *Gremlins,* an action-adventure film called *Explorers,* after River Phoenix and Ethan Hawke. Jason was awkward and shy and, frankly, a little off; he walked around with messy hair and scruffy clothes, like he didn't come from much, like his family didn't have money. But he was incredibly smart. Brilliant, in fact. The kind of kid who quite literally reads the dictionary for fun, who hangs back when others are deep in conversation, taking it all in, and only speaks his piece when everyone else is finished. I liked him instantly, and the three of us—Marty, Jason, and I—became practically inseparable.

One afternoon, Marty picked Jason and I up in his station wagon. I was riding shotgun, goofing around and being silly, doing character voices and generally sort of carrying on; Jason was in the backseat.

I can't remember what started it, whether it was an argument or good-natured teasing—I just remember Jason saying, "Shut up, Marty!" over and over—until, suddenly, he reached across the seat and whacked Marty over the head with his dictionary. Marty swerved, quickly corrected himself, but then he started breathing heavy, freaking out. I gripped the door handle, tugged on the seat belt strapped across my chest. I didn't understand what was wrong.

"Oh, God. I'm having an attack. It's gonna bring on an attack."

He steered the car onto the shoulder, reached for his wallet, and flung a card at us, a medical information card about epileptic seizures. "Read the card"—he coughed—"you'll know what to do."

Then he started shaking, convulsing. It was scary, but it somehow brought us all closer. Maybe that's why, a few weeks later, I agreed to sell Marty some memorabilia from *The Goonies*. Because forty dollars for the bicycle I rode all throughout production, and another twenty or so for my Members Only jacket, seemed like a good deal at the time.

In three months time, I went back to read for Joel.

By then, the field of potential actors who might play Edgar and Alan Frog, the comic book–obsessed vampire hunters of Santa Carla, California, had been narrowed down to a select few. I read for Joel, first by myself, with my new long hair and my new tough look, before he started pairing the actors off. I watched as Joel tried this Edgar with that Alan, that Alan with this Edgar, which is common in the casting process—matching actors with one another to gauge their chemistry, to see how they look on screen together, to confirm that their ages, sizes, physical characteristics, and temperaments seem to fit. Slowly, however, the other Edgars started falling away.

Next, I was paired with a number of different Alans. The third actor I read with was a kid named Jamison Newlander, and I knew right away that there was nobody else who could play that part; his timing was incredible. Anything I threw out, any ad lib or improvisation, he reacted to perfectly. It was as if he'd been in my living room with me, practicing for weeks. Before long it was clear—to everyone—that Jamison and I were the Frog brothers.

A short time later, I was at a wardrobe fitting with Joel at Warner Brothers. He showed me the costume department, the makeup department, introduced me to a lot of people with whom I would be working. We were figuring out my character's trademark costume, the camouflage, the red bandana, when the phone rang.

"Oh, it's very exciting," Joel started. "I have this beautiful cast. Oh, my God, so many great actors all together. We have Jason Patric, who's just *gorgeous,* and the great Dianne Wiest, and Jami Gertz, who's just this fabulously talented little actress. And all this fresh new young talent, Corey Feldman and Corey Haim . . ."

"Wait, what?" I blurted out. Joel waved me off, but I must have looked like a cartoon character, my eyes popping out of my head and steam coming out my ears. I hadn't met this Corey Haim character, but I'd been hearing about him for months. He had auditioned for Mouth, my role in *The Goonies.* He had won the role of Lucas, a job I had auditioned for and hoped would be my breakout role. And, just a few weeks earlier, he'd even moved in on my would-be girlfriend. There was clearly a new Corey in town, and he was starting to become a pain in my ass.

The Youth in Film Awards, now called the Young Artist Awards, are like the Oscars for child actors. I had been nominated every year since 1983, for guest roles in *The Love Boat* and *Lottery* and starring roles in *Gremlins* and *The Goonies.* It was backstage at the Ambassador Hotel that I met a beautiful little red-haired girl in a pink dress, cute as a button, with a spray of strawberry freckles on her face. Her name was Robyn Lively, and her entire family was in the business; her mother, Elaine, was a talent manager, her brother Jason was an actor, too (he played Rusty, one of Chevy Chase's kids in National Lampoon's

European Vacation); Blake Lively of *Gossip Girl* fame is Robyn's half sister. The moment we met, I was instantly in love.

Robyn and I spent hours on the phone after that—she had this adorable Southern accent, which made everything she said sound that much cuter—when, suddenly, she started talking about this Corey Haim.

"What's with this Haim kid?" I interrupted her. I had been planning to tell her how much I liked her; I was waiting for the right time to plant a kiss on her and make her mine, but this Corey Haim conversation was throwing a wrench in all that.

"Oh, my gosh, do you know him?" she gushed. "He's such a sweetheart, and so talented. I just love him. He even comes and visits me sometimes. Corey Haim, bless his heart. He's just the sweetest thing."

"So . . . do you *like* this guy?" I asked tentatively. "I thought you and I were . . . I thought we were sort of . . . a *thing*."

"You and I? Oh, honey, you're more like my little brother," she said gently. "But Corey Haim is somebody that I . . . we're sort of dating."

Whoever this Corey Haim was, I officially hated him.

It couldn't have been more than a few weeks later when I came home to find this message waiting for me on the machine:

Hey, man. It's Corey. Corey Haim. How are ya? Listen, I'm really excited 'cause I heard we're going to be working together on The Lost Boys. *That's really cool. And we have the same name, so we're probably going to end up being really good friends. Why don't we plan a time to get together, man? I'd love to get to know you. Maybe we could go to the beach, throw a football around? I'm staying with my dad here in L.A. Maybe we could meet up with you. Let's put something together, man. Call me.*

Damnit, I thought. This Corey Haim kid really *did* seem like a sweetheart. And it was really cool of him to make the first move and reach out. I didn't want to like him, but I could already feel him getting in.

We met at Paradise Cove on Malibu Beach—ironically, the very same place we would eventually shoot National Lampoon's *Last Resort*, our fifth film together—on a gloomy overcast day, our fathers in tow. It was the first visit I'd had with my dad in months, but it was as if Haim and I had known each other our whole lives. We had the same sense of humor, the same crazy ambition, the same interest in fashion, the same penchant for troublemaking, the same quest for adventure. It was an instant, electric bond. Even our dads got along.

After a few hours spent tossing a football on the deserted beach, we went back to Haim's apartment in the Valley, which is when I noticed that he was wearing a short gold chain around his neck, with a little charm that said "222."

"222? What's that?"

He fiddled with the chain at the base of his throat. "Oh, it's just a thing with me and my dad."

"What do you mean?"

"Well, 222. It's my favorite number. That's *my* number, man."

"Well, that's pretty weird," I said, "because *my* number is 22."

I have always had a passing interest in numerology. Twenty-two is considered a "master number" and sometimes called the "master builder"; it's somewhat sacred even, the most powerful of all the numbers. I had never met anyone else with the same interest and certainly hadn't met anyone else with a number so close to mine.

"No way," Haim said, amused.

"Yeah."

"*No way.*"

"Yeah."

"Wait a minute. Your name is Corey, my name's Corey. You're

Jewish, and I'm Jewish. You're an actor, and I'm an actor. And your number is 22, mine's 222?"

To two fourteen-year-olds, these coincidences—this cosmic connection—well, it all seemed very *deep*.

Haim started to confide in me, about some intensely personal stuff, very quickly after that. Within hours of our first meeting, we found ourselves talking about *Lucas,* the film he made in the summer of 1985, the role I had wanted for myself. At some point during the filming, he explained, an adult male convinced him that it was perfectly normal for older men and younger boys in the business to have sexual relations, that it was what all the "guys do." So, they walked off to a secluded area between two trailers, during a lunch break for the cast and crew, and Haim, innocent and ambitious as he was, allowed himself to be sodomized.

"So . . ." he said, "I guess we should play around like that, too?"

The thing about sexual abuse is that it's so taboo, so humiliating and depressing and generally difficult to comprehend, that it's not very often openly discussed. For these reasons, it's also often mischaracterized and misunderstood. Just because Corey wasn't held down and physically restrained doesn't mean he wasn't raped. Just because he technically "allowed it," doesn't mean the abuse was somehow his fault. And it certainly doesn't mean that he *asked for it.* Of course, this is a rather common defense among the accused—according to the *Los Angeles Times,* even Marty Weiss, sometime before his 2011 arrest, suggested that the defendant in his case "invited the sex" and that the Penn State scandal "was different because 'those kids didn't want it.'"

What researchers and psychologists understand now is that sexual promiscuity, sexual acting out, and an "inappropriate sexual knowledge and interest" are some of the strongest signs that a child has been sexually abused. And Corey talked about sex more than anyone I have ever known. He was abnormally sexualized. It was clear to me even then, on that first day that we met, that something had been done to him.

"No, that's not what kids do, man," I told him. "I'm a virgin, and I've never done anything like that. It's not . . . *normal.*"

"Well, that's what he told me. If you want to be in this business, you have to do these things."

"Naw, man. I don't know where you got that," I told him. "I don't think that's true."

In addition to being abnormally sexualized, Haim was also extremely hyperactive. He was constantly eating candy, or stuffing something else in his mouth, or talking a mile a minute, or rummaging through things, leaving a trail of destruction and clutter in his wake. Not long after his death, a costar or two commented on how hyper he had been during the filming of his final movie, how he seemed desperate for attention and affection. But he'd been like that for as long as I'd known him.

In the final weeks before taking off for Santa Cruz, which would provide the backdrop for the fictional coastal town of Santa *Carla* (apparently, the mayor of Santa Cruz was none too happy about his town being portrayed as the "murder capital of the world" in film; we took Santa Cruz and the neighboring town of Santa Clara and mashed them together), I was struck by the ways in which my life had become a kind of dichotomy. On the one hand, I had impressed Joel Schumacher and booked *The Lost Boys*, I had found a new friend in Corey Haim, and just two weeks before leaving town, I met a beautiful young actress named Katie Barberi.

I had been invited to participate in a charity event at Raging Waters, a water park in San Dimas, California, about a half hour east of downtown L.A. There were lots of young actors there that day—Alyssa Milano and Scott Grimes come to mind—as well as Katie, who had filmed an episode of *Kids Incorporated* and an episode of *Silver Spoons*, but was more or less new to the business. She had these big, thick Brooke Shields eyebrows and the widest, sweetest smile; we fell into flirting immediately. That progressed to hand holding, then to cuddling each other on various rides, then to making out under the waterfalls. It seemed like the height of romance, and I couldn't believe that I had finally found someone to love, who actually, unconditionally, loved me back (for Katie, my budding film career was irrelevant, my status in the business unimportant).

On the other hand, I wouldn't make it out of L.A. without one final run-in with Eric and one of his crazy friends, my tormenters from Stoneridge Prep. I had notified my school that I'd be withdrawing from classes early to go on location—about a month before the rest of the students would be let out for summer break. And it quickly became obvious, on the morning of my final day of class, that these guys weren't going to let me get away without first giving me a parting gift. All day they taunted me with threats about what might happen when school let out; they chanted and snickered and laughed, and kept whispering to each other about giving me a "swirlie." I had no idea what that meant.

At three o'clock, they pounced. They grabbed me from behind and pulled my jacket over my head; all I could see was the ground beneath me, the tiles of the linoleum floor. They dragged me down the hallway and into a bathroom—I clawed at the walls, clutched the doorframe to no avail—and they started to raise me high in the air. Suddenly, I was upside down. I could see the edge of the toilet bowl coming toward me. That's when I realized what a "swirlie" was.

As I screamed and flailed and kicked, I thought about all the movies I had made, my beautiful new girlfriend, Katie, and all the good things I surely had in store. *You are Corey Feldman*, I told myself. *You cannot be the kid that gets his head flushed down a toilet.* Then, something like an Incredible Hulk–kind of rage came over me—perhaps this was the well of rage Rob Reiner had been trying to tap into during the filming of *Stand by Me*. In an instant, I was able to kick and swing and fight my way out of their grasp, landing in front of them on my feet. All I could see was red. I ripped the jacket from my head, tearing it along the seam, and just started wailing. I don't even know what kind of damage I did—it was one of the first times I really stood up for myself, the first time I actually beat up another kid.

One of our teachers burst into the bathroom to break up the fight, and as he pulled me from the boys and restrained me, I stood there shaking, trembling, twitching, my cheeks bright red and blotchy, spit flying from the corners of my mouth. But once the details of the fight were pieced together, the principal of the school ended up blaming me. Talk about irony.

Thankfully, that was my last day at Stoneridge Prep. I left and never looked back.

CHAPTER 12

Not long ago I ran into Kiefer Sutherland at a restaurant in Los Angeles. I hadn't seen him in ten, maybe twelve years.

Kiefer and I were never close, despite having worked on two films together, back-to-back. In fact, when I was filming the sequel to *The Lost Boys* with his younger half brother Angus, I remember thinking that I felt closer in a matter of weeks to Angus than I'd ever felt to Kiefer, despite having worked together for nearly six months. Kiefer is—or at least was—a pretty introverted guy. Still, I tapped him on the shoulder. He turned around in his seat at the bar.

"Corey! Wow, man, how are you?"

We exchanged pleasantries, gave each other a hug, until talk eventually turned to our work together on the set of *The Lost Boys*.

"You had it rough, man. You went through a lot. I don't know if I ever told you this story, but I feel like I should . . ."

He proceeded to tell me about a night long ago, several weeks into filming in Santa Cruz. He had returned to the hotel from set, was sitting in his car in the parking lot polishing off a beer, when he saw me sitting on the exterior stairwell, my head in my hands, crying. He knew—he said—it must have something to do with my mother, who was once again acting as my on-set guardian. *Everyone* knew about the problems I was having with my mother.

Just a few days before the evening in question, I'd come back to the hotel to find she wasn't in her room. Several members of the crew, however, warned me that she was in the hotel bar, that I might want to help her back upstairs. I reluctantly made my way to the bar and found her, draped all over some greasy-looking guy, cocaine caked around the inside of her nostrils. She could barely stand up; I was mortified. I spent many, many nights after that sitting outside on the stairs, too embarrassed even to look at her.

"We all knew what a mess she was," Kiefer went on. "There were so many times I wanted to go down there, to shake some sense into her." Instead, he spent the evening with Jason Patric and Dianne Wiest, sharing a bottle of wine and surfing channels on the television. But every half hour or so, he'd pull back the curtains and peer out the window, checking on me, checking to see if I was still there.

Mark Marshall, Steven Spielberg's assistant and my chaperone on the *Goonies* trip to the Jacksons Victory Tour at Dodger

Stadium, was just finishing up work on *The Color Purple*. He was driving from North Carolina, and he told me he'd be making a pit stop in Santa Cruz on his way back to L.A. We were only a few weeks into filming on *The Lost Boys,* but it was welcome news—Mark had always been a calming influence, especially in the early stages of my friendship with Michael Jackson, when I spent an inordinate amount of time wondering when, if ever, Michael would return to the *Goonies* set. Mark was able, somehow, to keep me grounded, to keep me sane.

We had just transitioned to night shoots, working every day from 5:00 P.M. into the wee hours of the morning. When you're on a schedule like that, it's imperative to *stay* on it, even if you have a scheduled day off. You've got to stay awake all night and sleep during the day if you have any hope of making the transition back to work.

Mark didn't arrive in Santa Cruz until sometime after 2:00 A.M., the night before my day off. He was, not surprisingly, exhausted from the drive, and immediately went to sleep. I lay there for a while, my blankets pulled tight to my chin, but I was restless. I went back outside and resumed my regular place on the stairwell, resting my head in my hands.

Before long, a young Asian woman in a cowboy hat came and took a seat by my side. I recognized her at once; her name was Julie, she was an extra on set, and spent a lot of time hanging out at the hotel. I wouldn't be surprised if she was hooking up with someone in the cast. It's not unusual for extras to spend a lot of time hanging around the stars.

"I can give you something to make you feel better," she said, curling her lithe body against mine. "You don't have to be so tired, and so sad, all the time."

"What do you mean?"

"I have these . . . treats. I could give you some to help you stay awake."

"What kind of treats?"

"The same kind your mom uses."

I may have recognized Julie; I had not realized she was spending time with my mother. "What's that?" I asked.

"Cocaine. I have some. At my place. You wanna come over?"

So, I did. I hopped in her car, we drove to her house, and she spread out a little mound of cocaine, using a credit card to separate it into neat little lines on the coffee table. I snorted a line, sucked the excess off my finger, and felt wiped clean, like an eraser on a chalk-board. All of the things I had been depressed about were just gone. I wasn't sad anymore. In fact, I felt pretty fucking great.

"Come on!" She jumped up from her spot on the floor, next to the sofa. "I'm gonna teach you how to drive!"

We climbed back in her Volkswagen, a little white stick-shift convertible, and went careening over the hills of Santa Cruz—probably not the easiest place to learn how to operate a manual transmission, to say nothing of the added hindrance brought on by the coke. I kept slipping the gear, rolling the car backward, up and down the hills. But it didn't matter; I was watching the sun rise over the mountains, feeling the wind on my face, thinking we could drive anywhere, out of Santa Cruz, any place we wanted to go—until sometime around 7:00 A.M., when I suddenly remembered about Mark. Mark, who was going to wake up soon and find that I wasn't there.

"How long does this stuff last?" I asked her.

"Couple hours."

"So, it'll wear off this afternoon?"

"Eh, I don't know. You should be okay for a while. 'Til tonight."

"Well, then," I said, "you had better give me some more."

Mark was just waking up by the time I got back to the hotel, and I was wired, totally ready to go explore. We went to the beach, walked along the boardwalk, played video games, sat out in the sun, and had a grand old time, right up until my 5:00 P.M. set call.

What I didn't realize at the time is that when cocaine wears off, it wears off *hard*. And it wore off the moment I stepped foot on the set. I could feel it all coming down on me—the hours and hours without sleep, the vicious hangover that comes with having used hard drugs. *What have I done?* I thought, the panic already setting in. *Why am I doing this to myself?*

We were shooting a scene in the comic-book store. There were actually three of these sets altogether—an actual comic-book store located in downtown Santa Cruz, where we shot a lot of interiors; the storefront of a record store situated on the boardwalk, which was set decorated to look as though it housed comics; and a third interior set, which was eventually constructed on a Warner Brothers soundstage back in L.A., where we worked on pickups and coverage. I was supposed to be delivering my big speech about being a fighter for "truth, justice, and the American way," but I could not have been more ill prepared. I could barely keep my eyes open.

Of course, Joel came to set that day full of energy. I could see his mouth moving, but I could not, for the life of me, understand a word he was saying. Every few seconds, he'd be yelling at me for some new reason, because every few seconds, I was totally fucking it up. I'd say the wrong thing, or go to the wrong place, miss my mark or step on someone's line. I could not do anything right. And then I made the egregious error of asking my director for a break. Just ten minutes so I could "lie down."

"What's wrong with you?" Joel asked, his contempt for me at that moment only barely contained.

"Nothing," I muttered, rubbing my eyes.

"What do you mean nothing? You're obviously out of it. . . . Are you on *drugs?*"

"What? No. I just didn't sleep. My friend Mark is visiting and we spent the day together. I didn't think I would be this tired."

Joel was incensed. "You're out running around all day and night partying? This is a job, Corey. You're here to do a fucking job. Do you understand that?"

I nodded. "I didn't want to let my friend down."

"You're letting the whole fucking studio down! Do you have any idea how much money you're costing us? Because you're not prepared? Where the fuck is your responsible party?"

"I don't know."

"What do you mean you don't know? Who's here with you?"

"My mom."

"Well where the hell is she?"

I was exhausted, I was sick of hearing—even thinking—about my mother. So I let it fly. "I don't know, Joel. I saw her last night, she was totally fucked up. I was really depressed, so I went out. And I made a mistake. I fucked up. So, I don't know, Joel. I don't know what you want me to tell you."

"You know what?" Joel said, coming at me now, wagging a finger in my face. "I don't need this fucking attitude. Get the fuck off my set. I don't want to see your face anymore. I'm done."

For the second time in my life, I was fired.

I went back to my trailer and called my agent. She told me to sit tight. And the next day, thankfully, Joel called me into his office.

"I understand that you're going through a lot at the moment. But I have a film to finish. I'm going to do my job, just like you're going to do your job, okay?

I had never felt so relieved in my entire life.

"Now," he continued, "you should have some kind of responsible party here, and your mom's not cutting it. Is there someone who can come in and take over?"

I suggested my father, with the caveat that I hadn't seen him much, and he did agree to take over—but he wasn't in a position to drop everything and head straightaway to Santa Cruz. If we could find a fill-in, someone to act as my guardian for the remainder of the on-location shoot, then I could move in with my dad upon our return to L.A. He would take me to set while we wrapped up production at the Warner Brothers lot.

"Okay, who else is available?" Joel asked. "Who can we fly up here right away?"

We put our heads together. The best person—the only person—we could come up with was my old friend Marty Weiss.

"I need a girl. I need a girl right now. Can you call a girl for me? There's got to be somebody you know."

Haim was in one of his moods again. When he got fixated on an idea—any idea—there was no stopping him, no postponing him, no putting him off until later. He was going to drill you and drill you and drill you until he got what he wanted. It didn't matter if he was look-ing to smoke a joint, or score some crack, or find some girls—if he wanted a *hamburger*—once he fixated on something, it became all consuming. If that fixation proved to be an inconvenience to you, even if it pissed you off, well, he didn't seem to notice.

Despite our budding friendship, Haim and I didn't actually spend all that much time together during the filming of *The Lost Boys,* at least not until shooting resumed in L.A. Though the cast naturally broke down into cliques based on our respective ages—the younger kids, me, Haim, and Jamison; and the older actors, Kiefer, Jami Gertz, Brooke McCarter, Billy Wirth, and Alex Winter—Haim was able to move between the groups, probably because he was playing the younger brother of Jason Patric. Some of the older cast members had turned one of the hotel rooms into a sort of makeshift vampire lair, pushing the beds together and blacking out the windows with aluminum foil. I don't know if this was some attempt at going method, but I didn't like the vibe in there. I spent most of my time alone.

"Corey, we're in Santa Cruz. I don't know anyone here."

"What about that girl your mom hangs out with? The Asian girl?"

"I guess you can call her . . . ?"

"Can you call her for me?"

I set down the picture of my girlfriend, Katie, and sighed. "I really don't know her that well."

"Come on, man. I just need somebody to take care of me."

And then suddenly I remembered a story, something Jason Presson had told me about Marty, a month or so before I left town. Jason had spent the night at Marty's house; Marty was living, at the time, with his parents and his brothers and sister. At same point during the overnight, Marty had admitted to Jason that he was gay.

I'm not sure what made me think of that, or what made me say what I said next. It just sort of slipped out—it wasn't something I thought about, it wasn't something I meant to be in any way taken seriously. It was just a flip comment, a weak attempt at a joke.

"Marty's gay," I said. "Why don't you ask him?"

Haim looked over at Marty, sitting sheepishly in a chair in the corner. "Is that true, man? Are you gay?"

Marty was clearly flustered by this; he sat up a little, wiped his palms on his pants. "Well, uh, I mean . . . I don't know about *gay*. I don't really like to talk about it. I mean, I like boys as much as I like girls, but I don't know if you'd call that *gay*. . . ."

"Well, if you're gay," Corey said, not missing a beat, "then why don't you take care of me?"

They walked single file into the adjoining room—the room that had originally been intended for my mother. I heard sounds, banging, thumping. I felt my stomach flip-flop. I felt sick.

CHAPTER 13

"Your butt is mine."

"Hello?" I gripped the phone receiver tighter against my ear.

"Corey, it's Michael. Your butt is mine."

"What? What are you talking about?"

"Gonna make it right."

"What?"

"Do you like those words? They're the lyrics to my new song. It's called 'Bad.'"

Michael and I hadn't spoken in a few months, but his timing proved to be somewhat prophetic. Once filming on *The Lost Boys* resumed in L.A., bad is what I was gonna be.

As planned, I moved into my dad's apartment so he could take over as my official guardian. It was a one-bedroom in Hollywood, on the third floor of a seedy building on Cahuenga, and minimally furnished—there were a table and two chairs in what passed for a breakfast nook, plus a desk and a chair and a foldout couch in the little living room. This is where I slept. I was working on what would become my fifth hit film in a row (*Stand by Me* would open within weeks and become the sleeper hit of the summer); Haim and I were hanging out more, and "the two Coreys" was quickly becoming a "thing" in Hollywood; people everywhere assumed I was rolling in money, when really I was living in a rat-infested hole straight out of *Midnight Cowboy* and sleeping on the sofa.

One thing I can say for my father: he sniffed out Marty Weiss right away, told me I was no longer allowed to see him. "There's something not right about him. I don't want him around."

When, at my father's insistence, I severed contact with him, Marty went on to form a business partnership with my mother. Together, they created a talent agency for kids.

Meanwhile, my father had formed an agency, too. New Talent Enterprises, an acting workshop/management company, was located directly across the street from our apartment in a rundown three-bedroom house-turned-office building. My dad would place ads in the paper, and people would pay a couple hundred dollars to listen to him lecture about how he had built my sister's and my careers. (*The All-New Mickey Mouse Club* may have been a high point for Mindy, but she did continue to work throughout her teens and early twenties; she had a bit part in *Say Anything*, the Cameron Crowe–directed cult-classic starring John Cusack. She eventually left the business in order to lead a "normal" life.)

A few weeks after I moved in, my father took me with him to a friend's home in Marina Del Ray.

"Son?" he said, extending a freshly rolled joint, "do you want to smoke?"

I had admitted to my father that I was smoking weed shortly after his trip to Shasta to visit me on the set of *Stand by Me*. This wasn't exactly something I was afraid to reveal; my father was clearly a stoner, he'd never really attempted to keep his smoking a secret. In fact, when I told him I'd tried it, he actually seemed sort of impressed.

"Sure," I said, taking the joint from his hand.

My father was something like a used-car salesman in those days, or a slick game-show host. His hair was always perfectly coifed, brushed and parted and reeking of Vitalis, his plaid shirts always unbuttoned to mid-chest, revealing the glint of a gold chain, his pants always a bit too tight. Every time we walked outside together, he would tilt his head to the sky, forever at work on his tan.

He looked over at me then, through a haze of pot smoke, as if he had never been more proud. "You know, I've dreamed of this moment, when you and I would finally be able to share a joint. This is an exciting day."

I had to admit, I thought it was pretty great, too. Living with my dad was nothing like living with my mother. He was more like a friend than a father, and I was able to do more or less what I wanted. I could have friends over—my cousin Michael and Jason Presson became regulars at the apartment—and Katie and I were free to do as we pleased. She visited me on the set of *The Lost Boys*, I took her to the studio to meet Michael Jackson. It was my first real relationship, and I was hopelessly in love. After three months, we slept together. To me, it was tender, and romantic, and precious—even if I did lose my virginity on a pullout couch in a rundown apartment I shared with my dad.

Mere days after consummating our relationship, however, Katie informed me that she was moving to Mexico to live with her dad. Other than a role in *The Garbage Pail Kids Movie,* which premiered in 1987, she wasn't getting much work. Later, she would become a well-known star of Latin telenovelas, but I was shattered that she was gone. Anytime something good came along in my life, it seemed to be quickly snatched away.

I was back to working on the Warner Brothers lot.

The final scenes of *The Lost Boys* would be filmed on closed soundstages rather than on location, and—just like on *The Goonies*—we were shooting on more than one soundstage at a time. Though Joel was flamboyant and funny and fun, when he got angry, he got livid. By the time we returned to L.A., he was getting angry a lot. The demands and the pressure were mounting, and most of the cast was fairly stressed out.

The Lost Boys is, of course, a movie about hunting vampires. In the final stages of the film, most of the actors are covered in thick, gooey slime—Hollywood's answer to vampire blood. There were enormous vats of this stuff in the special effects department, and to it were added little chunks of Styrofoam to simulate guts; we'd get hosed down with this concoction, from what looked like a fertilizer sprayer one would attach to a garden hose.

There is a particular sequence of the film in which Haim, Jamison, and I are crawling through tunnels with the vampire gang of Santa Carla in hot pursuit. The tunnels themselves—merely crawlspaces, barely wide enough for us to pass through—were positioned high in the air, above the practical sets inside one of the soundstages; atop the tunnels was a complicated system of trusses, from which members of the lighting department could perch or, in this particular case, pelt us with "debris." As we crawled through, with Joel yelling, "Faster! Faster! This is no joke! These vampires are going to *kill* you," grips threw handfuls of dirt and bits of Styrofoam to simulate the crumbling nature of the caves. By the time we were finished, I was wet and cold and covered in slime, sweaty and weighed down by several layers of dirt-covered costume, my fingernails caked in grit and grime.

Movies, however, are rarely shot sequentially. One minute you might be filming such a scene, and the next you might be needed on another set, to redo a shot from the beginning of the film, pre-gore and guts, when you're supposed to be completely, angelically clean. Dick Donner had allowed us the use of the private shower in his office, so I would run across the lot to his bathroom, where I'd have to untie my laces, get out of my sopping vest, my harness, my flak jacket, my T-shirt, pants, and underpants, shower, then put the whole thing on again, strap up, lace up, boot up. Then I'd run over to makeup, where the ladies would wipe me down and make me back up again. And the entire time, Joel would be screaming for you, wondering why you still weren't on set. "I already fired you once," he would holler, "don't make me fire you again! What the fuck is taking so long? Stop being such a prima donna!" Meanwhile, I'd be finding unwashed bits of slime encrusted to my scalp, pulling my hair out in chunks.

In one of the best-known (and oft-quoted) scenes in the film, Brooke McCarter, playing the role of the vampire Paul, descends on the home of Sam (Haim) and Michael (Jason Patric).

"Garlic don't work boys," he says when he sees that we've filled a bathtub with about a thousand bulbs.

"Try holy water, death breath!" I shout, before splashing him in the face with my hands.

Brooke had on the makeup, the hair, and the contact lenses, he was snarling and chasing us, but no matter what he did, Joel was just not having it. He thought Brooke was expecting all the makeup to do his work for him.

"Get pissed! You need to get pissed! You want to *kill* these kids! You're a fucking vampire, for Christ's sake!"

We shot multiple takes, Joel got more and more angry, until finally he was full-on screaming at the top of his lungs. It put the fear of God in us.

If Joel was acting that way with the grown-ups on set, there was no telling what he might do to one of us kids. Things got much more serious after that.

Haim and I were back at the apartment. We had wrapped for the day, but my dad was still at the office. Corey pulled down our stash of triple-X magazines from their hiding place high in the cupboard, and before long he had an idea.

"Hey, do you know some girls? We're in L.A. now, man. I know you know some girls. Let's call some girls."

I hated when Haim was like this. These moods of his drove me crazy. "Dude, I just broke up with my girlfriend. I don't know any girls right now. I'm not Hugh Hefner, okay?"

"Okay, I'm sorry," he said, pacing around the apartment. A moment later: "But can you just call up some girls, please? I really need to hook up with a girl right now. I just need, like, five minutes. I just need someone to put her arms around me and hold me. It's not even about the sex. I mean, a blow job would be great. If you know any girls who would come over here and blow me, that would be awesome. Look at my dick, dude. It's hard as a rock."

I went to the fridge to get myself a soda. "That's great, man. I don't need to see your dick."

"I'm just showing you because this is how frustrated I am right now. I just want to get laid. Is that really such a bad thing? Is that really such a big deal?"

Before I even realized what was happening, he started in with, "Hey, why don't *we* just mess around, why don't we just touch each other?" I was used to his persistence; I was not accustomed to being hit on myself. I said no, I scooted farther away from him on the couch, I repeated that it wasn't "my thing" until finally, exasperated, I said, "Corey, are you *gay*?"

"I'm not gay, man. This is just what guys do. It's totally normal. Why don't we just do it?"

I yelled. We nearly came to blows. I smoked some weed of my father's, tried to settle myself down.

"Okay," he said after a long silence. "What about that one guy, Marty Weiss?"

I glared at Haim. "I'm not talking to him anymore."

"Why not?"

"Because he started a company with my mom, and my mom and I aren't really talking, and I think what happened in Santa Cruz was really fucked up and I just don't want to be responsible for that again."

"Okay. Don't you know anyone else?"

Actually, I did know someone. Every time I had seen Tony Burnham at one of Ralph's parties, he would be on and on about Corey Haim, about how good-looking Haim was and how much he wanted to meet him. At that moment, I wasn't thinking about the fact that Tony was an adult and Haim was a minor; I was thinking that I would do just about anything to get Haim to shut up, to stop him from hitting on *me*.

"Okay, who is this guy?" Haim asked.

"His name is Tony. He's older, and he's kinda fat. He's really not at all attractive."

"Have him come over."

"Are you serious?"

Haim raised his eyebrows and gave me a frustrated nod.

"Look, I don't feel comfortable with this," I told him. "Why can't you just go out and get yourself laid like everyone else?"

"Just call him up, man. Just please do me a favor and call him."

Whatever happened between Tony and Haim that day, I cannot tell you—they went off to the laundry room in my father's building. Next thing you know, Tony was always at Haim's side, driving Haim around town, hanging out with Haim's mother, passing himself off as a friendly big-brother type. Looking back, I think Tony must have thought of Haim as his boyfriend. I think he believed they were having a real relationship. I didn't understand that what he was doing was wrong, or what it would eventually do to Corey Haim. I just thought that if Haim seemed to be okay with it, I should learn to be ok with it, too.

I probably should have been prepared for the strangeness of fame when, a year or so earlier, I got a call from Steven Spielberg's office. Drew Barrymore, apparently, had a crush on me and someone had finally decided, on her behalf, to intervene. She had been calling in to Amblin regularly, begging someone to give her my phone number.

"Isn't she a little young for me?" I had asked at the time. She was ten. But Hollywood agents and producers love to arrange these little meet-cutes; it's like casting a movie, but with real-world results.

Drew's mother, Jaid, had called me to arrange the meeting. It was all very innocent, of course. Drew and I went to a movie; her mother drove. Despite her age, though, Drew was already a huge star; the fact that *she* had wanted to meet *me* was quite the ego boost.

This, however, was different. By the time *The Lost Boys* wrapped, you could tell that things in my life were really starting to change. And it happened fast. Almost, it seemed, overnight.

The first indication was the fan mail. I had received fan mail before, especially after *The Goonies* premiered in the summer of 1985, but it had trickled in to my agent's office, a letter or two at a time. Now I was getting bags of it, delivered to me twice a week. Nearly half of the contents were from Japan; I knew that some of my films had been big overseas, especially *Friday the 13th: The Final Chapter,* but that still didn't explain what I was supposed to do with the giant box of plastic sushi someone sent me from the other side of the world.

Next were the billboards. Just like the fan mail, there had been billboards before, too, including a giant one for *The Goonies,* with moving parts that swayed in the breeze, perched high above Sunset Boulevard. But there were more now—billboards, newspaper ads, including a full-page "For Your Consideration" ad in the back of *Variety,* lauding the success of the newly released *Stand by Me.* The film was distributed, at first, in limited release, playing in only a few theaters in New York and L.A. When those showings sold out, it was clear that *Stand by Me* would become the sleeper hit of the summer—within four weeks we were number one at the box office.

The rise of "the two Coreys" was even more surreal. You could sense that people were excited to see us together. The paparazzi had started paying attention to us, following us around, asking us questions—"You're both named Corey? And you're both actors?"—snapping our pictures whenever we went out to eat. The very next day you'd see the snapshot splashed across the pages of magazines. Fans had not yet started to stalk us, but that would come soon enough.

My father had taken over as my manager, and was practically drowning in publicity requests, for personal appearances, photo shoots, interviews. Suddenly, I was invited everywhere, L.A. opened itself to me like a flower. The Comedy Awards—where someone snapped a photo of Shari Belafonte and me, wearing Groucho Marx–style fake glasses, with the mustache and the oversized nose; it ran in practically every entertainment and teen magazine—the American Music Awards, the Grammys. I was invited to ride in the Hollywood Christmas parade, where I got to meet Stevie Wonder. And everywhere I went, my father was right there with me, introducing himself as my dad. "Hi, I'm Bob Feldman, Corey Feldman's father"—that was his opening line.

I may have been the burgeoning teen heartthrob, but dropping my name was getting him laid.

Anytime anybody asked me to do anything, my father would book me, without hesitation. I was doing a photo shoot or an interview—most often for one of the teen magazines—practically every day of the week. Having strangers ask me about my personal life was unsettling. I had no intention of speaking plainly about the realities of my life at home, so I kept things nice and fluffy; told them my favorite color, told them my common nicknames. Even back then, at age fifteen, I was conscious of wanting to stay positive, to affect people positively, so I aimed a lot of my spare time at doing charity work, showing up for pediatric cancer fund-raisers, cooking for the homeless at soup kitchens, making appearances at the children's hospital, becoming a spokesman for the "Just Say No" campaign. I had watched Michael Jackson navigate this side of fame; this was, of course, long before his first brushes with scandal, when he still had an almost unimpeachable reputation and had become one of the most philanthropic of all entertainers. I was consciously molding that part of my career after him, albeit on a much smaller scale.

I hadn't seen Michael in months, but we finally made plans to get together. He picked me up in his Mercedes—Bill Bray, his longtime security chief, was driving—Michael and I sat in the back. He was location scouting in preparation to shoot the video for "Smooth Criminal"; we were headed to 20th Century Fox to check out one of the sets for *The Two Jakes*, the sequel to *Chinatown*. He thought he might get inspired, since what he wanted for *Smooth Criminal* was a 1930s gangster-era vibe.

Being friends with Michael had its difficulties—either no one believed me (at least no one outside the entertainment industry; the kids I knew from school tended to be rather skeptical), or everyone wanted me to arrange an introduction. On that day, I had brought with me a little tape recorder. I put it in the pocket of my parachute pants.

"What is that?" he asked as I climbed in the car.

"What?"

"It looks like you have a brick in your pocket."

"Oh!" I had already almost forgotten it was there. "It's a tape recorder. I was wondering if I could record some of our conversation today, just to have it? You know, just to keep?"

"Sure," he said, without a second thought, without a care in the world about being recorded. During the hour-long drive from Encino, talk shifted from the abuse I had suffered at school and at home, to the abuse he went through with his parents (at nearly thirty years old, he was still absolutely terrified of his father), to, suddenly, matters of business. He started grilling me about my management, about things I had never even thought of, let alone knew anything about. Did I have a lawyer? An agent? A business manager? Who was my accountant? What kind of instructions did I give him? What kind of percentage were these people taking from me? Where was my money invested? Did I have a portfolio? I remember laughing; I thought it was funny, like he had forgotten that I was still just a kid. What the hell did I know about business managers and portfolios? I wish I had thought a little more about what and why he was asking.

At some point, conversation shifted to a discussion of his upcoming sixteen-month, fifteen-country world tour, which would launch the following summer. "After the tour, I'm done," he said.

"What do you mean?"

"I'm changing everything. I'm going to have a whole new look. No more glove. No more hat."

"What do you mean no more glove?" I asked. "You can't get rid of the glove!"

"I have to, Corey. I can't keep doing the same thing forever. You have to keep changing and evolving. That's the magic of what we do. You can't be predictable. The second your fans think they know what they can expect from you, you become uninteresting. You have to keep moving forward."

"That makes sense," I said, playing with the tape recorder in my lap. "You still have to wear the glove, though. At least wear it when you sing 'Billie Jean.'"

"You think?"

"If you don't wear the glove for 'Billie Jean,' your fans are going to be disappointed. *I'll* be disappointed. You have to at least wear it for that one song."

He thought about that for a while. "Okay, what I'll do is, I'll do all the other songs. Then at the end, I'll pull out the glove, and everyone will know what's coming."

"They sure will."

"Okay, I'll do the glove and the hat, but only when I sing 'Billie Jean.'"

Ralph Kaufman was moving up in the world.

Gone were the days of hosting young actors inside his modest home in Hollywood; he teamed up with a businessman based in New York and grew the parties in scale and size, relocating them to penthouse suites or ballrooms at Hollywood hotels. On the surface, "Ralph Kaufman's club" was a private social space for famous teens; in reality, it became a promotional tool to popularize a new brand of soda. The soda came in a lot of kid-friendly flavors—strawberry, bubble gum, cream soda—and exploded in popularity, thanks to its unofficial endorsement by those who frequented the club: Sean Astin and his brother Mackenzie, Scott and Heather Grimes, Ke Huy Quan, Alfonso Ribeiro, Drew Barrymore, Ricky Schroder, Harold Pruett, Christina Applegate, David Faustino, Tina Yothers, Corey Haim, and

Alyssa Milano and me; Ralph asked Alyssa and I to cohost the first of his flashy new parties.

At the outset, Ralph's club was very exclusive, aside, perhaps, from the presence of photographers and members of the Hollywood press; it proved to be a safe and comfortable, age-appropriate place for all of us to hang out with one another (no alcohol was ever served, neither officially nor even in secret, and most of the kids there—at least in the early days—were more or less still sober). Ralph's club could also reasonably take credit for bringing together a number of young Hollywood couples. Haim, in particular, began dating a string of ingénues; first Kristy Swanson (star of *Flowers in the Attic* and, later, *Buffy the Vampire Slayer*), then Alyssa Milano, and finally Nicole Eggert, of *Charles in Charge* and *Baywatch*. But as more and more celebrity kids showed up, the pressure to expand began to mount. Ralph's quickly morphed from smallish get-togethers of about fifty people, to elaborate affairs with two hundred or three hundred guests, relocating along the way from private suites to expansive roof decks and, eventually, to warehouse-size ballrooms.

I was too naïve to know that all of us should have been compensated with appearance fees; Ralph and his promoters were able to charge for tickets, sell out of soda, and pack the place with kids who were trying to break into the business. None of our parents were savvy enough to discern this, either. As the parties grew, however, the atmosphere started to feel exploitative. I felt like I was being clawed at. What had been a respite from the madness was fast becoming the primary cause of it. Ralph's stayed popular for nearly two years, but I outgrew it fast. By age fifteen, I was ready to enter the world of adults.

By late 1986 or early 1987, my father had hired a man I'll call Ron Crimson, a young, good-looking guy in his early twenties, to work in the offices of New Talent Enterprises. Every time I walked across the street to talk business with my father, Ron would saunter over and manage to say something outrageously funny. We hit it off immediately.

It was almost eerie how similar we were. It was as if he had studied me and was copying my every move. Before long, he was spending most of his time at the apartment, or driving me to restaurants and clubs around town.

One night we headed to dinner at The Palms. Just as I was opening the doors, out walked Sam Kinison, wearing his trademark beret. *Back to School,* the 1986 film he starred in with Rodney Dangerfield, had just come out; I recognized Sam immediately from the late-night talk-show circuit. We had never met, but we bumped right into each other.

"Hey," I said, startled, "you're Sam Kinison, right?"

"You're Corey Feldman!"

"Yeah?"

"I'm a big fan. You're fucking awesome. You're a great actor."

"*You're* fucking awesome," I said, delighted that he knew who I was.

"Hey, do you ever come down to The Store?" The Comedy Store, the legendary comedy club on Sunset Boulevard, would end up being one of three or four places in Hollywood that would actually let me in, even though I was only fifteen. "Why don't you come check out my set?"

The Comedy Store was inherited by comedian Pauly Shore's mother, Mitzi, after her 1973 divorce; she also owned Cresthill, a Spanish-style mansion in the hills above West Hollywood. It's a massive four-bedroom home with panoramic views of the Sunset Strip, but in those days it was just a big empty shell of a house, used to accommodate up-and-coming comedians when they traveled to L.A. to perform. Richard Pryor, Robin Williams, and Jim Carrey have all stayed at Cresthill. By mid-1986 Sam had moved in, along with friend and fellow comedian Carl LaBove. I became a regular at both places.

On any given night you might find as many as ten or twelve comedians at Cresthill, crowded around the massive oak table, in the center of which was a mountain of cocaine. This was my introduction to the bacchanalian nature of Hollywood nightlife—half-naked women draped over fat, out-of-shape funny men, booze and drugs flowing freely. I was offered coke nightly, but after what happened on the set of *The Lost Boys*, I felt more comfortable sticking with what I knew: marijuana and alcohol. What I was interested in *trying* were hallucinogenics. Taking a tab of acid and seeing imaginary characters and dreams come to life sounded like magic to me. Within weeks, I would have an opportunity to try acid and much, much more. And the opportunity would present itself right inside my very own home.

I was rifling through my dad's things one afternoon, hoping to score some weed. In the back of his closet, on the floor, hidden behind piles of clothes, was an old leather briefcase with a shoddy combination lock. It didn't take long to figure out the combination—000—perhaps it had never been properly set. I snapped the briefcase open; inside was a veritable treasure trove of drugs, an entire block of blond hash, a bag of mushroom crumbs (plenty enough to get high on), and a gallon-size Ziploc of pills, all different shapes and sizes. I held the bag up to Ron. I didn't know what any of them were.

"Oh, man. *These* are a score," he said, pulling out the pills marked 714. "These are Quaaludes. These are amazing." He continued picking his way through the bag—"These are uppers. These are downers. These are painkillers"—easily identifying each drug, its manufacturer, and its probable effect.

Quaaludes were my favorite. I felt like I was drinking without actually being drunk. I felt like the Stay Puft Marshmallow Man. High on Quaaludes, Ron and I went back to The Store.

Sam was there, outside the club with a motley crew: Tommy Lee, still in the early stages of stardom (to me he just looked scary—supertall, hair down to his ass, eyeliner, piercings, and completely covered in tattoos), a number of comedians, a circle of girls, and Ron Jeremy, who I immediately recognized from his movies. Jeremy was nicer than I would have expected; I had imagined all porn stars would be sleazy and sort of low class. Jeremy seemed like a regular guy. We chatted for a bit, until he pointed to a girl in the crowd.

"See that girl? Do you think she's cute?"

She was a petite blonde with Farrah Fawcett curls and full red lips.

"She's gorgeous," I said. "Probably a little too old for me, though."

"Well, she really wants to meet you. She's a big fan."

Jeremy took her by the hand and led her over. "Corey, this is one of the biggest stars of adult entertainment. This is Ginger Lynn."

Ginger, then twenty-four (nearly a decade older than me), seemed sophisticated and sweet. The fact that she was flirting with me made her intoxicating. We exchanged phone numbers. A week later, she picked me up in her silver Porsche and blew me in the parking lot of a drive-in theater.

I felt like the luckiest kid in the world. I was the opposite of a Lost Boy. I was a fifteen-year-old already grown up.

CHAPTER 14

There is a photograph, which was taken at my fifteenth birthday party, hanging up in my home office. It is part of an elaborate framed collage, just one among many different pictures taken over the span of several years. It is flanked on the left by a photo of Michael Jackson and me, on the right by another of me with Muhammad Ali. The fact that it's part of the collage is the only reason I haven't taken it down.

I had thrown the party at New Talent Enterprises, my father's management firm. All the usual characters were there: Alyssa Milano and Scott Grimes, plus Majestik and E'Casanova, the famous Michael Jackson impersonator. (For weeks my friends begged me to invite the real Michael; E'Casanova was the best I could do.) But the picture in question is of Corey Haim and me. We're both staring intently at something just off-camera. Surrounding us are three of our closest friends: Ralph Kaufman, Tony Burnham, and Ron Crimson. Somewhere in the background are Marty Weiss (arrested in 2011 for committing lewd acts on a child) and Bob Villard (indicted in 1987 on child pornography charges—though the conviction was later overturned—and convicted in 2001 of a misdemeanor for child pornography possession; pleaded no contest in 2005 to committing lewd acts on a child). It is, frankly, rather creepy. I wish I had understood the significance then, before everything that was about to happen.

My resolve not to do coke didn't last very long.

I was spending countless nights at the Cresthill house, but practically everyone in Hollywood was doing loads of cocaine (it was, after all, 1987). Plus, Ron and I were going out four or five nights a week, and he kept telling me that I just had to try it. I had never told him about the night in Santa Cruz, or the fact that cocaine had more or less gotten me fired. And I didn't feel comfortable trying it again in front of so many people, so I pulled Sam aside and asked if he'd break me off a little, allow me to take some home.

"You sure you're okay with this?" he asked. "I don't want to be a bad influence or anything."

I was fifteen years old, getting coke from a famous comedian. "Bad influence" might have been a bit of an understatement.

Cocaine is hypnotic. It gives you a sense of power, fills you with false confidence. For the first time, everything I said seemed important. I felt laser focused, like I could communicate more clearly, like my words were transcendent. "Ron," I remember saying, "you were right! Cocaine *is* the answer."

I was sitting on the couch at my dad's. I had taken some pills, some concoction that Ron had made up. In the span of a few months, he had become like my personal chemist, feeding me a mix-match of pills from the dwindling supply in our Ziploc bag. I was reclining, my eyes closed, feeling the high wash over my body in waves, when Ron came over and sat down next to me, a triple-X magazine in his hands— Haim and I had bought the magazine together; we kept a stash of porn in the cabinet above the fridge. I began idly leafing through the pages when Ron started touching me, reaching across my thigh to the crotch of my pants. I froze, felt my breath catch in the back of my throat.

"Is this okay?" he whispered in my ear.

I had so many hazy thoughts rolling around my drug-addled brain, floating across my eyelids like clouds. Haim was doing it. Loads of boys in Hollywood were doing it. It wasn't okay. I was petrified. But I didn't want a confrontation with my new, close friend.

He unbuttoned my pants, and took out my penis.

"We shouldn't be out here, in the living room," he said.

He grabbed my hand and led me into my father's room. He pushed me on the bed and took me in his mouth. I was immediately revolted, but I tried to tough it out. I told myself I could do it, that a lot of other people were doing it, that I should stop fighting and go with the flow. I ignored the nausea that gripped my stomach. I tried to imagine that I was somewhere else. That it wasn't real. That it wasn't happening.

In the gray light of the morning, though, I was disgusted and full of shame. I wasn't sure if I had dreamed the whole thing. I went across the street to my dad's office. I knew Ron would be at work. I had to look in his eyes. I had to know if the nightmare had actually happened.

Ron seemed completely and totally normal. I chalked it up to being crazy, to boozing too hard, and I buried it. Pushed it way down and tried to forget. Told myself it was a drug-induced dream.

That was the beginning of a cycle I didn't know how to break.

My father just wasn't around much—he spent most of his time at work or was busy pursuing his own social life, so Ron and I continued hanging out, continued spending nights together out on the town, as if nothing ever happened. We went to Club Hollywood, where he introduced me to the owner, a wise-guy type, with a crooked nose, a face full of pockmarks, and what little hair he still had sculpted into a greasy bouffant. His massive belly brushed the edge of his desk, his shirt was unbuttoned to reveal tufts of curly black chest hair and an enormous, gaudy gold chain. In front of him were rails of cocaine. We stayed up partying for two days straight.

I finally went to sleep in my father's bedroom. Ron passed out on the couch. But when I woke up, he was on me, touching me, tugging on the zipper of my pants. I realized it was happening again. I told myself that it was a dream, if I told myself it was only a dream, he would stop. He put his mouth on me again. I pretended to be asleep.

I don't know why I couldn't confront Ron, but I was consumed with guilt. I felt like the whole thing was my fault. If I hadn't have said yes that first time, then what he was doing would clearly be wrong. But I did say yes, so he must have thought it was something I wanted. When I would feel him climb into my bed at night, I started rolling on my side or kicking around in my sleep, as though I were dreaming. I would abruptly roll over, pulling the covers tight to my chin, but he would creep around and come at me from the other side. I desperately wanted him to stop, but I was scared of losing my friend.

After months of this, I knew I needed a night away from Ron. So, when Ralph Kaufman invited me over to his place, I went.

Ralph had recently moved out of the house he shared with his father, all the way across town, to an apartment just a block away from my house. Harold Pruett was there that night; for some reason, he was staying with Ralph for a few weeks. Harold and I stayed up late doing cocaine (Ralph wasn't much of a drug user to my knowledge), until Ralph put on a porno. He took a seat next to me on the couch.

I had been hearing rumors that Ralph might be gay, even that Ralph might be into young boys, but he had never made an advance aimed at *me*. He had always seemed fairly normal, in fact, like someone I could trust. When he put that porn film on, though, I felt my chest tighten, my stomach seize.

"Too bad we can't get some girls over here, right?" he said, smiling.

I grunted. There wasn't anything else I could say.

"Does this turn you on?" he asked.

I knew where this was going. I convinced him to turn off the tape, told him that I was just really tired. Nothing else happened that night. A few nights later, however, something did.

Harold and I passed out on the bed. When I woke up, Ralph was on me, exactly the way Ron had been. This time, I was able to deal with it more directly. I pulled up my pants and ran across the street, back to my dad's apartment, and cried for the rest of the night.

For reasons that I still don't completely understand, I have a hard time telling people no, a hard time recognizing when someone isn't to be trusted. I desperately want to see the good in people. I desperately wanted to believe that all of these people in my life were loyal and true friends. Because what would it mean if they weren't? What would that say about my life? Slowly, however, over a period of many years, I would begin to realize that many of the people I had surrounded myself with were monsters.

Ralph used to tell us that he'd gotten his big break starring as the little kid in *The Jungle Book*, the old live-action movie, filmed some years before the animated Disney version, that Bill Kaufman was actually his step-dad, the one who had helped get Ralph into the business. None of that turned out to be true. Bill Kaufman wasn't Ralph's step-dad; Bill Kaufman was Ralph's lover. Together, Ralph and Bill had been working together, coercing young men into their home. I was just the latest in a series of boys to be groomed.

I was shattered, disgusted, devastated. I needed some normalcy in my life. So, I called Michael Jackson.

Michael Jackson's world, crazy as it sounds, had become my happy place. He was adamantly against drugs and alcohol, he was extremely straightlaced; I couldn't even swear around him. Being with Michael brought me back to my innocence. When I was with Michael, it was like being ten years old again.

"Let's do something fun," he said. We were sitting in the dining room at Hayvenhurst. We had just finished dinner. It was a rare night, since no one else was home. "Do you have any ideas?"

"You tell me," I said. "It's your house."

"Should we go to Disneyland?"

I looked out the window. It was dark outside, already after seven o'clock. "Don't we need all your security?"

"Let's not tell anyone that we're going. It'll just be you and me."

We jumped in his Mercedes and took off for Westwood, to a high-rise apartment building on Wilshire. "We'll just stop in for some disguises," he said, pulling the car into an underground garage. I didn't even know Michael *had* an apartment. We took a private service elevator to the penthouse, walked inside, and I realized the place was empty. There were a desk and a chair in the middle of the room, a small dining table in the corner, but that was it. The closet, however, was full. He picked his way through wigs, mustaches, clown makeup, fake noses, hats. Sometimes he would put on these eccentric costumes and attempt to go out in public and blend in with everyday people. As he continued rifling through his closet, I started to look around.

He had a full-length mirror hung on the wall; scrawled on the mirror, in crayon, was a list—song titles, tracks he was considering for his upcoming album. At the bottom he had written: "Does this equal 100 million?"

Michael was fairly obsessed with the notion that *Bad* needed to outsell *Thriller*, even though many in the business would have explained that that was an impossible task. (More than thirty years after its initial release, *Thriller* remains the bestselling album of all time.) Next to the mirror—all over the walls—were Post-it notes, self-affirmations. I couldn't believe even the King of Pop sometimes struggled with self-doubt.

I pulled my hair into a ponytail and donned a fake mustache and a pair of aviators, while Michael put on a fake nose, sunglasses, and a giant afro, and we strolled into Disneyland like two regular guys. (Though Michael was still wearing his trademark penny loafers, white socks, and white V-neck shirt peeking out from his red button-down. I don't know how we made it through unnoticed.) We wandered through gift shops, all throughout the park, until we ended up at Videopolis, a five-thousand-square-foot outdoor dance club for teens. There we were, Michael Jackson and Corey Feldman, in the mid-eighties, standing amid a thousand oblivious teens. A Madonna song was playing. I told Michael I wanted to dance.

"Are you crazy?"

"Oh, come on," I said. "It'll be fine."

"Do you realize what would happen if they find out we're here?"

"Well, don't do the whole Michael Jackson routine," I told him. "Just dance like a normal person."

"Corey." He raised an eyebrow, and I realized he had a point.

We stayed at Videopolis, tucked out of the crowd, near the back, until the park closed down sometime around midnight. Only Michael didn't feel like making the long drive back to Encino. We decided instead to stay the night at the Disneyland Hotel, but when we approached the desk, the attendant told us they didn't have any available rooms.

"I would really appreciate it if you could help us out," Michael said. He was kind and casual, not at all egotistical or demanding, as one might have expected from someone so famous.

"I'm sorry, sir. We're completely booked."

Michael looked over at me and sighed. "I didn't want to have to do this." Then he reached for his wallet and pulled out a California driver's license and an American Express card printed with the words "Disneyland" and "Michael Jackson" in giant gold letters. He set them both on the desk. I thought the hotel attendant might choke to death; his eyes popped right out of his head.

"Uh, I'm sorry, sir," he said, fumbling around with some papers. "Uh, just one moment. Let me see what I can do."

I don't know if they threw some poor people out in the middle of the night or what, but a few minutes later we were directed to a small room on the second floor, roughly the size of a shoebox. You would think Michael Jackson would have insisted on something more grand, an elaborate, multiroom suite maybe, but he wasn't at all bothered by the casual accommodations; he was just happy to have a room. When he realized, however, that there was only one bed, he immediately picked up the phone.

"We're gonna need a cot."

He insisted that I take the bed.

I had spent the night at Hayvenhurst before, but I was usually ushered out early the next morning. So I was surprised when Michael woke up, looking perfectly put together, like he hadn't slept at all, and said, "What do you want to do today? Let's have another adventure."

Unfortunately, I had to go home.

"My dad's got me doing these side jobs, just to bring in some income," I said. "I have to film a game show today."

Michael looked at me strangely. "What kind of game show?"

"*Hollywood Squares*."

"Corey! No! You can't do that. That's a huge mistake!"

"What do you mean?" I asked.

"Shows like that are for people at the end of their careers. They're for people who don't have anything else going on. You're at the beginning of your career. You need to be focused on serious, important projects. Please don't do that show."

I had to admit, he made sense. "But it's not up to me," I said. "It's up to my dad. My dad is my manager now."

"You have to talk to him."

"Well, maybe if *you* talked to him, my dad would listen."

"All right," Michael said. "Call him up."

That's how Michael Jackson ended up giving my father career advice. I was floored, however, when my father didn't take it. He explained that he had already committed me to an appearance. "I made a commitment that my son would be there, so he's going to be." I could hear him, his voice crackling over the static-filled phone.

Michael handed me the receiver with a look that meant, Well, I tried.

He dropped me off at the apartment, and I did the game show as planned. It was the last time I spent any quality time with Michael Jackson. I would still see him, of course, many more times over the next several years, but we never shared another night like that, hanging out, having fun, just the two of us.

Hollywood Squares was only the latest in a series of bad decisions my father had made concerning my career. I was, after all, living in a one-bedroom apartment, sleeping on a sofa bed, and being molested by a man my father had hired, while he was booking me on every low-rent game show on television and ignoring career advice from the most successful entertainer of all time. To top it off, I'd come down with mono on the way home from a publicity trip to New York. The drug use, the incessant partying, coupled with a non-stop schedule of photo shoots, interviews, and appearances, had literally made me sick. I needed a break. But if my father had any say in the matter, I wasn't going to get one.

"There's this PBS movie called *The Frog*," he told me one afternoon at his office. "They're interested in you for the lead, but you'll have to go in and audition."

"You want me to audition for a PBS movie?"

"It's a really good opportunity."

"Oh, yeah?" I said. "How's that?"

"It's a starring role, Corey. It'll be your breakout performance."

It was true that every role I had played up until that point had been part of an ensemble cast, that I'd been looking for a project in which I could be the solo star. I had been hoping that film would be *License to Drive*. I had already auditioned for the lead role of Les, though each time I went in, the producers were slow to respond, or would suggest that I come in "one more time," before they made a decision. After my fourth audition, talk had turned to the idea of having me read for the secondary role of Les's friend, Dean. I wanted my next role to be a starring one, but a PBS movie about a talking frog clearly wasn't what I had in mind. I needed to be focusing on big-budget studio films with reputable directors attached.

"I think we should wait for *License to Drive*," I told him.

"Well, they're not budging. They're not convinced you can carry the movie. Now, I've got you booked to sign autographs at a baseball game this afternoon, so go get yourself ready and I'll come over to pick you up."

I went home, sat on the couch, and thought. Michael Jackson was right. My previous four films—*Friday the 13th: The Final Chapter* (number one at the box office), *Gremlins* (number two), *The Goonies* (number two), and *Stand by Me* (number one)—had already grossed nearly $300 million; *The Lost Boys* (number two) would gross another $32 million on top of that. Now, right when I was starting to pop, my father wanted me to audition for PBS. He was, it seemed rather obvious, on the verge of ruining my career. When he got back to the apartment that afternoon, I told him no. I was going to pass on the frog movie.

"Well, I'm your father and your manager, and I say you need to do this movie."

"Dad, I'm sick and I'm tired. If it's not a big-budget studio film, I'd rather take a break. I need the rest."

"Son, I am telling you, as your father and your manager, *this* is what you need to do."

To be honest, I wasn't all that surprised by his response. I took a breath, and went ahead with my prepared speech. "Dad, I don't want you to manage my career anymore. I love you, and I'm happy to be living with you, but you're more like a friend than a father and you don't know how to manage me. I don't think you're choosing the right things. I don't think you're taking my career in the right direction. I think it's time I found new representation."

He looked at me coldly. "So, that's how it is?"

"Yeah."

"So, you're in control, then?"

"Dad, I'm just saying this is the way it has to be."

"Let me tell you something," he said, staring me right in the eye. "If I'm no longer your manager, then I'm no longer your father. You can pack your bags and find a new place to live. Now, get the fuck out of my house."

I called Tony Burnham. He was the only person in my immediate circle who wasn't molesting *me,* but who was also old enough to drive a car.

By then, Haim and his mother had moved into an apartment in Tony's complex, so while I was sleeping on the sofa, Haim was living just five feet from Tony's doorstep. It was a ridiculous arrangement. At some point amid this chaos, Tony, Ron, Haim, and me all did blow together, even though I was laid up with mono, sick as a dog, and sometimes couldn't stay awake for more than an hour or two at a time. If it wasn't the first time Haim experimented with cocaine, it was definitely one of the first. That knowledge has been exceedingly difficult to live with, knowing that I helped influence his drug use and, ultimately, unwittingly contributed to my best friend's demise.

In the mid-eighties, very few child stars had filed for (not to mention won) legal emancipation from their parents. Laura Dern, Courtney Love, and Juliette Lewis come to mind, but the maneuver was more often employed to flout child labor laws than it was to recoup squandered earnings or to sever all ties to the parents themselves. The most famous of all legal emancipations, those of Drew Barrymore (1991) and Macaulay Culkin (1997), wouldn't happen for several more years. So when Ron suggests I get myself a lawyer, I don't at once know exactly what he has in mind.

Carol Warner, my eighty-year-old attorney, explains the realities of legal emancipation—it'll mean controlling my own business, writing my own checks, and living in my own apartment. It sounds like a brilliant—and perhaps the only—way to gain real control over my life. During the lead-up to the hearing, however, I'll have to continue staying at Tony's (since he seemed like a responsible guardian, at least in the eyes of the court), demonstrate that I can be self-sufficient, and prove that I'll have the ability to earn income. My agent goes about looking for film deals, while I round up a business manager to add to my management team.

The entire process, despite its potentially drastic and serious repercussions, lasted only a few months, and by the time I arrived at the courthouse on the day of the hearing, I had my regular cast of crazies in tow—Ron and Tony were there, plus Mark Rocco, who was now prepared to hire me for his film *Dream a Little Dream*, as well as a few producers from *License to Drive*, for which I'd now officially signed on (I'd play the supporting role of Dean, since Haim had snatched the lead); all are prepared to testify that I could be independent. Not only did I have the potential for work, I had already locked down two films.

From my seat at the front of the courtroom, I turned around and watched as my entire family filed in. I had had virtually no contact with either of my parents since getting kicked out of my father's home, and now they were actually *holding hands*, parading around like members of the Brady Bunch. These were two people who had barely spoken in eight years, and what little they did say was usually about how much they hated each other. According to my mother, my father was a deadbeat who wrote child support checks, photocopied them to show me as evidence, and then cancelled them before my mother could collect the funds. According to my dad, my mother was a lying sack of shit. Now here they were, united together against me.

Ironically, parental consent is sometimes required to grant a legal emancipation; the rules vary from state to state and from case to case. After several hours of testimony, the judge called the key participants into his chambers, and explained that my parents would actually have to sign off on the decision we reached here today. By then, my mother had already checked out; she had more or less given up. My father, however, was a bit more persistent.

In preparation for the hearing, my lawyer had given me some

homework: I was to find out exactly how much money I had made, and exactly how much money I had left. I was able to track my career earnings through the Producers Pension, Health, and Welfare plans (operated by the Screen Actors Guild); by 1987, I had earned a little more than one million dollars.

My father was convinced that by stepping in during filming of *The Lost Boys* and managing my career for the previous six to nine months, he had neglected his own business and should therefore be compensated for the loss. An appropriate payout, he suggested, would be approximately $40,000—which was interesting; $40,000 was exactly how much I had left.

The judge granted my emancipation, and I wrote my father a check. I was fifteen years old, and—just like that—completely on my own, not to mention flat broke. But at least I was finally free.

CHAPTER 15

Ron and I are on our way to Arizona.

He left his job at New Talent Enterprises and I hired him as my assistant, though a good half of his "official" duties were drug-related. I was also more or less living with him, in the apartment he shared with his mother. It was closer to 20th Century Fox than my sister's place in Woodland Hills, which is where I had moved immediately following the emancipation (emancipated or not, the judge ordered me to live with another legal adult). But Mindy and I—pitted against each other since childhood—had never gotten along, and I knew the living arrangement wouldn't last. She had to know about the blow; I was out of my mind on coke round the clock. Plus, Ron was still having his way with me, and that wasn't something I wanted her to ever know.

Like so many times before, we had been up for several days straight when we came back to Mindy's apartment to crash. Like before, I woke up to find him crawling all over me, yanking at the waistband of my pants. But on this particular night, he was drunk, and more aggressive than usual. I could smell the booze on his breath, feel the roughness of his stubble against my skin. He kept trying to cuddle me, to *hold* me. He was being blatant about it. And then I felt him take off his pants. I felt his penis rub up against my back.

The time for subtle communication was over, but I have neither the strength nor the courage to confront Ron directly, so I'm thrashing my legs and yanking the covers over me and violently flip-flopping from side to side. It was enough for the night; Ron seemed to get the picture. But I was mortified that all this was happening with my sister asleep in the next room. What if she found out? What if *anybody* found out? I packed my bags, but the only place to go was to Ron's. The fact that he shared the apartment with his mother made me think I'd be afforded some kind of protection (I wouldn't), because surely Ron wouldn't attempt to sodomize me with his own mother in the house (he would).

Now, only weeks later, we were driving to Arizona, ostensibly to visit Ron's father, a sheriff in a town somewhere near Phoenix. Really, the trip is an excuse to drop acid and take a drive through the wide-open expanse of the desert. Road trips on acid have become one of our new favorite pastimes.

"What's this music?" I ask, leaning back against the headrest, sinking low into the seat.

"This is Pink Floyd," he says. "This is a real treat. There's nothing like Pink Floyd when you're on acid."

He cranks up the music. I had always thought Pink Floyd was some kind of hardcore, death-metal band, but these instrumentals, this orchestration—it feels profound. Listening to Pink Floyd on acid is like putting on 3-D glasses—I'm convinced that I can *see* music, that I can feel colors. I feel like some unknowable doorway has opened deep within my mind.

Under Ron's tutelage, my drug use has progressed quickly. I'm doing coke constantly, with Ron, with my newly formed entourage of hanger-on friends, and, of course, with Corey Haim. I'm up to an eight-ball every two days. I have dry and cracked nostrils, but I love the rush, the parties, the high.

Meanwhile, Sam Kinison and I have forged a tight friendship. Sam's brother, Kevin, committed suicide in the spring of '87, and I've kind of slid into place, filled that void, helped him get over some of that loss. Since then, we've been living the *Lost Boys* mantra together—"Sleep all day. Party all night." He's visiting me on the set of *License to Drive* and we've got clouds of weed smoke billowing out of my trailer. At night we're having regular coke-off challenges, daring each other to see who can stay up the longest, who can do the most rails. And there are always new and different celebrities to party with. We're hanging out with guys like Michael J. Fox and Billy Idol. I feel like part of an elite, exclusive group.

Within months, Ron is pushing me to try crack and, eventually, I do. He takes me to some rundown apartment in the Valley—supposedly we're there to buy coke—but this guy is sitting amid an elaborate collection of glass pipes and some kind of jerry-rigged cooking station. I've never even seen crack. I don't know anything about it, I'm not even familiar with the paraphernalia. "You ever done whip-its?" the man on the floor asks.

"Of course," I tell him, with a smart-alec smirk.

"If you've ever done whip-its, it's just like that."

I inhaled, and immediately got what's called a ringer—everything went quiet; all I heard was a high-pitched tone before dropping fast to the floor. It was engulfing, all encompassing. It was like having an orgasm and being punched in the face at the same time. Crack literally took me off my feet. After that, Ron continued pushing the envelope, always trying to get me to try something new.

I quickly decide that I need my own place—and a lock on the door to my bedroom—so, at fifteen, I get my first apartment at the Oakwoods, the outpost in Studio City. It's fully furnished, so I can move right in, and the two-bedroom immediately becomes the staging area for elaborate nights with all of my friends. We're having "mushroom parties" or putting on *Dark Side of the Moon* and doling out the acid. Haim, too, is over all the time—we're in the thick of shooting *License to Drive,* our second film together, and it's during this period that we solidify our bond, that we become like brothers. What we don't yet realize is that we're both terribly self-destructive, and toxic for each other.

It must have been right after Christmas, because my apartment was loaded with sandwiches. I'd thrown a party and ordered about a hundred foot-long vegetarian specials from Subway, even though I only had maybe thirty guests in attendance. I've got boxes and boxes of them stacked around the living room now. Haim and I are high out of our minds, reclining on the sofa, when he looks over at me with a one-eyed, quizzical stare.

"Dude," he says, "what are we going to do about all these sandwiches?"

I come up with the brilliant idea to feed the homeless, so we somehow manage to drive ourselves downtown and dole out leftover submarines to the indigent residents of L.A. That must have taken up an hour or two, so we come back and do some more rails. Next thing you know, it's four in the morning and we're due on set in three hours. Real sleep is no longer an option, so we decide to send Kevin, my resident "couch surfer," out for another eight-ball—we'll use this in lieu of morning coffee—and take a little nap. "Make sure you wake us up by six thirty," I call out as Kevin disappears into the night.

I feel like I've just shut my eyes, but Kevin is already back, hovering over my face, shoving a picture frame at me with three quarter-gram lines drawn out on the glass. I nudge Haim, we snort the lines, and I get up to take the phone off the receiver, because it's now ringing off the hook. That's when I glance at the clock. It's 9:30 A.M. We're already more than two hours late.

"What the fuck?" I shout at Kevin. "You were supposed to wake us up three hours ago!"

Kevin starts in on a long, rambling story about traffic and naps and stopping at his apartment, while I start forwarding through the seventeen messages that have been left on my answering machine. The first one is from the second assistant director, and he sounds pleasant enough, just a friendly message checking in, since at that point I was about five minutes late and oh, did I happen to know where Corey Haim might be? They couldn't get a hold of him, either. Then, the messages got a little less friendly, as they're being left by people higher and higher up the ranks of the production team. The last one is from the executive producer, and he's screaming into the phone, "You pieces of shit! Do you have any idea how much money you are costing me? You are a pair of fucking fools . . . jackasses!"

Haim and I practically choked on our cigarettes after that one, thought for sure we'd both be fired. It's a miracle they didn't shut down the whole production. Despite our shenanigans, *License to Drive* will gross more than $22 million, and is considered a box office success.

Whenever things got heavy in the years that followed, Haim might shoot me a look, lower his breath, and whisper: "Pair of fucking fools . . . jackasses."

We'd burst into laughter, mutually amused at our ridiculous past.

Dream a Little *Dream*, a sort of surrealist rom-com about a high school slacker, the object of his affection, and an elderly professor on a quest for immortality, is exciting for a variety of reasons, not least of which is the fact that it's my first starring vehicle. This one is *my* movie. For the first time, I'll be top-billed. I won't be part of an ensemble cast.

Director Mark Rocco, who at the time had only made one other movie—a tiny independent production starring, coincidentally, Joe Pantoliano, one of the evil Fratelli brothers in *The Goonies*—is all about making a serious, art-house film. This, too, seems fortuitous. I'm trying to transition out of teen movies. I'm tired of doing prepackaged, commercialized family films.

The acting seems like it'll be a welcome challenge. *Dream a Little Dream* is like an endlessly more elaborate version of *Freaky Friday*; half the time I'll be acting as though my body has been inhabited—in a kind of metaphysical, meditative dream state—by the spirit of Coleman Ettinger, a character the great Jason Robards is playing. I'll also be allowed to act as a sort of uncredited, unofficial producer; I'll have a say in the casting process. And I'm getting an opportunity not only to write an original song for the film, but to choreograph an on-screen original dance. By early 1988, I've developed a little reputation for being able to mimic the moves of Michael Jackson. I've been hard at work on my singing, too. Prior to the emancipation, I was spending hours at Recording Star, a sort of do-it-yourself recording studio in Westwood, bringing demo tapes home to my dad. I hadn't been any *good*, but I desperately wanted to be. Now I was going to have my very own single, which would be released on the *Dream a Little Dream* soundtrack.

It's a lot of firsts. With all of the added pressure and the mountains of responsibility, I decide to curb my drug use. I'm not ready—or willing—to give up partying completely, but I make an effort to slow things down.

A few weeks into casting, we've already zeroed in on a trio of young actresses to play the role of Lainie Diamond, the fourth lead and my on-screen high school crush. The frontrunners are Meredith Salenger, from the Oscar-nominated Disney movie *The Journey of Natty Gann*; Ione Skye, who in a matter of months will have her breakout with Cameron Crowe's cult classic *Say Anything*, a movie that also stars my sister; and a virtual unknown named Jennifer Connelly. She's only done a few films, most notably *Labyrinth*, the campy vehicle for David Bowie, but she's got my vote. She's not only a stunning beauty, but obviously immensely, insanely talented. Unfortunately, she wants too much money. Meredith Salenger wins the role. I find—to my delight—that we have incredible chemistry.

I go away for a few days to attend to some business, and when I come back one of the producers informs me that he's got some good news.

"Oh, yeah?"

"Lala is doing the movie," he says. Lala is Laura Sloatman, Frank Zappa's niece and Corey Haim's current girlfriend. They've been having a torrid love affair, attached at the hip since *License to Drive*, but their relationship is a dysfunctional ball of drama. I'm not too keen on introducing that dynamic to this film. "Why is that good news?"

"Because Lala only agreed to do the film if Corey Haim agreed to do it, too."

Now, I love Corey Haim like a brother, but I'm wary of doing another film with him, especially on the heels of *License to Drive*. I'm trying to clean myself up, to branch out, to work on my music, and in two days' time my breakout film has been turned into another "Two Coreys" movie. It's suddenly clear that I never really had any say in it at all.

———

Dream a Little *Dream* is filming in Wilmington, North Carolina. I've already been here once, to assist with location scouting, but now I'm back, checking into my room at the Shell Island Resort. Ron is with me, still acting as my assistant. By the time filming ends, he'll have scored his second cameo in one of my movies—I managed to get him a small role in *License to Drive* as well.

As we're nearing our first official day of shooting, I get an unexpected call from one of the producers.

"There's a problem with Haim," he tells me. "He might have to back out at the last minute."

"What? Why?"

"He's had an accident. He broke his leg."

Apparently, Haim had been attempting to teach his mother, Judy, how to ride a motorized scooter. We each own one—I actually purchased the exact Vespa that Haim's on-screen sister, Natalie (played by Nina Siemaszko) rode in *License to Drive*. But Judy, still a shaky novice, had run Haim's scooter into a brick wall, injuring herself and breaking her son's leg in the process.

We're able to write Haim's injury right into the script, so that he—and his cast—can still be in the movie, but to my knowledge this is his first experience with prescription painkillers like Percocet and Vicodin. While I don't have any evidence that Haim is *abusing* these drugs, he does manage to play up his injury, to the point that we're forced to take an insurance day or two. This isn't the first time he has managed to shut down an entire production, and it certainly won't be the last. But looking back, I think those few weeks marked the beginning of what would be, for Haim, a lifelong battle with prescription drugs.

Tony Fields was one of the dancing zombies in "Thriller," so I know he knows a thing or two about Michael Jackson–style moves. We begin our work together, choreographing the now-famous scene in which I dance my way down the bleachers, performing for Lainie Diamond, who at this point in the film has been inhabited by the mind of Coleman's wife, Gena. I'm looking forward to showing the world what I can really do, but the scene itself calls for some interesting concessions.

Technically, my body has been inhabited by the spirit of Coleman, so I'm merging the spritely dance style of a teenager—heel spins and freezes reminiscent of Michael Jackson—with vaudevillian-type moves with which an elderly Coleman might be familiar, like Fosse-esque jazz hands and Broadway-style balance checks. This is an awful lot to convey within a two- or three-minute dance sequence—the sheer complexity of it should have probably signaled a problem within the script. But I'm too excited about showcasing my dance moves to realize we've wandered into the territory of the esoteric. I can't see that the script is muddled, and deciphering all of these nuances is going to be a problem for the average moviegoer. It's one of many cues—or clues—that I am about to miss.

Back in L.A. I get a call from Joe Dante's office. I haven't seen him since our days on the set of *Gremlins* but he's interested in having me read for a part in a new film starring Tom Hanks. I've gotten my driver's license, but I don't yet own my own car. So, I ask my neighbor, Chris, if I can borrow his. Chris lives across the hall from me at the Oakwoods, and he operates with immunity as the complex's unofficial coke dealer. All I have to do is knock on his door; a few hours later, he'll discretely slide a little package underneath my door, and I'll deliver him the cash. It's incredibly convenient, which makes the arrangement exceedingly dangerous.

Chris owns a burnt orange Chevy El Dorado, a real '70s-era junker that's completely falling apart. This is what I'm driving when I pull into the Universal Studios lot to audition for *The 'Burbs*. I haven't seen Joe in five years, not since I was a clean-cut, precocious twelve-year-old. Now I've got ratty black hair extensions, a too-cool-for-school attitude, and a coke problem I'm trying to keep under wraps. Plus, I'm driving a beater. It must have been a shocking transition, but my new burnout persona is a perfect fit for Ricky Butler, the long-haired, loud-mouthed resident of Mayfield Place, the fictional setting for Joe's campy take on a Hitchcockian send-up. I've got enough of a chip on my shoulder to be miffed that I'm not being offered a starring role, but I'm excited about working with Tom Hanks and Princess Leia.

In the interim, I hire a new assistant. I keep Ron around as a friend—I'm still too afraid of being alone to completely cut him out of my life—but I don't want him working for me anymore, not after he made a crack in Wilmington about missing "play time" together; it was the first time he had ever verbally acknowledged the abuse. So, Tony Burnham hooks me up with Gary Hayes, a no-nonsense kind of guy with a girlfriend. Ironically, he appeared to have a problem with gay people. I figure he'll be a safer, more appropriate fit.

Fresh off an official offer to star in *The 'Burbs*, I feel like I'm moving up in the world, so I buy myself a BMW and send Gary out to look for houses. I don't even bother looking at the one he suggests, a "perfect house with a view on Picturesque Drive." I rent the place sight-unseen. It's a craphole, a one-bedroom shack with a kitchenette instead of a kitchen, but it does have an impressive view of the Valley. My cousin Michael drops out of school to move in with me—rent-free. Michael and Ron (who I'm also allowing to squat) configure a sort of apartment for themselves in the screened-in portion of my cliff-side balcony.

I may look like shit—skinny and wiry and drawn—but I'm more or less sober. Which is why it's frustrating that Joe Dante and Carrie Fisher have insisted on taking me aside on the set of *The 'Burbs* and talking to me about what they're calling my "spiraling drug problem."

"What are you talking about?" I shout, probably a little more forcefully than is necessary. "I'm not even doing drugs anymore. I mean, I do them once in a while, for fun. But it's not like I'm an addict or anything. I barely even do coke anymore. You should have seen me last year on the set of *License to Drive*."

Carrie and Joe do not agree. Joe tells me he's very concerned, reminds me that he's known me for years. He points to Carrie, and explains that she's dealt with her fair share of pain and addiction. Her semi-autobiographical novel, *Postcards from the Edge*, has just been published; her struggles with alcohol are widely known.

"Please, listen to me," she says. "You are such a talented actor, but if you keep going down this road, you're going to throw it all away. You've got to stop before it's too late."

"I really appreciate you guys taking the time," I say. "But you're completely off base with this."

And when I said that, I really believed it. Because only a month earlier, my circle of friends had convened a meeting to address the fact that we were all getting a little out of control. As a result, Haim and our friend Kevin had checked themselves into rehab; Ron went off to get sober (supposedly) in Arizona; and Alfonso and Ricky had told their parents everything, they were no longer allowed to hang out with the rest of us. I felt like we had each done what was needed. I may not have been going off to rehab, but if all of my friends were getting sober, I imagined I'd wind up sober, too. It's not like I had any intentions of partying by myself. I was past all that, and almost a little annoyed that Carrie and Joe couldn't see it. Then came the last day of production, when, for the first time, it occurred to me that they might be right.

It's the middle of summer and we're working at the Universal lot, in broad daylight, trying to get a tight shot on my face. Joe wants to catch the Klopeks's car in the reflection of my sunglasses, but I'm so coked out, I'm having a hard time holding still.

"Corey, you have to stop twitching," one of the crew members is whispering in my ear.

"I'm sorry," I say. "I, uh, had a lot of caffeine today."

Sometime after we finished filming, Joe Dante gave an interview, in which he talked about how much I had changed since our days together on the set of *Gremlins*. He said that filming *The 'Burbs* was the only time in his career that he dreaded coming to work in the morning, because he had to deal with Corey Feldman.

The 'Burbs will debut at number one, but it will be my last starring role in a major studio film for a long, long time. My career is about to take a plunge, but I'm too far gone to stop it.

CHAPTER 16

I'd been dating Charlie Spradling, a quint-essential B-actress and wannabe *Playboy* pinup, since we met on the set of *License to Drive* (she has a small, uncredited cameo, where she makes out with Heather Graham's on-screen boyfriend). It was a whirlwind romance, full of drama and fighting and lying and suspicion—rumors are swirling that she's been cheating on me with Charlie Sheen; people seem to love seeing "Charlie and Charlie" together, even though she's been living with me. Now, our relationship has crashed and

burned; only a month or two after moving in, she's on her way out.
Seeing as how she had been living with her previous boyfriend, Dave
Mustaine, the lead singer of the metal band Megadeath, at the beginning of our relationship—I actually went to Dave's house to help her
pack up her things—I probably shouldn't have been surprised when a
van full of long-haired musicians, all part of some new rock band I
haven't yet heard of, pulled up outside my home on Picturesque Drive.
She announced that she was now "dating the band"—as in, *all* of
them—and that they were there to help her move out. Still, I'm devastated by the breakup. When Ron and Michael return home (the
four of us had been cramming ourselves into my tiny one-bedroom
house), I'm sulking, alone, on the balcony.

"I know how to make you feel better," Ron said. "Let's do some
coke."

I sighed. "Coke will just make me stay up all night talking about
her. I don't want to talk about Charlie. I don't even want to *think*
about her tonight."

Ron put his hands in his pockets and shrugged. "We could do acid?"

"I'm fucking depressed, man. If I take acid I'll just have a really
bad trip."

"Well," he said, "how about heroin?"

"*What?*" I looked at him like he was crazy.

"We could do heroin," he said again.

"I'm not going to put a needle in my vein, man. That's disgusting."

"You don't have to shoot it."

"What are you talking about?"

"You don't have to shoot it. You can snort heroin, just like cocaine."

That was interesting. I'd always thought heroin was an intravenous-
only type drug. "Well," I said, "what does heroin . . . *do?*"

"I've only done it once, but it's sort of like pain medicine."

"I don't know," I said, shaking my head. "Where would we even
get any?"

"You just go downtown. All the Mexicans sell it. It's called *chiva* in Spanish. You just drive downtown, stick your head out the window, and say *chiva*."

For someone who had supposedly only done heroin once, he was starting to sound pretty familiar with the process. "I really don't think we're going to be able to drive downtown, stick our heads out the window, yell *chiva*, and expect someone to run right up."

"Trust me."

"All right, fine," I said. "I think you're crazy, but I'll try it."

Ron turned out to be right—it really was that simple. Back at the apartment, latex balloons in hand, we just sort of stared at each other until finally someone broke one open. Inside was a gooey, tarlike brown slime. It smelled a bit like burnt sandalwood. "How are we going to snort this?" I asked.

It also turns out that your microwave has all kinds of convenient and unexpected uses. Nuke some *chiva*, and it becomes hard enough to crush into powder and snort.

Heroin wasn't anything like what I imagined. It didn't give me the psychedelic, hallucinogenic high of acid, wasn't as in-your-face as the knock-me-to-my-knees force of crack. I felt a warm, slightly tingly sensation pass over my body, like an internal heat wave. I was a little itchy, and felt the temptation to keep scratching my skin. But I couldn't believe this was the effect of big, bad heroin, the *worst* drug in the world, the scariest stuff you could do. I felt relaxed and at peace. Thoughts of Charlie were gone with one quick snort.

The effects of heroin, at first, are subtle; in the past I've described it as a delicate flower. It seems harmless, because it takes awhile to consume you. It was months before my flower had become a Venus flytrap, eating me from the inside out.

———

We've hired the singer and soap opera star Michael Damian (best known for playing Danny Romalotti on TV's *The Young and the Restless*), to produce and record "Rock On," a cover of the David Essex song, for the *Dream a Little Dream* album. In addition, he'll be working with me on my song, which is to be featured in the film as well as on the soundtrack. It's a tight deadline, and we get to work right away, throwing out ideas and playing with melodies in the living room of my home on Picturesque Drive. The work we do here lays the foundation for "Something in Your Eyes," which is to become my first original single.

The transition to music seems like a no-brainer, a natural, even obvious next step in my increasingly successful career. The release of *License to Drive* had brought with it the first glimpses of what the press would eventually dub "Coreymania." Even as far back as filming, Haim and I had once found ourselves locked in a trailer—a screaming crowd of frenzied fans was pounding, chanting, literally rocking the trailer, as if they were trying to shake us out. We had looked at each other in disbelief, and asked ourselves, Is this real? Is any of this really happening? Overnight, the two of us together had become a security team's nightmare. We brought with us total pandemonium. It was as if I had woken up one day and started living Michael Jackson's life. It was as if I had wanted so badly to be famous that I had willed it into fruition. And as much as this new reality was completely surreal and insane—in many ways, I still felt like the shy, awkward outcast who was made fun of at school, ignored by girls, and getting a cup of spit overturned on his head—I ate it up.

With all the attention, as well as all the press I'm doing for my new single—I'm telling everyone it'll be on the soundtrack—a number of opportunities arise. I'm invited to be part of an all-star lineup of teen actors at a charity event in Idaho, where I'll get yet another chance to sing "Something in Your Eyes." I decide to invite Haim, not to make it an official "Two Coreys" trip, but because by now, I'm worried about him. He's been living with Brooke McCarter—vampire Paul from *The Lost Boys*, who's acting as some kind of combination manager/life coach—but I know Haim is now heavily into crack. Whereas I have lined up and filmed *The 'Burbs*, Haim hasn't booked anything in months. He's on some kind of self-imposed hiatus, the results of which can't be good. I think bringing him with me to Idaho might help him reconnect with his fans, might encourage Haim to straighten himself out.

The concert is being held at a local high school—I believe it's a Mothers Against Drunk Driving event. Everyone gets checked in to the hotel and then I'm off to rehearsals. I've got "Something in Your Eyes" ready to go, plus two or three other originals.

The whole week is a blur—there's a local mall appearance, at which I was trapped in my limo in the parking lot, surrounded by fans and guarded by cops in what looked like riot gear. There are girls collapsing and crying hysterically. I don't get to spend too much time with Haim, since he's technically not in the show. But all in all, the trip feels like a success. I'm excited about what I believe is a burgeoning music career. We take the private jet back to L.A. At home, I turn on the news.

The headlines are everywhere—"Two Coreys Disaster!" "Two Coreys Disappoint Fans!" Every channel is airing footage of Haim and I disembarking from the plane in Idaho; they're running it over and over, in slow motion no less, like we're two criminals being paraded out for a perp walk. I was dumbfounded. What in the world was going on?

What I hadn't known was that, while I was busy with soundchecks and backstage preparations and performing, Haim had gone on a full-fledged one-man bender. He was at the *high school*, asking local kids where he could score crack; he commandeered the limo and picked up a truckload of strangers, boozing it up and joyriding around town, and then decided to go full rock-star and trash his hotel room.

Starry-eyed and self-absorbed, I was completely oblivious. The bad press is the first sign of an impending "Two Coreys" backlash. It registers, but not seriously enough.

In an attempt at damage control, I sign up for an episode of *CBS Schoolbreak Special* called *15 and Getting Straight*. This is perhaps ironic, since I'm doing anti-drug awareness television at the same time that I've got a festering drug problem. I'm still experimenting with heroin, but I think I have it under control, and I've managed to keep it well hidden. I sign on to do the show with two other kid stars, Drew Barrymore and Tatum O'Neal.

Drew and I haven't seen each since our "date" all those years ago, and she's not ten anymore. She's fifteen now, and a firecracker. She's flirtatious and coquettish, she oozes sex appeal, she acts like a woman much older than her actual age. We have instant chemistry. Plus, she's really hamming it up, flirting and cooing and touching. And so begins yet another whirlwind romance, which the press seizes on from the start.

By the spring of 1989, press junkets—two- or three-day publicity tours that usually take place in posh hotels or resorts—have become old hat. For *Dream a Little Dream*, we've been put up at the Four Seasons—Haim, the director Mark Rocco, and myself are each given our own enormous penthouse suite. After we've convened as a panel and fielded questions from as many as thirty to fifty journalists and entertainment reporters, these rooms will be used to conduct one-on-one interviews with individual members of the press. Publicity is part of the job, but junkets are generally laborious, monotonous affairs; you spend your days trying to come up with a fresh, exciting way to answer a question you've already heard fifteen times before, and it can be a struggle to remain focused and attentive and gracious. But when it's finally over, the studio will often let you keep the room for one final night. "Relax, take a bath, have a massage, order room service," one of the executives tells me. "The bill is open, incidentals are on us. Thanks for all your hard work."

I looked around my gorgeous, enormous, empty suite at the Four Seasons, and did what any seventeen-year-old would do. I called a few of my friends. Unbeknownst to me, Haim was busy doing the exact same thing over in his room, as was Mark down the hall. Within an hour, the three of us had packed the top floor of the hotel with nearly a thousand "guests."

Coming off my first starring role and now hard at work on my song for the soundtrack, I'm still trying to keep my drug use under control. So, in an epic display of responsibility and maturity, I decide to stick with booze for the night. I emptied a bottle of Stoli into an ice bucket, tossed in some orange juice, and carried that around the party like my own personal Big Gulp; the whole time I'm hollering to people—many of whom I don't even recognize—about how no matter how much I drink, I can't seem to get drunk. "I can't get drunk," I shout over the music, pointing down at my "cup." "It's amazing"—gulp, gulp, gulp—"I can't get drunk!" I'm drinking, and drinking, and drinking, and not feeling much of anything, or at least that's how it seemed.

An hour or so in, things are already spinning out of control. Room service is on speed dial—bottles of Dom Perignon, liters of vodka, food trays, and crudité platters are being sent up one right after the other; I have no idea who's even placing the orders. I look over to my right, just as someone knocks on the door. It's the cops, but don't worry, Ricky Schroder will handle this. He's got the door barely cracked ajar, trying to explain to the officers that there's been some kind of mistake, we can't *possibly* be responsible for disturbing the peace. I'm watching all of this with my bucket of alcohol, thinking, *Oh, my God, what have I done?*

Meanwhile, I wander into one of the bathrooms to find a pile of burnt washcloths and towels—for some reason, someone has started setting the linens on fire—and butter smeared across the mirror. I'm looking at weird butter messages and a pile of smoldering towels, realizing that my impromptu wrap party has turned into some kind of nightmare circus. Over in the master on-suite, I find my cousin Michael and John Preston standing in the shower, fully clothed but soaking wet. In between them, wedged into the bathtub, is the small refrigerator from the minibar.

"Fuck you, man! *I'm* getting the last bottle of vodka!" Michael and John are holding each other by the shirt collars, screaming at each other through the shower stream.

"No, fuck *you*! It's mine, you asshole."

"I found it first! Possession is nine-tenths of the law, man."

I drag them out of the shower, they're slipping and sliding all over the place, and yell, "What the fuck is *wrong* with you people?"

Michael starts in immediately. "He's being an asshole and trying to take all the booze"—before turning to face John directly—"That's not cool, man."

I give John a shove as he rises from the bed. "You guys, it's *my* booze. It's *my* room. Do you have any idea how expensive minibar snacks are? You've got the whole refrigerator shoved in the shower!"

Of course by then, the bill for the minibar was going to be the least of my worries. I have vague memories of throwing everyone out at some point. I know I went to sleep by myself.

In the morning, as I made my way through the lobby, everyone in the place was giving me the evil eye. Mark stumbled downstairs, bowing his head in shame. There were three executives from the studio standing around the front desk, ogling a bill that was clearly several pages long. One of them turned to me with a bright-red face and a pinched mouth. He was completely and utterly pissed.

"Well, I hope the party was good."

"Party? What party?" I said as casually as I could muster. "I mean, we just had a few friends over. Nothing big."

"Nothing big? Perhaps you can explain how we ended up with a bill for ten thousand dollars?"

I looked sheepishly at Mark and Haim. "Well, uh, that couldn't possibly be just for my room."

"It's for all three rooms. But still, we told you to get a *massage*, not feed the fucking army."

Within hours, the story broke in the press—every sordid detail about the crazy party the "Two Coreys" threw at the Four Seasons, including some that seemed grossly exaggerated, was splashed across the pages of the tabloids. If they're to be believed, televisions were tossed out of windows, Haim and Ricky Schroder hosed down a stripper with Champagne, and kids went streaking down the halls of the penthouse, pandemonium into all hours of the night. I have no idea how much of that may have been true—maybe it's all true. All I know for sure is that I don't remember much.

I had been concerned about the marketing campaign for *Dream a Little Dream* from the start. Giant wall-size posters had been pasted up in malls across America and kids everywhere were eating it up. The problem is that *Dream a Little Dream*, at least as I had envisioned it, was supposed to be a more mature, thinking-man's piece. That's part of the reason we reached out to more mature, well-established stars—acclaimed actors like Jason Robards, Piper Laurie, and Harry Dean Stanton. We were trying to attract an older, post-adolescent audience, but the marketing team had put together a poster that looked like a tear sheet from a teen magazine. Together, Haim, Meredith Salenger, and I look like characters in a John Hughes film, and the result is total confusion—expecting a typical "Two Coreys" caper, teens are walking out of theaters all over the country, wondering exactly what the hell this is.

Dream a Little Dream opens at number five and plummets. Within three weeks, it's yanked from the theaters. I've never been part of a flop before, and it stings, but I take it as further proof that the "Two Coreys" are due for a break.

To add insult to injury, Haim has chosen this same month—March 1989—to make an appearance on *The Arsenio Hall Show* and to announce publicly that he's got a craving for crack. Why he's decided to do this I have no idea—none of this is really public knowledge and nobody's been arrested yet, but Haim has taken the reins and thrown his carefully calibrated public image directly down the toilet.

At the same time, I've gotten a phone call that we've missed the cutoff for inclusion in the *Dream a Little Dream* soundtrack album, too (we'd already missed the deadline for inclusion in the film itself), even though I've been out promoting "Something in Your Eyes" for months. The studio promises to release the track as a single, but eventually discussion on that subject ends completely and I'm too deep into a drug haze to really care. (It wasn't until sometime in 2009 or 2010 that I discovered "Something in Your Eyes" *was* released on vinyl—my assistant at the time, Jake, came across the record on a Canadian eBay page and brought it home to show me because I was convinced he was making things up. I have no idea if the record was ever released in the United States. Regardless, I never saw a dime and have no way of tracking down how many copies were ultimately sold.)

To top everything off, Drew and I—once hot and heavy and totally in sync—are unraveling after only a few months of dating. I'm angry because she had discussed some intimate details of our relationship with her agents. It's a perfect storm of bad press and personal problems. Signs are everywhere that the carefully placed pieces of my life are about to break apart. Still, I ignore them, because I know I've got the Academy Awards coming up.

In an attempt to spice up what many fear has became a staid, stoic affair, this year's Oscars will do away with a number of traditions: there'll be no official host, but there will be a dearth of live musical performances, including an elaborate thirteen-minute number featuring eighteen young actors—the "stars of tomorrow"—called "I Wanna Be an Oscar Winner." It'll be written by the great composer Marvin Hamlisch and directed by choreographer Kenny Ortega, who's riding the wave of *Dirty Dancing* success and will go on to do extensive work with Michael Jackson (he directed three of his world tours, This Is It, HIStory, and Dangerous). I'm excited to work with the greats, and to sing and dance on one of the world's biggest stages.

Drew is getting ready at a hotel not far from the Shrine Auditorium. Despite the fighting, we're committed to staying together through awards season. (Only days earlier, we had presented one to our matchmaker of sorts, Steven Spielberg, at the Directors Guild.) It's my job to meet the limo and pick her up at the hotel. We're only a little ways down the road, but with the miles-long caravan of limos (this is, after all, years before towncars became the preferred mode of chauffeured transportation), it will take over an hour to drive roughly five hundred feet. Finally, after what feels like a year, I take her hand and help her climb out of the car.

I've been to award shows before, the MTV Awards, the American Music Awards, but I've never seen anything like this. The red carpet stretches the length of two city blocks—it feels *miles* long—and is flanked by a wall of photographers, journalists, reporters, and members of both the domestic and foreign press. There are flashbulbs and publicists and microphones and cameras and fans and screaming and shouts of "Drew!" "Corey!" "Drew!" "Corey!" It's exciting and intimidating and Drew and I are holding on to each other for dear life.

Suddenly, amid all the chaos, I feel a tap on my shoulder. I turn around to face a tall, skinny, gaunt-looking guy with a shock of blond hair covering half his face. It's River Phoenix. I haven't seen him in years.

We're exchanging pleasantries when I notice he's holding hands with his girlfriend, a grown-up Martha Plimpton. It's completely surreal—four kids that started out in the business together, standing together ten years later on the red carpet at the Academy Awards. Not only that, but River's up for an Oscar. He's been nominated for Best Supporting Actor for his work in the Sidney Lumet film *Running on Empty*. But he doesn't look good. In fact, he looks loaded. But I brush it off. I'm not going to let anything cloud the day.

People have often asked if I was nervous, knowing that I'd be performing live in front of something like fifty million people. But it's not the fifty million people I'm worried about, it's the few thousand gathered together in this one room. From my place on the elevated stage, I'm staring down at Tom Hanks, Steven Spielberg, Tom Cruise, Billy Crystal. Every giant star and entertainment industry bigwig is staring back, and I know that any one of them could make or break the rest of my career. All I'm thinking, as the opening chords of our dance number ring out, is *Don't mess this up, don't mess this up, for the love of God, don't mess this up.*

The performance seems to be going okay—the audience laughs and applauds in all the right places—and it's over in the blink of an eye. Unfortunately, the 1989 ceremony has been categorized as one of the worst broadcasts in the history of the Academy Awards. It started out with a famously bizarre performance by Rob Lowe in some sort of dystopian Snow White number, and it just goes downhill from there. As for the "Oscar Winners of the Future," the Academy might have been a tad off the mark—none of us have won an Oscar (at least not yet), although Blair Underwood, Patrick Dempsey, and Joely Fischer have been nominated for Golden Globes, and Chad Lowe has an Emmy.

Drew and I make the after-party rounds, stay out late, and attend the Governor's Ball. It's been fun, but we both know that it's over. By the end of the night, our short-lived relationship has flamed out.

CHAPTER 17

Present-day Los Angeles is a whole-foodies'
mecca—it's brimming with health food stores, farm-to-table restaurants, vegan groceries, and cutting-edge raw cuisine. But Los Angeles
circa 1989 doesn't have much to offer a die-hard vegetarian in the way
of restaurant fare. There are only a few shops that cater to veggie-
lovers, and I'm at one of my favorites, a place called Veggie Cuisine on
Ventura. As I approach the counter, I spot a stunning, achingly beautiful girl with a mop of curly brown hair. She is mesmerizing. I am

floored by her, in fact. As I take my place in line, she turns to her right—she seems perplexed by the menu—and casually asks me what I'm having. Eventually, she asks my name, too.

"I'm Corey Feldman."

"And what do you do?" she says. There's not a trace of name recognition.

"Uh, I'm an actor."

"What kind of an actor?"

I can't believe she doesn't know who I am. I don't know if she's really never heard of me, or if she's playing some kind of high-stakes cat-and-mouse game, but I'm used to screaming tweens ripping at my hair and clothes, literally throwing themselves at me. This, therefore, is refreshing.

"I'm in . . . you know, movies and stuff."

"Oh, yeah? Like what?"

Suddenly, I'm being forced to recite my entire résumé, which makes me feel like a heel. I manage to get her phone number, but she's aloof. As I watch her walk out into the Southern California sun, the owner of Veggie Cuisine leans over from behind the counter. "Don't even waste your time," he says. "You should see her *last* boyfriend."

I raise my eyebrows in anticipation.

"He's an Adonis."

"Huh." I shrug. "What's her name?"

I call Vanessa Marcil repeatedly, but she remains coy. She gives me the I-just-want-to-be-friends routine. Still, I'm persistent. And when my agent calls to tell me about an offer to go to Australia, I hatch a plan.

The 'Burbs is opening in Australia in June, just a week after *The Fox and the Hound* is due to be rereleased in theaters. I'm going over to do press for both, but I've also been invited to perform a series of concerts promoting my new single. Some insanely popular Australian dance troupe will be the opening act, and the whole production is sold to me as a massive tour; supposedly, we'll be playing thirty thousand- and forty thousand-seat stadiums. The trips seems like a great way to advance my music career, not to mention—since it'll be an all-expenses-paid, first-class trip—an excellent way to impress a pretty girl. I somehow convince Vanessa to go with me, but only after promising to get her her own hotel room, and not to "expect anything." It's the first time in my life I lied to someone I loved.

The Australia trip turns into something of a disaster. The publicity portion goes fine—I do Australia's version of the *Today* show—and we're put up in penthouse suites with impressive views of the harbor and the Sydney Opera House, but then confusion sets in. Two days before I'm scheduled to appear on stage, my publicist informs me that the entire show has been cancelled, something about disappointing ticket sales. Then we discover that our hotel rooms—paid for by the concert promoters—haven't actually been paid for at all. Neither have our first-class transpacific plane tickets. I get my uncle Merv on the phone (since, as a successful concert promotor, he's been bringing groups like the Beach Boys to Australia for years), and he pulls some strings to get us home safely. I would have been devastated but, despite her insistence that we remain "just friends," Vanessa and I are officially together. Amid the chaos, romance had bloomed.

Vanessa and I are inseparable. I take her everywhere with me. Which is how, two months after we met, we're in Vegas—in town for the Consumer Electronics Show—drunk, and talking about getting married.

"How much do you love me?" she cooes, downing another glass of Champagne.

"More than anything," I tell her, and I mean it. I've always been a fall-in-love-fast, love-at-first-sight kinda guy, but what I feel for Vanessa is unlike anything I've ever known.

"Enough to marry me?" she asks.

"Yes."

She seems satisfied with my answer, which gives me the confidence to return the question. "Do you love me enough to marry me?"

She nods.

"If you would marry me right now," I say, "I would marry you. You are everything I've ever wanted."

She sets down her glass. "Okay. Let's do it."

Next thing you know, we're at the Silver Bell Wedding Chapel picking out a wedding package. It's hokey and ridiculous. We're an Elvis impersonator short of total Vegas cliché, and I can't stop giggling.

"What's so funny?" she says.

I tell her I'm just really happy.

The next morning, hungover and a little worse for wear, we're back on a plane to L.A. We're coming in for a landing, I can see the runway at LAX from my window, when Vanessa rests her head on my shoulder. "I can't wait to tell all of our friends," she says. "This is going to be so funny."

"I know, right? No one is going to believe us." As I'm picturing the looks on all of our friends' faces, it occurs to me that we shouldn't share news of the wedding with the fans. I'm afraid having a wife will be bad for my image, since my fan base is made up entirely of love-struck, fanatical teens.

"Oh, I'm totally fine with that," she says. "I mean, it's not like this is a real marriage, anyway."

I turned to face her abruptly. "What do you mean?"

"I mean, we're not *really* married."

"Of course we're really married. We got the license and everything."

"Yeah, but it's not like we're going to live together or anything. We did it as a joke, right? For our friends?"

Her words take the wind out of me. I remembered, vaguely, laughing about how our friends would be shocked, but I didn't think the entire marriage was a joke. I had meant it when I told her I loved her.

"We'll keep dating and everything," she continues, "but I'm not going to move in with you. We have to be practical. We've only known each other a few months."

I thought it was a little late to be thinking practically. "What are you saying?"

"I'm saying, if you're going to take this whole thing so seriously, maybe we should just get it annulled right now."

I don't want an annulment. So I agree, against my better judgment, to take things slow.

Back when all the bad press started, I had signed on to do a Disney movie. Image in trouble? Sign up to work with the Mouse. The film is called *Exile*—it's loosely based on *Lord of the Flies*, and it'll air on NBC's The Wonderful World of Disney series, as an original Sunday-night movie. We'll be shooting on the deserted side of Catalina Island, and I already know I'm not going to be able to find drugs there. I've only been doing heroin for a few months—Vanessa doesn't even know about this yet—but my appetite has proved voracious; I'm already up to ten balloons a day. In order to make it through the one-week on-location shoot, I figure I've got to detox. So, I gather the strength to tell Vanessa that her young "husband," if you can even call me that, has a secret heroin problem. She is livid, she feels duped, but she agrees to stick by me. Then, I have my cousin Michael and Tony Burnham sweep me off to the Pasadena Recovery Center. Tony is so worried about me he's got tears in his eyes. "I don't want to lose you," he keeps saying. "I'm afraid you're going to kill yourself."

I assure him that it's not that bad, but this is just one more lie in a web I've built up around me. I had lied to Drew during the course of our entire romantic relationship—at fifteen, she'd already been in and out of rehab, twice, and had gotten herself sober, while I was off doing heroin and crack cocaine behind her back. I lied to Vanessa, let her get swept off her feet by a closet junkie. And I'd lied to the whole world by starring in *15 and Getting Straight,* and preaching about the dangers of drugs. I was terrified of rehab, but I knew it was where I needed to be.

I think I lasted about ten hours.

Since the emancipation—even before that, really—I've surrounded myself with a surrogate family. Sure, many of them are molesters, abusers, and addicts themselves, but the result is that I've never, *ever* spent even one night alone. (At least, not one I can remember.) And now I'm in a hospital gown, hooked up to an IV, and I'm terrified. I can't take it. I'm yanking IVs out of my arm and throwing a total, meltdown-style tantrum. I sign an involuntary discharge notice, and get myself back home.

Back on Picturesque Drive, Ron's managed to score some Quaaludes. "We haven't done these in forever, man. Not since the days with your dad." Jon thinks the Quaaludes will be a great way for us to avoid doing heroin. I eat a few, and my body instantly turns to mush. I'm laying across the steps that descend to the sunken living room, too drugged up to really move. Somehow I manage to stumble into bed. An hour later, I wake up. Ron is at me, tugging on my pants.

"You motherfucker!" I lunge for him, but I'm so fucked up, I fall out of bed, flat on my face. I'm screaming at him, "If you ever come back here, you're dead. I'll kill you. I will fucking kill you!" I'm screaming at him from the floor.

Ron is finally gone for good. One week later, I get a call from the check-cashing place down the street. Ron had been stealing checks and passing himself off as me. Despite the theft and the betrayal, my cousin Michael remains friends with him. I can't understand it, even though it's the exact same situation with me and Corey Haim and Tony Burnham. I'm still friendly with Tony because I'm too screwed up to connect the dots, to make that mental leap.

I move into a three-bedroom apartment in Beverly Hills. Vanessa stays over often enough, but I can't get her to move in with me. Therefore, I'm jealous, I accuse her of lying and cheating, I hear vague rumors about her dating other people, I'm convinced that she's started a relationship with Prince. I somehow make it through *Exile*, but by the end I'm going into withdrawal cold turkey. I feel like I'm actually dying.

It's a spectacular tailspin. I'm flaking on meetings right and left. I'm supposed to audition for *Toy Soldiers*, which will feature my friends and fellow costars Wil Wheaton, Keith Coogan, and Sean Astin, but I blow off the president of Island Pictures. On our second meeting, I flub all my lines. Vanessa and I are a mess; I'm lazy about hiding my habit, and she's finding balloons shoved under the carpet and crack pipes half-buried in the trash.

By the time *Rock 'n' Roll High School Forever* comes around at the dawn of 1990—my first direct-to-video movie—I'm in a freefall. We're on set one day when the first assistant director comes over and discretely tells me to wipe my nose, because I've got brown gunk leaking out of it. Instead of thanking him and taking care of the problem, I make a huge production. I spin an elaborate story about a blown tire, subsequent work on my car, and engine grease—it's the engine grease that's rubbed off on my nose—while the crew looks at me with disgust.

Soon, I'm running out of money. I've got a three-hundred-dollar-a-day heroin habit, and I'm spending money as fast as I make it. In lieu of cash, I start hawking my personal belongings to dealers on the street. Before I know it, I'm selling my CDs on a corner in exchange for crack rocks. Still, I haven't hit bottom.

———

In another attempt to salvage an unsalvageable relationship, I decide to take Vanessa on a three-day trip to Big Bear; it's a two- to three-hour drive up to San Bernardino County. Of course, I'll need enough heroin to get me through the long weekend, so I make another stop downtown on my way to some audition at 20th Century Fox. I've never had an official connection; I know the right streets, where to find the Mexican gangbangers I usually buy from. These guys keep balloons in their mouths so that if the police roll up, they can swallow them. I find my guy, and he spits out what I need. I buy twenty-five balloons, well over two grams in total.

On the way to the audition, I tear one open. The heroin tastes like cocoa powder, and I realize that I've been sold bunk. I'm on my way *back* downtown, in an attempt to haggle a trade, when I see an unmarked car flip its lights. I pull over and watch the uniformed officer approaching through my rearview mirror.

"Have you been drinking today?" he asks as he fingers my license and registration.

I'm actually genuinely surprised by the question. "No, sir."

"Why is there an open bottle of alcohol in your car?"

I look over at the passenger seat. In the well, rolling around the floor, is a half-drunk bottle of tequila I hadn't even realized was there.

"I'm going to need you to step out of the car."

I've got twenty-five balloons of heroin stuffed into one of my socks, and I'm terrified. I take a seat on the curb and watch as a second officer opens my glove box and pulls out a joint. An open bottle and marijuana are already enough for an arrest, but they soon find a single balloon that's fallen beneath the driver's seat. Every other time I've dealt with the cops, I've managed to talk my way out of trouble. I've already avoided an arrest for possession, and even got one officer to *return* my confiscated weed. But these guys are loving it; they are reveling in the fact that I'm up against the wall and I can tell, no matter what, that I'm completely and totally fucked. Still, I'm not above begging.

"Please, sir. Give me a chance. This is going to ruin my career."

"Your career?" he snorts. "What's your career?"

"I'm an actor."

"An actor? What movies have you been in?" Now he's looking me up and down.

"Uh, *The Goonies*? I was in *The Goonies*."

"*The Goonies*?" I think I recognize a flicker of recognition in his face. "Is that the one with a whole bunch of kids, and they ride around on their bikes and find a pirate ship or something like that?"

"Yep, that's it," I say. I feel something that's not quite relief flood over my entire body. Maybe this is going to work.

"Never heard of it," he deadpans. My stomach sinks right back down, so low it feels like it's in my feet.

"What else?"

"Uh, *Stand by Me*?" I offer half-heartedly.

"*Stand by Me* . . . what's that one about?"

"Four kids that go looking for a dead body? Please, sir, have some mercy on me."

"Wait, is that the one with the kids walking along the railroad tracks? It was a Steven King book?"

"Yes!" I say.

"Never heard of that, either."

I'm handcuffed now, sitting in the backseat of the unmarked squad car. There's another guy back here with me, with a ratty beard and tattered clothes. He looks homeless. I watch as the cops continue searching my car, when the man turns to me and says, "Tough break, huh? Well, you gotta deal with it. You gotta pay the price."

"I've got to get out of this," I tell him. "This is going to ruin my life."

I manage to lift my foot high enough so that, handcuffed, I can reach into my sock, retrieve the balloons, and shove them, one by one, behind the seat. "Please don't tell," I say to my companion.

"Don't worry, man. No problem."

When we pull into the station, I watch as the bearded man gets out of the car and whispers something in the officer's ear.

"Really?" the officer says. "Thanks for the tip." Then he turns to his partner. "Looks like we're gonna hafta pull out the bench. Our friend here's left us a little present."

I'm booked on suspicion of possession with intent to sell, on account of the large amount of heroin I'd been carrying.

On the very same night, all the way on the opposite coast, somewhere down in Daytona Beach, Florida, another former child actor has gotten himself into trouble. Danny Bonaduce has been arrested for attempting to purchase cocaine, and the twin arrests explode in the press. By the time Vanessa bails me out, sometime after 4:00 A.M., I'm deep into withdrawals, scared shitless, and convinced that I've completely destroyed my career. I think about all the kids that watch my movies and think I'm somebody cool. I know I've let absolutely everyone down. I figure my friends will bail on me. I'm sure that Michael Jackson, with his still squeaky clean image, will never speak to me again.

I know I'm going to need some serious firepower in the courtroom. Dick Donner, in a spectacular display of compassion, hooks me up with a lawyer, Richard Hirsch, and even fronts me some money for my impending legal fees. Richard, in turn, introduces me to Bob Timmins, the drug counselor with a proven track record of helping downtrodden celebrities get themselves clean. Bob immediately sits me down and talks about getting me straight.

"The first thing we need to do is get you into rehab," he says. "We need to prove that you're taking this seriously and seeking treatment before the court demands it of you."

"Yeah, that's fine," I tell him. "Just as long as it's not a long-term thing."

"You really need to be somewhere for something like six to nine months."

"I can't do that. I can kick this myself in three weeks."

"You'll have to go to AA."

"Yeah, yeah, fine. But three weeks is the most I can do."

Bob sets me up at Exodus, a private rehabilitation center in Marina Del Ray, but it's like rehab for rock stars. Dave Navarro and Joseph Williams, the lead singer of Toto, are my two roommates. Down the hall is a girl I recognize from the cover of a Jane's Addiction album; Perry Farrell is her boyfriend. I end up sending my cousin Michael out to score for me, but there's nowhere in rehab where I can cook up the heroin in order to crush it. So, when Perry comes for a visit, he and Dave convince me to try it their way. Together, they proceed to shoot me up.

At the arraignment, I plead not guilty to two felony counts of possession with intent to sell; each carries a maximum penalty of up to four years in prison.

Funny thing about being an addict: when you finally get sober, when you feel clean and strong and something that seems awfully close to normal, you immediately begin contemplating the idea of partying again. Because you're fine now, right? You just needed to get all that craziness out of your system. Now you can party *responsibly*. It's the disease talking, but he sounds a lot like yourself.

My next project, which will film while I'm out on bail, is the exceedingly violent, action-adventure film *Edge of Honor*. We'll be shooting in Washington state, and I'll be reteamed with Meredith Salenger, but there's no way anyone will insure me without a protective clause in my contract. I'll be required to submit to regular drug tests; fail one, and the whole production will be shut down. It's a lot of pressure, but I'm not being drug tested *yet*—shooting is still several weeks away—so I decide I'll just smoke some weed, because this being-totally-sober thing, I know, is not going to work out for me. At the time, someone I'd met in rehab was trying to convince me to commit to long-term rehab instead of doing the movie.

"No, no, I'm fine," I tell him. "I'm just smoking weed and drinking. I'll be fine."

"So, you're just changing seats on the *Titanic*?" It's a mantra that gets thrown around in rehabilitation circles all the time, a warning against the dangers of switching or substituting addictions, but I'd never heard it before. "Huh?" I ask, no doubt with plenty of attitude.

"You can fool yourself if you want, but the ship's goin' down either way."

"Listen," I said. "I know myself. I got this. I'm cool."

By the time I make it to Washington, I'm in full relapse, driving several hours to downtown Seattle to score crack rocks. I narrowly avoid another arrest (the cops pull up just as I'm approaching a possible dealer). Then, for some inexplicable reason, my mother decides to send my younger siblings on a plane, alone, to visit Vanessa and me. By now, my mother's had another child with a different man; Brittnie is about three, Devin and Eden are ten and nine.

Vanessa and I are a wreck, fighting constantly, so I escape back downtown. A bum approaches me, asks me to rent him a hotel room; amazingly, I do. In exchange, he shoots me up. And this is the saddest moment of my life: I was three hours late getting to the airport, and now I'm driving my siblings around while I'm high on heroin. It occurs to me that I'm doing the same shit my mother used to do to me, I'm doing the same things I hated her for. And I hated myself, but I couldn't stop.

Back in L.A., I do a few talk shows, try to convince everyone that I'm clean and sober, but then I'm right back downtown. I have almost no money, not enough for the two balloons of heroin and the crack rock I so desperately need, so I stiff a dealer. I drive off before he can see that I slipped him a five-dollar bill instead of a twenty. In the rear-view mirror, I can see his friends gathering, emerging from back alleys and dark street corners, when suddenly the back window explodes. I look behind me—there's a brick sitting in the middle of my backseat.

I'm at Vanessa's apartment building, buzzing and buzzing and buzzing, but she's not letting me in. I don't know if she's out or if she's hiding from me, but I'm sitting in a car with a shattered rear window when the cops roll up and ask me what I'm doing.

"I'm here to see my wife."

There's some concern that I've actually stolen the car in which I'm sitting, which of course I haven't. I do have three outstanding traffic warrants, however. I'm arrested again, and the cops find three balloons of heroin in my shoe.

I'm back at Exodus for another thirty days, but this time I want to get sober. I'm starting to see that maybe AA can work. People are checking in as addicts and walking out as fully realized people, no longer shadows of their former selves. I feel faint glimmers of my spirituality coming back, remember what my life was like when I believed in God and all He could do. I'm praying on a regular basis. They call this the "pink cloud," the sense of euphoria that comes with new-found sobriety. I'm starting to think, maybe I can do this.

My counselors want me to check in at Cri-Help, a no-frills, non-profit rehab facility in North Hollywood, immediately after my thirty days at Exodus are up. Cri-Help is like a military boot camp with mountains of rules, including no communication with the outside world for the first month. I'm terrified, but I decide to go. My hope is that by doing so, the judge will drop all the charges.

Vanessa takes me to check in. It's dark and dingy and not

air-conditioned. There's no swimming pool or Jacuzzi. It's nothing at all like what I'm used to. It's like prison. But I say good-bye to my wife. I resolve to attend every group therapy session and every meeting. By now I've even got my first sponsor, who also happens to have been one of my costars on *Gremlins*—it's a strange convergence of my two lives, that of movie star and down-and-out drug addict.

The first few days at Cri-Help pass uneventfully, but then I experience a hiccup: Vanessa has been leaving me tokens and gifts, like love notes or a pair of her panties, stashed secretly beneath empty crates kept out back by the trash. This is in complete violation of the rules, and we've been caught. As punishment, I'm being kicked out of rehab, and the only way to get myself back in is to attend thirty AA meetings in the next thirty days; if I can do that, Marlene, the head counselor at Cri-Help, will be willing to back me in court when asking the judge for a second chance.

I take this in stride, go to the meetings, get the vouchers signed, until the thirty-day probationary period is up. That's when I decide I need just one more night of partying before they let me back in. Just one more chance to have some fun before I get locked down for good.

I'm in a seedy section of Hollywood, idling outside some apartment building trying to score and, apparently, blocking a driveway, when the cops show up. I give them some song and dance about how I'm just "dropping off my maid," but they run my plates. I'm arrested *again*, this time for additional outstanding traffic warrants and driving with a suspended license.

Three days later, on December 10, 1990, I appear in court and plead no contest to all three felony charges. I'm fined five thousand dollars, given four years probation, and ordered back to live-in rehab. I go back to Cri-Help, knowing that it's my last chance.

CHAPTER 18

After nine months of treatment and little
to no interaction with people in the actual, outside world, I earned my
completion certificate from Cri-Help. I was sober. I was happy. I was
ready to get back to work.

I was also in debt—for legal fees and rehab expenses (I'd borrowed
nearly $30,000 from Richard Donner alone)—to the tune of $180,000.
My reputation as a rising star in Hollywood had been eviscerated. My
name, once associated with a slew of number-one hits, was a punch

line. I had just turned twenty-years old and I was starting all over. Again.

By the fall of 1991, there hadn't been many instances of downtrodden or drug-addled celebrities successfully reinvigorating their careers. This was a full five years before Robert Downey, Jr. became mired in the fallout from the first of his high-profile arrests—for speeding down Sunset Boulevard while in possession of heroin, cocaine, and a .357 Magnum and, one month later, for wandering into a neighbor's home and falling asleep in one of the beds; more than ten years before he would make what many consider to be the most successful comeback in Hollywood history. Drew Barrymore, once a fanfavorite and critical darling, was also still struggling—it would be another four years before she started landing the roles that ultimately salvaged her career; nine years before her production company's reboot of *Charlie's Angels* re-established her as a genuine, bankable star.

Without any kind of roadmap to follow, my agent and I go back and forth on how best to move my career forward. And within days of my release from Cri-Help, he brings me offers for two different films: *Round Trip to Heaven*, starring my old video game–playing costar Zach Galligan, and something called *Happy Campers,* in which I'll play a summer camp waterskiing instructor. Both are silly, schlocky scripts, but my agent convinces me to take them. "They'll forgive the fact that you're doing B-movies if you can show up on time, do good work, and prove that you're a professional," he tells me. "That's what Hollywood needs to see from you right now."

I don't understand the potential long-term effects of doing lowbudget, straight-to-video movies. So, instead of playing the long game, of waiting for a quality project I can really sink my teeth into, I choose roles based entirely on my dire financial situation. Together, *Round*

Trip to Heaven and *Happy Campers* will earn me $200,000. That's not such a bad deal for someone with a mountain of debt.

Despite being a campy T&A comedy, filming on *Round Trip to Heaven* goes smoothly; people in the business seem genuinely happy to have me back. Soon, there's even chatter about reprising my role as the voice of Donatello in the upcoming *Teenage Mutant Ninja Turtles* movie.

The original *Teenage Mutant Ninja Turtles* was brought to me in the fall of 1989, when I was already pretty deep into my heroin haze. It was an independent production, a tie-in to the comic-book series and the successful Saturday-morning cartoon, but to me it looked cheap and cheesy. Still, it was quick work, necessitating only a couple of days in the studio, for which I was paid scale (the minimum amount allowed for members of the Screen Actors Guild). *Teenage Mutant Ninja Turtles* went on to gross more than $130 million at the box office, making it the highest grossing independent film of its time.

Coming back to work on the second sequel (*Teenage Mutant Ninja Turtles II: The Secret of the Ooze* was filmed when I was in rehab) felt a little like redemption.

It was late fall, 1991, and we were shooting *Happy Campers*, a raucous comedy about a lakeside summer camp, at Bass Lake, a laid-back tourist hot spot not far from the south entrance of Yosemite National Park. While the other young actors spent their downtime drinking and partying—in a setting that reminded me an awful lot of filming *Friday the 13th*—I retreated to my cabin or sought support at daily AA meetings. My costar Jack Nance was also a recovering addict; together, we kept each other focused and on track.

I was leaving one of these meetings when Kris Krengel, one of the film's producers and an assistant director, pulled me aside. She had just finished shooting a film called *My Own Private Idaho* and she was worried about River Phoenix.

"I wouldn't normally say anything, but I know you were a heroin addict," she said, before taking a long, dramatic, deep breath. "And that's what he's been doing."

I couldn't believe it. It was true that I had only known River long ago, back when we were just children, but even then he was so dedicated, so driven, so devoted to his craft. More recently, he had been making a name for himself as a budding activist and philanthropist. He might have seemed out of sorts at the Oscars, but heroin didn't seem like something River would be about.

"Trust me," she said. "I know what I'm talking about."

Kris encouraged me to call him. She knew I was dedicated to my sobriety, and she thought my experiences with addiction might somehow be of help.

The phone rang and rang and rang, until finally River picked up. He sounded like he'd been asleep, though it was probably four in the afternoon. He sounded out of it, and I could tell, right then, that what Kris had said was true. I told River that I had heard some things, that I was concerned about him, and that when I was back in L.A. we should meet up and talk things through. He seemed amenable. We made loose plans, said good-bye, and hung up.

River and I played phone tag for a while after that, but never did get together, and I never saw him again. Less than two years later, on October 31, 1993, he would die, in a convulsing, overdose-induced fit, outside the Viper Room, a nightclub owned by his pal Johnny Depp. He was just twenty-three-years old.

As production dragged on, I used the weekends to escape to L.A. and work on repairing my relationship with Vanessa. I was renting a new home in Venice, though I still couldn't get her to move in with me; even with my newfound sobriety, our relationship was still very much on the rocks. It was when I arrived back from one of these weekend trips that I discovered the film's producers had cut a last-minute deal. The movie I'd signed on for, *Happy Campers*, would now be called *Meatballs 4*.

I had actually been sort of excited about *Happy Campers*. It wasn't exactly Shakespeare, but the director, Bob Logan, had just done the campy spoof *Repossessed* with Linda Blair and Leslie Nielsen; I thought we'd virtually be guaranteed a theatrical release. Now, *Meatballs 4*—a film I never would have agreed to make—was destined for a straight-to-video release. People sometimes have the misconception that actors have any real control over their destiny. In reality, the fate of your career is very often in the hands of those you sign on to work with.

In January, Vanessa and I traveled to Ixtapa, Mexico, for a charity golf tournament. It was our final attempt at saving the relationship, as well as our last public appearance together. By the time we got home—after nearly three years of ups and downs, of lying and cheating and suspicions and jealousy—we were over.

Despite all the drama, there's one thing I can say I did for Vanessa Marcil: I got her a meeting with one of my agents. By the close of 1992, she had snagged the role of Brenda Barrett on *General Hospital*, a role she would play off and on for the next twenty years, and for which she would win a Daytime Emmy. She has also starred on *Beverly Hills, 90210*, and NBC's *Las Vegas*. She was even named one of *People* magazine's 50 Most Beautiful People. She's done well for herself, and I wish her the best.

Back in L.A. and single, I plunged headfirst into sober life.

I had been thinking a lot about the way we teach drug awareness in this country—the message of programs like D.A.R.E. is fear-based; we use scare tactics to keep kids off drugs. We preach about the evils and dangers, wind them up until they think that recreational drug use or underage drinking will turn them all into homeless junkies. To me, this is the biggest mistake.

As anyone who's ever experimented knows, your heart won't explode after snorting a single line of cocaine. You won't become a high school dropout just because you took one puff from a joint. So, when a kid who's been taught to irrationally fear drugs sees his friend smoking pot—and quickly determines that his friend isn't on a downward spiral; he's actually turning out just fine—he starts to think, perhaps I've been lied to. He starts to wonder: hey, maybe drugs aren't so bad after all.

The truth, of course, is that drugs won't kill you on impact. In fact, recreational drug use can actually be a lot of fun—why else would so many people partake? But therein lies a bigger truth, as well as a bigger problem: addiction isn't immediate, but addiction can ruin your life.

I wanted to change the public discussion. So, in addition to attending as well as hosting regular AA meetings, in addition to acting as a sponsor and being sponsored myself, I also started lecturing at universities about the dangers of drugs but, more important, about the misconceptions that exist around their consumption. I also wanted to use the negative experiences in my life and, by helping others, turn them into positives. It wasn't a particularly profound or even an original goal, but it worked for me. At least for a while.

I also dove back into my music career. Whereas before I had been entirely focused on pop stardom, using movies to drive the success of my music, trying to get my singles inserted into my movies, now I just wanted to write songs for me. I hooked up with a drummer friend of mine, as well as Mark Karan, then an independent producer (now, he's best known for his work with Bob Weir, formerly of the Grateful Dead). Song writing, particularly in the months following the split with Vanessa, became cathartic. And soon, I would have a new tragedy to work through: in April, I got the call that Sam Kinison was dead.

Just as Sam and I had once competed in coke-off challenges, wagering to see who could stay up the longest, in more recent years we'd begun competing to see who could keep themselves sober. He was battling his own demons, had been in and out of rehab like me, but he had been doing really well in previous months. Which made it all the more ironic that he was killed by a drunk driver.

Sam was a dear friend. We weren't always the best influences on each other, but I loved him like a brother.

CHAPTER 19

One of the things I very quickly discovered is that going on auditions stone-cold sober is much harder than going in when you're lit. I hadn't successfully completed a sober read since childhood, when I'd fearlessly rambled on for Joe Dante or done shameless impressions of the Fonz for Richard Donner. So, when I scored an audition for a new film starring Al Pacino, I was nervous, to say the least.

Pacino, though it's perhaps cliché to say so, was easily one of my favorite actors, and I was a huge fan of the Godfather films. (Another cliché—though I was perhaps lucky that *The Godfather III* hit theaters when I was in rehab.) I studied like mad, prepared for weeks, but by the time I walked in, I was a wreck. I was consumed with fears, and way too busy wondering what the people gathered in that room were thinking. Did they really believe I was sober now? Did they even think I could act?

Right in the middle of the read, I felt my left eye start to twitch. Then, my lip began to quiver. I lost complete control of my body. It was such an incredible opportunity—a brilliant script (written by Bo Goldman, two-time Academy Award winner for *Melvin and Howard* and *One Flew Over the Cuckoo's Nest*), an accomplished director (Martin Brest)—and I watched it slip right through my fingers. The role of Charlie Simms in *Scent of a Woman* would go to a young Chris O'Donnell.

I continued auditioning, but that big break just wasn't coming. I had managed to pay off a large chunk of my debts, but I wasn't yet out of the hole. And so, I made the mistake that so many young, impatient actors make: instead of trying to reinvent myself, I went back to doing what "worked." Corey Haim signed with my agent, and we agreed to a three-picture deal.

The reunion, however, quickly became awkward, and not just because I had misgivings about a reteaming of the "Two Coreys."

Nearly a year earlier, I had come home to find a man dressed as Donatello from the *Ninja Turtles* waiting for me on my doorstep. I'd never received a singing telegram before, and I just sort of stood there, dumbstruck, as the turtle danced and sang and then handed me a VHS tape. I went inside, inserted the tape in my VCR, and watched as the turtle removed the head of his costume. Inside the suit was Marty Weiss, wishing me a happy birthday. (Apparently, he was doing kids' parties now.)

I thought the gesture was more than a little creepy, and when I told Haim about it, he insisted we beat Marty up. We made a plan to lure Marty to a nearby park and jump him.

This sounds much more sinister than it actually was—I don't believe either of us actually hit him, we just sort of dragged him to the ground and swatted at him for a bit. But for Haim, it was a way of communicating just how much Marty had affected him. Several months later—around the time we signed our three-picture deal—I moved to Encino, and Tony became my roommate. Haim took this as a kind of betrayal. Looking back on it now, who can blame him?

Whether it was denial, or the fucked up way your brain works when you've been a victim yourself, I just didn't think of Tony as a bad guy. I still thought, erroneously and ridiculously, that because Haim "wanted it," the abuse had not been Tony's fault. While Haim tolerated the arrangement and the two remained civil—Tony even scored a small role in one of our upcoming movies—it was clear to me that Haim could no longer stand him.

Despite the awkwardness, the first of the three new films Haim and I would make together seemed promising. *Blown Away* was an erotic thriller, kind of a *Basic Instinct* for a younger generation, costarring Nicole Eggert (who would later become Haim's fiancé). Haim and I were both attracted to the script because it afforded us an opportunity to break sharply from the kid-friendly roles we were used to playing. The film sold to HBO as a first-run feature in April 1993, where it premiered to pretty great ratings.

The second film on our schedule, National Lampoon's *Last Resort*, proved to be a little less promising. Haim and I were expecting to shoot a movie with a budget of between $4 and $5 million; we showed up on the set of what looked like a rinky-dink student film operation. The camera equipment was second-rate, the lighting packages were exceedingly cheap, and we were among a skeleton crew. We looked at each other that first day, wondering what we had gotten ourselves into.

Working under the umbrella of National Lampoon, we *thought*, would guarantee a relatively high production value; unbeknownst to us, a low-rent company had recently merged with National Lampoon in order to cash in on the name. It was the second time I'd become a victim of a last-minute bait-and-switch. It was also around the time I noticed Haim was popping Valiums and Somas (a muscle relaxer) by the handful.

As production dragged on, we began shooting at Paradise Cove, the same beach where Haim and I had played football all those years ago, on the day that we first met, when a dust particle or a grain of sand flew into my eye. The pain and the throbbing soon became unbearable, and filming became impossible—I had a steady stream of tears rolling down my face. (How ironic, when I had been worried about crying on cue all those years before—now I couldn't stop!) I found out that I had an infected tear duct, for which I would need surgery. After nearly two years clean and sober, I was faced with the prospect of taking prescription pain medicine.

I wasn't keen on putting any foreign substance in my body, especially after catching a glimpse of what Haim was up to. And had the operation been my only health hurdle, I perhaps could have made it through without medication. But within a few months, I would have four impacted wisdom teeth removed, then a slipped disk in my back, and then came the first stages of what would become a two-year struggle with aching, unexplained stomach and groin pain. I was able to keep my prescription pill use under control; at first, I used them only as directed. That would become more and more difficult, however, as the months dragged on.

By the beginning of 1995, things seemed to be looking up. The last of my three films with Haim—*Dream a Little Dream 2*—was in the can. It would be another straight-to-video release but, hey, I was working regularly and ready to move on to new things. I auditioned for a Warner Brothers television pilot—a mainstream project with quality people—and, incredibly, I got the job. We shot the pilot for *Dweebs*, a sitcom about brilliant but socially inept computer geeks (not unlike the premise of today's smash hit *The Big Bang Theory*), and CBS picked it up. On the heels of that news, Richard Donner—who had become something of a guardian angel in my life—snagged me a role in his upcoming film.

I had already done an episode of his successful HBO series *Tales from the Crypt* (that was after he got me a very small cameo in the 1994 blockbuster *Maverick*, starring Mel Gibson). Now, he was gearing up to make the second *Tales from the Crypt* movie in what was intended to be a trilogy of films. Both the television series and the films were helmed by some real Hollywood heavyweights, including producers Robert Zemeckis and Joel Silver. *Tales from the Crypt: Bordello of Blood* would be a great opportunity to work with major players in the industry. I felt like I was finally back.

Dweebs premiered in the fall to excellent reviews; the (now defunct) Viewers for Quality Television called us the "biggest surprise" of the season. But as is so often the case, we struggled to find a wide enough audience. This was, after all, a show about computer nerds; in 1995, *cell phones* were still something of a rarity, and Facebook wasn't even a glint in Mark Zuckerberg's eye. We were, perhaps, a little ahead of our time. As a result, *Dweebs* was cancelled after only six episodes. A few months later, *Bordello of Blood* tanked at the box office. (It probably didn't help that the film's star, comedian Dennis Miller, went on television and told audiences not to bother even seeing it.)

The sting of two failed projects was one thing. The unexplained pain, with which I was still struggling, was another. All those things combined, however, lead to a catastrophic moment of weakness, one I have never before admitted to publicly: by the end of 1995, I was gobbling twenty double-strength Vicodin a day. I was still going to meetings, still trying to live the sober life, but I was no longer really buying into it.

I had heard of using marijuana as a way to mitigate pain (again, this was 1995; "medical marijuana" hadn't yet hit the mainstream), and I thought marijuana might be better than prescription pill abuse. So, I smoked a joint. The joint led to an eight-ball. And the eight-ball led to a full-fledged relapse.

I tumbled downhill faster than I ever had in my life. My car—a flashy Mercedes I had purchased with my network sitcom money—was repossessed. The beautiful home in Encino, right around the corner from the Jackson family estate, I could no longer afford. I moved to an apartment in Woodland Hills and, at first, both Tony and my cousin Michael came with me. But soon neither of them could stand watching me ruin my life. Again. Eventually, they both moved out.

I found myself wandering through Chatsworth Park one night, the same park where I had gone climbing with Tom, my mother's old alcoholic, abusive boyfriend. I was terrified. I couldn't believe—after all those months in rehab, and all the hard work in recovery—I had allowed myself to go careening off track. It ended up being one of those cry-your-eyes-out, howl-at-the-moon kind of nights, and I had a kind of spiritual awakening, a "moment of clarity," as it's often referred to in sobriety circles. I had to admit to myself that I was out of control, had to give it all up to God, so to speak.

I vowed to no longer be overcome by the negative. My relapse only lasted a little more than a month, and I never had another hard drug again.

After two years of living with undiagnosed and unexplained pain,

I passed the first of several kidney stones. I also found a doctor who was able to further explain my problem: some people, for some reason, have overactive kidneys, and may pass many microscopic stones, in addition to the bigger, visible ones. These are undetectable to the naked eye, but can still cause irritation, pain, and even blood in the urine. The diagnosis was a welcome discovery; it had just come a little bit late.

During the filming of *Dweebs*, I started toying with the idea of putting together a psychedelic rock band, something a bit reminiscent of Pink Floyd. I had become a huge fan of their music, had traveled all over the world to see their shows, I had even become friendly with David Gilmour after meeting him backstage at a show in L.A., around the time I was shooting *License to Drive*. I pulled together my previous collaborators, Mark Karan and David Dunn, brought on some new artists, and together we formed Truth Movement.

I finished the first album near the end of 1998. It was a dark, intensely personal, autobiographical piece, with songs like "Hopeless" and "Spiraling Downward," essentially a suicide note set to music. But the process, again, proved cathartic. And whereas my solo album had been universally panned, and certainly never got a distribution deal, *Still Searching for Soul* did a little bit better. We even scored a deal for placement in record stores.

Truth Movement started playing small shows around L.A. for virtually no money—sometimes we even had to *pay* to play—but within a year or so we were setting out for a cross-country tour. It was a modest affair, sure, just seven guys stuffed in a van with a bunch of gear and a trailer hitch, and in Seattle, right in the middle of sound check, I completely lost my voice. (Luckily, it's a psychedelic rock band; we were able to improvise a lot of instrumental intermissions.) But hearing promos for our shows on the radio, seeing fans show up in their *Goonies* T-shirts, was actually, *oddly*, encouraging. It's not like I didn't know that some people were there for the spectacle. But I didn't need to sell out a stadium. I was happy if anyone at all wanted to hear us play.

CHAPTER 20

I needed to blow off some steam, which is how I found myself at Las Palmas, a trendy nightclub at the north end of Hollywood. I was scanning the room when I locked eyes with a pretty brunette. She was different from the girls I usually dated, but there was something about her. There was something sweet, angelic even, about her face.

I wasn't looking for a relationship. I wasn't even really interested in having a fling. I'd fallen into an all-too-familiar pattern with women, ever since my breakup with Vanessa: meet someone with whom I thought I might have a future, move her in within three months, get engaged in six, and by nine months—when I would invariably discover that I was being lied to or cheated on, or both—everything would fall apart, and then I'd be on to the next. By 2001, I wasn't sure if I could trust anyone. I had more or less given up. I was just about to call it a night when the pretty brunette sidled over.

"Excuse me," she said, "are you Corey Feldman?"

"Yes."

"I'm so excited to meet you! I've been a fan of yours all the way until . . ."

"Until when?" I interjected.

"Well, until today!"

Being recognized by a fan at a nightclub isn't usually the way to a love connection, but I thanked her, offered to buy her a drink at the bar, and before long she was pulling me on the dance floor. The girl had chutzpah, I had to give her that. She wasn't afraid to take charge. She knew how to get what she wanted.

Susie Sprague and I slept together that very night, and within days I had told her everything about my life—everything about the abuse, the drugs, the scandals, and the recoveries. I confided in her about my insecurities, my jealousy, and my inability to trust. I even told her I didn't know if I knew *how* to have a relationship. I wasn't sure if I really knew how to love, or how to be loved back. Susie had been hurt before, too, but she was still willing to give it a shot. So, we decided to try things differently than either of us had before in the past. In order to build trust and to restore faith in ourselves as partners, we would have an open relationship. If we had an urge or a fantasy, we would share it with each other.

We fell in love quickly. With Susie, there was no fighting, no bullshit, no jealousy, no lying, no cheating, and no drama. We were just happy— every single day. I recognized it as the start of a new kind of life.

Nearly a decade earlier, when I first heard that Michael Jackson had been accused of child molestation, I almost laughed—it seemed so ridiculous. Then I got a call from the LAPD; a sergeant and a detective wanted to talk to me about my friendship with him.

The audiotapes have long since been leaked to the press—I clearly stated that Michael never touched me, never acted in any way inappropriate. What's incredible about them, however, is that I admitted that I *had* been molested; I even named my abuser. The sergeant peppering me with questions, Deborah Linden, breezed right past that. She didn't seem the least bit interested.

Over the next several weeks, I made a few informal comments to the press and declared that Michael was innocent of the charges. (I was still living in Encino at the time; the paparazzi often made the two-minute drive to my house once they'd grown tired of staking out Hayvenhurst.) Michael was appreciative that I had spoken out on his behalf, and as a thank-you—several months after he settled the case out of court—he invited me up to Neverland Ranch.

I took Corey Haim with me, since he had never actually had an opportunity to meet Michael face-to-face. We rode go-karts. We giggled as Michael told us stories about Madonna, his date to the 1991 Academy Awards. (I think she intended to make a man out of him, but Michael wasn't ready for all that.) We ordered movies to watch in his theater. Together, the three of us screened *Dream a Little Dream*.

But I didn't see much of Michael in the years after that. He called once when I was in the hospital, still seeking treatment for my as-yet-undiagnosed kidney stones. I called his camp in 1995, after word came that he had collapsed—from "exhaustion"—in New York a few days before he was due to film an HBO special, *One Night Only*, at the Beacon Theater. It was obvious even then that his physical health, perhaps even his mental health, was deteriorating. Still, I wanted to see him. So when I was invited to attend the celebratory concerts in honor of the thirtieth anniversary of his solo career, I leaped at the chance. The Jackson camp secured my tickets, while I proceeded to make travel arrangements for Susie and me to fly to New York. I had us booked at the Millennium Hotel, adjacent to the World Trade Center, until Majestik convinced us that we should stay with him, nearer the family, uptown.

The first of the two performances, held at Madison Square Garden, was the evening of September seventh. Susie and I arrived early, walked the red carpet, and took our seats in the stadium—the whole thing was great fun; Whitney Houston, Slash, 'N Sync, and Destiny's Child were all part of the star-studded event, but Michael's performance was lacking. He seemed out of it, not quite present, like he wasn't even enjoying the occasion. That was odd; Michael loved to perform. I was having trouble reconciling the man on stage with the man I had grown up idolizing.

When the concert ended, sometime around eleven o'clock that night, Susie and I hopped in a car with some of the family and rode as part of a lengthy caravan through the city streets. Michael was hosting an elaborate "Champagne and Caviar Dinner" at the renowned Central Park restaurant, Tavern on the Green. The whole place was a who's-who of Hollywood and the music industry; everyone from Gloria Estefan to Elizabeth Taylor to Marlon Brando was there. At some point, Sean Lennon offered to take a photo of Susie, Michael, and me. It would be the last photo he and I would ever take together.

We spoke briefly about spending a little alone time together that weekend. Of course, Michael had a jam-packed schedule, so we decided it would be most convenient to meet at Madison Square Garden again, on Monday afternoon, a few hours before the start of the second concert. Susie and I said good night and headed back to the hotel. Everything got really weird after that.

Susie and I were supposed to pick up our passes and credentials at the VIP Entrance, but when we arrived on the afternoon of the tenth, there weren't any passes to be had. I had been to a number of Michael's events before; they were always impeccably organized and usually ran smooth as silk. Something about this felt mighty different. After milling around outside for a while, I ended up getting separated from Susie, led down two elevators and several dimly lit hallways, and shoved into a tiny dressing room. I must have waited in there for an hour. Each time I poked my head out, to inquire about my girlfriend, or about when Michael might be showing up, two burly security guards would direct me, brusquely, back inside. "Just wait right here, sir," they kept saying. "Please stay inside the room."

I felt like I was being held hostage. It wasn't even clear if Michael was expecting to see me or not. Finally, he showed up and walked, alone, into the room.

"I need to talk to you about something." He was all dressed up in his concert attire, and he seemed jittery. Nervous, even. "You know I love you, right? You know I want to believe what they're telling me isn't true?"

"What who's telling you?" I asked. "About what?"

"Please promise me you're not going to write this book."

"What book?"

"They're telling me you're writing a book about me, and you're planning to say all these terrible things."

It's true that I had had offers before, had even toyed with the idea of writing a memoir about my life, but I had never actually moved forward, never gotten anything off the ground. Regardless, why would I write a book *about* Michael Jackson? Stranger still, why would I write "terrible things" about him? Michael and I were *friends*; we had never before had anything even resembling a fight. Which is what I told him, as we stood next to each other in that small dressing room.

"Okay, I want to believe you," he said. "I really do. But you're going to have to talk to my mother."

We walked out of the dressing room and he sort of shoved me in Katherine's direction; she had apparently been standing outside the dressing room, in the hallway. I turned to speak to him, to ask him, again, what was really going on, but a crowd of security guards enclosed around him. With that, he was gone.

Katherine gave me a hug and told me not to worry; she didn't seem to share Michael's concerns, and mumbled something about people trying to take advantage of him, that it was difficult to know whom to trust. But I soon discovered that there weren't any passes or credentials available for Susie or me; it was obvious that we were no longer welcome backstage. So, instead of attending the concert, we wandered out into the night. I let our tickets fall from my hands, landing in a muddy puddle on the street. I couldn't explain what had just happened, I wanted to get the hell out of town.

The next morning was September 11.

I had actually called a bellhop to come and collect our luggage; Susie and I were preparing to take a cab to JFK. That was moments before the first plane hit. After that, everything just sort of stopped—until Majestik rushed in and suggested we meet up with the family. "If anyone's going to make it out of New York, it's the Jacksons."

Like it did for so many, many people, the day dissolved into a blur of fear, panic, terror, and sadness. We spent most of the morning schlepping our luggage over to the Plaza hotel, where a large portion of the Jackson family was staying. (Joe and Katherine were at a different hotel down the street; Janet and Michael were at a third hotel around the corner.) Jermaine spent most of his time on the phone, speaking to someone about maybe renting a bus. And at 4:00 P.M., after hours of sitting around in a state of shock, we were boarding.

As I climbed aboard and got Susie settled in one of the seats, I saw Majestik shoot me an odd look. Then, Randy appeared behind me, and said he needed to have a word. I followed him and Jermaine back off the bus, to the sidewalk.

"I'm afraid you can't come with us," Randy said.

"What are you talking about?"

"I don't know what happened between you and Michael, but he doesn't want you on that bus."

I couldn't understand it. First, the strange confrontation about a book that didn't exist; now, I was being kicked off what was literally the only ride out of town—all of the tunnels and bridges were closed. I was going to be stranded in New York for apparently no good reason. I was embarrassed, but also insulted and hurt. Eventually, Jermaine agreed to let us travel with them, as long as I promised never to tell Michael he had allowed us to get back on the bus.

The next few days were bizarre, to say the least: riding on a bus with the Jacksons, stopping at fast-food restaurants and more than one Cracker Barrel. (I don't know if it's still official policy, but at the southern-style restaurant, celebrities used to eat free.) Somewhere outside Nashville, when it became possible to secure ourselves a rental car, Susie and I disembarked, thanked the family, and headed back home by ourselves.

Back in L.A., I tried to put what had happened with Michael behind me—but not before including a thinly veiled song about the experience, "Megaloman," on my third album. Within weeks of its release, I was sent a cease and desist letter from Jackson's attorneys, claiming that the song was defamatory. I responded with my own letter; of all people, Michael Jackson should understand the importance of creative freedom. (It's not like he hadn't written skewering songs of his own.) The letters stopped after that, and the song stayed on the album.

I went about promoting and performing, and Susie and I moved in together. On Valentine's Day, 2002, we got engaged. But Michael and I would never reconcile. We never spoke to each other again.

———

I first noticed it in 2002, when I was touring to promote my third album.

It used to be—back in the '80s and '90s—that, as a celebrity, you could anticipate when and where you would be expected to interact with the press. If you attended a film premiere, for example, or an event with any kind of red carpet, reporters and film crews would certainly be there. If you hosted a fund-raiser or a charity gala, you might even *call* the press in order to secure coverage for your event. But you didn't expect to be bombarded by cameras on a random week-night, if you went out for an anonymous night on the town. You didn't expect to see paparazzi loitering outside a restaurant when all you wanted was a quiet meal with your significant other. By 2002, that had changed. And suddenly, the only film offers I was getting were to play some version of myself.

Bikini Bandits was the first project in which I starred as "Corey Feldman." It was a ridiculous premise and a poorly written script. I regretted it, but I needed the money.

Next, I got a call from Wes Craven. I was a huge fan—I had already made several horror films, and Craven is an *auteur* of the slasher. He had even revived more than a few stalled-out careers: Drew Barrymore had a small part in the 1996 blockbuster *Scream*; it was one of her first roles on the road back to mainstream stardom. I took a meeting with Wes for his new film called *Cursed,* and we talked all about my proposed character. I was stoked—I thought it was the call I'd been waiting for. But when the script came back nearly six months later, I saw that I'd been given a two-page cameo and, again, I was being asked to play myself.

"I don't understand," I told one of the producers. "We talked about playing a *character*?"

"Well, the script has changed. But Scott Baio's in it—he's also playing himself."

I passed. They offered me more money. Again, I said no. Again, they increased the offer. Finally, after they agreed to pay me, per day, an amount equivalent to my weekly rate, I agreed. (Lucky for me, the movie encountered massive production delays, was rescripted and partly recast, and my footage ended up on the cutting-room floor.)

The third such offer was for a film called *Dickie Roberts: Former Child Star.* David Spade called me himself, and told me he wanted to put me in a poker scene with Leif Garrett, Dustin Diamond, Danny Bonaduce, and Barry Williams. Again, I turned down the offer and, again, I was offered more money. The clincher was when they agreed to let me provide a song for the soundtrack.

On one of the last days of filming, a slew of former child actors—including Gary Coleman, Florence Henderson, Jeff Conaway, Todd Bridges, Christopher Knight, and Maureen McCormick—was assembling to sing a sort of "We Are the World" parody, a celebrity-studded song called "Child Stars on Your Television" that would play during the film's closing credits. I wasn't sure I wanted to be a part of it, but then the producers told me they'd secured a cameo with Corey Haim. At that point, I hadn't seen him in ages. Against my better judgment, I signed myself up.

I was walking through the parking lot that morning when I heard someone call out from behind me. "Core! Core, man. What's up, bro?"

A particularly unkind reviewer once referred to a bloated, over-weight Haim as looking like a "fat lesbian." It was a cruel thing to say, but it wasn't entirely untrue. By 2002, Haim was puffed up and swol-len; he was, in fact, unrecognizable. I had walked right past him without even stopping.

The final offer to play myself—that old nail in the coffin—was for a Big Brother–type reality show, to be filmed with a cast full of "ma-jor" celebrities. The pitch came from Mark Cronin, whom I had worked with back in '92, not long after news broke of Sam Kinison's death. A number of my friends told me to tune in to Howard Stern that day; Stern was devoting an entire radio show to Sam's legacy, playing old clips of Sam's appearances. I felt compelled to call in, which lead to an appearance on Howard's short-lived Channel 9 television show (on which Mark Cronin was a staff writer) to perform my single "What's Up with the Youth?"

I didn't know much about Stern's television show; I was told it was a little like Club MTV. It was closer to a surrealist, David Lynch–inspired acid fest. I ended up dancing on a stage next to a topless little person dressed in a grass skirt while Howard stood in the audience, wearing a bald cap and something akin to a Brazilian-cut bikini, batting around blow-up dolls as if they were beach balls. The whole thing—which, unfortunately, will live forever on YouTube—might be the most uncomfortable five minutes in television history. So, when Cronin came calling, I probably should have hung up the phone.

The Surreal Life was pitched to me as a positive show. The point wasn't to portray all of us as hapless has-beens, or to make fun of our respective careers. Still, I declined. Again, I was offered more money. And again, against my better judgment, after many rounds of negotiations and a meeting with one of the top execs, I agreed to play myself.

Before filming began in earnest, in the fall of 2002, each of the seven cast members—Vince Neil, MC Hammer, Emmanuelle Lewis, Gabrielle Carteris of *Beverly Hills, 90210,* Jerri Manthey of television's *Survivor,* Brande Roderick of *Playboy* fame, and, of course, myself—participated in some initial interviews; the footage would be used to build the opening credits and to establish our "characters" on the show. I sat down in front of a camera, and a producer asked me a question. "So, Corey, you've been around for so long. You're really more than an actor. You're an icon, an industry. How does that make you feel?"

"Uh, well, thanks," I said. "But I don't know if I agree with all that. Really, I'm just happy that I'm still making movies after all these years. I'm happy that I'm still working."

"Okay, that's great, but it doesn't really incorporate the question. Please repeat the question and restructure the answer accordingly."

Have you ever noticed, in those interview segments on reality shows, that the cast members almost always begin by speaking in complete, well-constructed sentences? You know why, right? The cast member is being asked a series of questions by someone positioned off-camera. But no one wants to hear the producer talking, so the cast member is encouraged to repeat the question so that the viewer will be able to follow along at home.

I balked. "I don't really want to say those words. I mean, that sounds pretty egotistical."

The producer and I haggled back and forth, until finally I said something like: "Okay, I'm more than an actor, I'm a musician, and a producer, and a dancer. And it's wonderful if people think that I'm an icon, an industry, but really, I'm just appreciative of the fact that I'm still working."

I left the session feeling more than a little uncomfortable.

There's a special editing term used in the world of reality television: it's called the "Frankenbite," as in, the piecing together of disparate sound bites to manufacture story, to create drama, and, sometimes, to make it appear as though someone said something they really didn't. I don't want to be one of those people who blames the editors for the fact that their reality television portrayal turned out to be unflattering, but when I watched the opening credits of that first episode, and heard myself say, "I'm more than an actor. I'm an icon, an industry," I knew I was in trouble.

I don't blame people for being turned off by what they saw on *The Surreal Life*. I sounded like a pompous, egotistical ass. Even *I* sat there every week, cringing in front of the television, screaming, "Shut up! You sound like a total idiot!" It was the single worst professional experience of my life. It was also the first time I was able to see—with the advent of the Internet—viewer's reactions in real time; I have never heard the word "asshole" used more times in reference to myself.

It's not like people had never had negative things to say about me before. For years, people have made ridiculous, off-color comments about my relationship with Michael Jackson—that we had "matching monkeys," for example. (I don't even have to mention what some people have come up with based on his problems with molestation accusations and my history of abuse.) For the most part, I don't care about stuff like that. People can say whatever they want. But what killed me was the construction of that "icon, industry" quote. It shows up everywhere, it's listed on several professional Web sites as one of my "famous quotes"; it will forever be attributed to me. I *am* proud of my career, and I am proud that I continue to work as an actor, but that quote is never something I would have said. It's not how I feel about myself.

There was one positive thing to come out of *The Surreal Life,* though I never thought I'd get married on a reality show, and it certainly wasn't my idea. The producers approached Susie and I three days into filming (she was around a lot behind the scenes)—everyone knew we were engaged, so they pitched us the idea of getting married on the season finale of the show.

I said no way, told the producers I thought they were crazy. But they kept increasing the proposed budget for the wedding, kept promising more and more perks. Even though my entire family advised against getting married on television, I knew I couldn't afford to give Susie the wedding she deserved—if I agreed to get married on the show, the network would provide us a wedding planner, fly in our family from all across the country, and Susie would be able to pick the dress of her dreams. It's perhaps also helpful to point out just how draining a show like this is—it's long hours, lots of stress, and zero privacy. Eventually, you just get worn down. I ended up selling myself on the idea.

Susie was a stunning bride, and despite all the chaos around us, I was able to block out everything and focus solely on her. After the wedding, we took off for our honeymoon in Bora, Bora. I felt calm, and at peace. I was married now, and deliriously happy. But after *The Surreal Life*, I also knew things would have to change.

I moved management. I vowed to turn down every single offer to play myself. I only wanted to work in challenging, artistic, redeeming roles. If that meant that I didn't work for a while—if it meant I never worked again—that was going to have to be okay. I was going to have to swallow my pride. I would have to take a leap of faith.

Above: On the "Rock On" music video set: Michael Damian and *Dream a Little Dream* costars Meredith Salenger and Corey Haim, 1988.

Left: Alfonso Ribeiro and I kicking it old school after performing "Dirty Diana," 1988.

Jeff Hoefflin and I watch as Michael Jackson poses with his wax figure at Hayvenhurst.

Majestik, Muhammad Ali, and I, circa 1986.

[Left to right]: Jeff Hoefflin, me, Michael, Emmanuel, and LaToya in Michael's theater at Hayvenhurst.

Sir Paul McCartney and I come together backstage at The New World Tour, 1993.

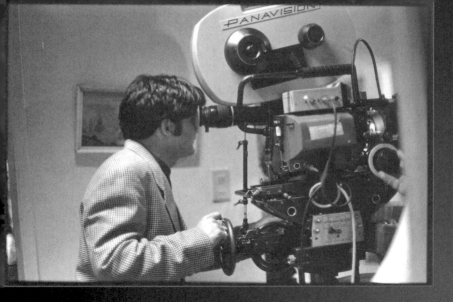

Behind the camera producing *Dream a Little Dream 2*, 1994.

The final photo: Yoko Ono, Susie, Michael, and I, photographed by Sean Lennon. Tavern on the Green, September 7, 2001.

Backstage with Pink Floyd's David Gilmour.

Miraculous moment: With baby Zen on the day of his birth, August 7, 2005.

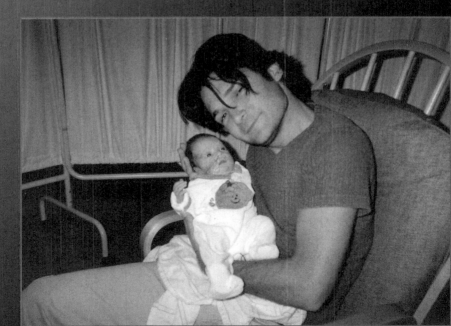

Lone soldier: In my Edgar Frog costume again for *Lost Boys: The Thirst*, South Africa, 2009.

Corey and his mother Judy were closer than ever in his final days.

Me, baby Zen, nephews Ashton and Dorion, and sister Mindy at a Goldstein family dinner.

Soul survivors: Cousin Michael and childhood friend Ian, showing off baby Zen.

Above: Richard Donner and I, celebrating on my tour bus at *The Goonies* 25th anniversary concert, June 2010.

Right: My proudest achievement: A happy and healthy Zen.

CHAPTER 21

In February 2004 I read a quirky script for
an independent film from an up-and-coming Spanish director. As
soon as I leafed through it, the characters, the camera direction, all of
it immediately leaped from the page. It was a wildly ambitious project, and my role, that of the sheltered, socially inept Norman For-
rester, was the acting opportunity I had been waiting for.

I spoke with the director, a then-twenty-six-year-old Eugenio
Mira, and quickly discovered that he was charismatic, full of energy,

and—like me—an unabashed lover of film. He also had big plans for the production: not only would the film be shot in "real time," but my character would be in every shot of the movie. Not every *scene,* mind you—every single shot. It was a huge amount of responsibility, but Susie and I were stoked and we agreed to travel to Spain for the three-month shoot. It was the second piece of good news we had received that year. By the spring of 2004, Susie and I discovered that we were going to have a baby.

Barcelona is an incredible, vibrant, cosmopolitan city. It's the home of Park Güell and Sagrada Familia, two of the most famous works by the surrealist architect Antoni Gaudí. It's also a city of small hills; our hotel suite was perched at the top of one, and we had an incredible view from our fourth-floor balcony. Of course, living in Barcelona for three months also came with its challenges. In 2004, Spain still felt very much like a country of smokers; people lit up just about everywhere, which can be a little uncomfortable when you're traveling with a pregnant wife. Drinking, of course, is also part of the culture—it's completely acceptable to drink during lunch; in fact, there was *always* a bottle of wine on our table. And if you know anything about Spanish food, well, it's not exactly vegetarian-friendly. Susie and I carried around a little tourist's guidebook, which was supposed to point us in the direction of the city's few meat-free restaurants. We went to one—an Italian-style bistro—and were shocked to find "horse steak" on the menu. (So much for vegetarianism.) Still, filming *The Birthday* was one of the most exhilarating and exciting professional experiences of my life.

The Birthday performed well on the festival circuit—it won Best Art Direction and was nominated for Best Film at the Sitges Film Festival in Sitges, Spain; *I* won Best Actor at the Luxemburg Film Festival—and earned a theatrical release in Spain. But, as so often happens with small independent productions, it failed to secure American distribution. Eugenio Mira has a bright future—he was a second unit director on the brilliant 2012 film *The Impossible*, starring Naomi Watts and Ewan McGregor and his newest film, *Grand Piano*, has been called one of the most anticipated releases of 2013. His film *The Birthday* is one of my proudest achievements as an actor. I dearly wish more people had seen it. My hope is that, one day, they will.

After three months in Barcelona, Susie and I were back stateside, making preparations for the baby. I had also signed on to do another film (it was schlock, but I was trying to build my nest egg), which would shoot for three weeks in Bulgaria. We decided we would both go to Europe—Susie and I didn't like being apart, especially when she was with child—and by the time we returned home, she would have another month or so left in her pregnancy. As the saying goes: if you want to make God laugh, tell Him your plans.

Just a few days before we were scheduled to leave the country, we attended a friend's wedding in Palm Springs. (I actually became ordained online, at the couple's request, in order to officiate the ceremony.) It was August and it was hot, the temperature had been averaging well over a hundred degrees. Still, we wanted to stay through the weekend, turning the trip into something of a mini-vacation. Besides, Susie was planning on getting a maternal massage, and she needed it; she'd been struggling with pretty severe back pain for the past several months. The morning after the wedding, though, I woke up and reached across the bed for her. Susie wasn't there.

That part wasn't unusual. Susie has restless leg syndrome, which frequently kept her up at night. She often left our bed in the wee hours of the morning, in an attempt to get comfortable, and in an attempt not to disturb me. I woke up many mornings to find her curled up in random spots throughout the house. I looked around our hotel suite, and found her in the sitting area, laying on her back with her feet stretched straight up in the air.

"You okay?"

"I haven't slept," she said, visibly exhausted. "My back is killing me. Maybe it's the heat?"

We went about our day as planned, lounging poolside, relaxing and unwinding before we would make the long ride home, host a baby shower, and then make our way across the Atlantic. But all throughout the afternoon, she kept saying she just didn't feel *right*. She felt off. And then she told me that she hadn't felt the baby move in a while.

"What?" I shouted, the panic already creeping in.

"I haven't felt the baby move since yesterday. I think that's why I was up all night."

I insisted we head home. I wanted to get Susie nearer to her doctor. It didn't make sense to stay in Palm Springs, even if nothing was really wrong. We packed up the car and started the two-hour trek, and as we entered L.A. county, she suddenly felt the baby kick.

"There he is!" she shouted, breathing an audible sigh of relief.

"You still want to call the doctor?"

"No, I'm sure everything's fine," she said. "I think we panicked for no good reason."

Now that we were back home, a day earlier than expected, we decided to go out for a quiet dinner and a movie. But as we left the theater later that evening, again Susie said, "I haven't felt him move."

"What are you talking about? I thought everything was fine now. I thought you said he moved earlier."

"He did," she said. "But I haven't felt anything else since then."

"Well, that's it," I said. It was time to call the doctor.

We checked into Tarzana Medical Center, and Susie was immediately hooked up to all kinds of equipment and fetal-monitoring machinery. We were shocked to discover that—at just thirty-two weeks along—she had gone into preterm labor. More terrifying still, the ultrasound tech poked and prodded Susie's belly, but the baby still wasn't moving; she couldn't get him to respond. On the fuzzy black-and-white monitor, the baby looked almost frozen. Then, as they moved the wand across Susie's belly, they discovered a little white blip on the baby's brain. No one could explain what had caused it, only that, at some point, the baby had suffered a "loss of oxygen," which had been caused by some kind of "traumatic event." That's when the doctor dropped a bomb, the single scariest sentence ever uttered to expectant parents: "Your baby may not turn out . . . *normal*," he told us. The baby's chances of being born with MS were great. He might never run, laugh, or play. The options were laid out before us: leave the baby in and "see what happens," or take the baby out and hope for the best. We prepared for an emergency C-section.

I stood next to Susie's head, behind the giant blue surgical curtain separating the top half of her body from the bottom, and when those first few, gentle cries rang out we were both flooded with relief. But then the baby went stiff again, and started turning blue. He was immediately placed in some kind of oxygen tent—it looked like a scene straight out of *E.T.*, the doctors all standing around him in their surgical masks, poking and prodding and pumping. Susie was hysterical. She kept screaming out, "What's wrong?" So, I lied to her, told her that everything was fine, and prayed harder than I ever had. I begged God to let my son turn out all right. Finally, he started to cry again, more robust now. I could hear him crying his way back to life.

Zen was carted off to the NICU. I stayed with Susie while the doctors stitched her up. But, after the dramatic birth, she was understandably exhausted. I left her to sleep, and crept out of the room to go see my son.

Zen was nestled in another oxygen chamber, intubated, hooked up to wires and monitors, with a little visor-like contraption covering his eyes (he had jaundice, which is common in premies); he looked like a little robot baby. As I bent over to stare at him, a nurse appeared at my side. "Would you like to hold him?"

I hadn't even realized that would be possible.

She unhooked him from all the machines, wrapped him up like a little burrito, and placed him in my arms. He was just shy of three pounds. His entire head fit neatly within my palm. I had never seen anything so tiny in my life. I was petrified. But as I pulled the visor from his eyes, Zen looked right at me. He zeroed in, as if to say, I'm okay, Dad. I'm a fighter, and I'm going to be just fine. I kissed him. I was going to give my little boy all the love that I had missed.

Leaving my wife and my newborn son to shoot some ridiculous movie in Bulgaria—three days after his traumatic birth—was one of the most difficult things I've ever done. But we arranged for a friend to stay with Susie, and by the time I got back to L.A., Zen was able, finally, to come home.

Still, Zen's first few months of life were tough. He had difficulty sleeping, terrible cramping and gas, and two hernias, for which he would eventually need a small operation. Like all new parents, Susie and I barely slept. We eventually began taking turns; I'd be up most of the night on dad duty, Susie would take over by morning. I spent most of those first six months terrified that something would go wrong. It was amid this sleepless haze, and a mountain of dirty diapers, that I got a call from the journalist Martin Bashir.

In the spring of 2003, Susie and I had watched the devastating footage that made up the ABC News special *Living with Michael Jackson*. It aired more than a year after Michael and I had had our public falling out, at a time when I was no longer a child, someone who blindly idolized the self-professed King of Pop. I was an adult, and a soon-to-be father, as well as someone who had been abused. But as I watched the show—and just like so many millions of people, there was footage that I found disturbing—I couldn't help but feel sorry for him. I remember asking Susie, how could he have allowed this to happen? How could he have been so easily taken advantage of again? It wouldn't be long before I found out.

Almost immediately after the show's airdate, Tom Sneddon, the Santa Barbara D.A., launched an official investigation. By November of that year, Michael Jackson had been arrested. And the first time Martin Bashir came calling, almost two years after taping the interview that started it all, I turned him down. Bashir, however, was persistent. He kept calling me, as well as my agent.

In the weeks that followed, Bashir convinced me that he hadn't attempted to defame Michael Jackson when he first descended on Neverland Ranch. That seemed plausible. Surely, he and his crew had simply unearthed some uncomfortable information, and the rest had unraveled from there? In the meantime, I had entered talks to star in an off-Broadway play in New York, and was hard at work on my next album. A little publicity certainly couldn't hurt. And all along, Bashir had claimed that he only wanted to ask me a few Jackson-specific questions; the proposed *20/20* special, on the whole, was supposed to be an hour-long retrospective on my life. I thought it would be a chance to debunk some myths and misconceptions, to show the world who I really am. In the end, he appealed to my ego. I'm not proud of that, but it's true.

Before I actually sat down in front of the cameras, I insisted that none of the footage be used as part of another Jackson exposé. Of course, that's exactly what happened.

The interview aired in February 2005. As soon as I saw the promos—*Child Actor Corey Feldman Speaks Out Against Michael Jackson*—I had a sense of what I was in for. At the same time, I immediately began racking my brain. I couldn't remember saying anything that seemed all that groundbreaking. I did admit that Michael had once shown me a book filled with pictures of adult genitalia affected by venereal disease—that happened at his apartment in Westwood, en route to our overnight, undercover adventure at Disney. And I did say that, as a father, I would never have agreed to send my kid to an overnight at Neverland Ranch. At the time, I actually didn't believe this was a particularly controversial statement.

I don't have any evidence that Michael ever molested any child, and I have always insisted, emphatically, that he never did anything to me. But he obviously had issues. His health was rapidly deteriorating; anyone who followed the tabloids could easily attest to that. Plus, I had witnessed first-hand his issues with paranoia, had interacted with people in his own camp who perhaps didn't always have his best interests at heart. It wasn't the first time such accusations had been lobbed in his direction. And, child molester or not, Neverland Ranch had become a center of controversy, gossip, and rumor. Why would anyone drop off their kid in the middle of all of that?

Not surprisingly, the interview immediately exploded in the press. It looked like an attack piece, which is never what I intended. But I certainly should have been smart enough to predict how this would play out. Not long after the interview, I was subpoenaed to testify in the case; it was widely reported that, come March of that year, I would be taking the stand not in defense of Michael, but on behalf of the prosecution.

When members of the Santa Barbara County sheriff's office searched Neverland in the fall of 2003, they seized reams of pornography, but found absolutely zero child porn. They confiscated alcohol, but the notion that Michael had ever plied children with drink—or "Jesus juice," as it came to be known in the press—was certainly never proven. The D.A. tried to present these artifacts as "evidence" of Michael's transgressions, because he knew their very existence would be at odds with Michael's public persona and that, in turn, might "prove" his guilt.

By indulging his inner-child, by building a sprawling home and calling it Neverland Ranch, Michael had become, by the early aughts, a caricature of himself. In that infamous interview with Bashir, he even admitted that he often thought of himself as a real life Peter Pan. When you think of Peter Pan, you don't imagine that he's got some porn and some booze stashed out back in his shed. Sneddon knew this, and he sought to exploit that disconnect in order to win his case.

But the truth is that Michael wasn't a cartoon character. He was a grown—if spectacularly misunderstood—man.

There was one unexpected perk from having agreed to the Bashir interview: because I had gone on the record so many times before in support of Michael Jackson, and because it seemed as though I had suddenly changed my mind, neither the defense nor the prosecution believed I would be a viable witness. Instead of being compelled to testify, I would move to New York with my family and watch the trial unfold from afar.

CHAPTER 22

Fatal Attraction: A Greek Tragedy was an off-Broadway spoof of the 1980's cult film starring Glenn Close and Michael Douglas. It's a hilarious concept and a wacky script; I played the lead role, a character called—wait for it—*Michael Douglas*. A "traditional" Greek chorus provided the narration, a ridiculous combination of ancient text and not-so-ancient quotes from the original movie.

The play ran from July to August 2005, and though it was a small production, I earned some of the best reviews of my entire career. My stage debut had been a success, and I returned to L.A. with newfound focus.

I had actually been planning on doing more work behind the camera when I got a call from the producer Greg Goldman, who pitched me an idea for a show. It was a scripted sitcom, but it would be filmed to look like a documentary, kind of like *The Office*. It would be a bit like *Three's Company*, but Haim would play the bad-boy bachelor to Susie's and my domesticated, drama-free marriage. The working title was *Three's a Crowd*.

Corey and I had been approached many, many times with ideas for shows and movies over the years. Back in the early '90s, we shot a pilot for a sitcom that never got picked up. In the early aughts, I even took a meeting with Jeff Cohen, Chunk from *The Goonies*, who had grown up to become a successful entertainment attorney. By the end of 2005, however, it was like everyone in Hollywood had suddenly gotten the memo—ideas for ways to reunite the "Two Coreys" were flying in from every direction. Some pitches weren't half bad, some were outright ridiculous—someone actually pitched the idea of dressing us as Mounties (the pitch came from Canada), and having us host a cooking show. Of all the ideas I had heard, *Three's a Crowd* was easily the best of the bunch. I just wasn't sure that I wanted to go there. In the last few years, Haim had turned into a mess.

Haim often stayed with Susie and I, whenever he was in town, whenever he needed a place to crash for a few days to get on his feet. He stayed with us in the fall of 2001, not long after Susie and I returned from New York, and he stayed with us again in 2003, shortly after we filmed *Dickie Roberts*. That's when he was at his worst. His hair was thinning, he was close to three hundred pounds, his body was falling apart—still, I had no idea how bad things had really become.

A day or two before he arrived, I got a call from his mother.

"If he's going to come and stay with you," she said, "you'll need to be prepared. So, you should go to the pharmacy and pick up a bottle of charcoal tablets."

"*What?*"

"Charcoal tablets. Buy a bottle, and whenever you see him overdosing—which will probably happen on a daily basis—you're going to take a handful of pills and shove them down his throat. If he's foaming at the mouth, or if his eyes roll back in his head, or if he's so inebriated that he can't put a sentence together, if he's not making any sense, that's when you'll know to do it."

"What if he's choking?"

"If it's so bad that he can't swallow, you'll have to call the paramedics. But hopefully you can get to him before things get that bad."

It was the most surreal conversation of my life—and I starred on a show called *The Surreal Life.* It was as if we were chitchatting about vitamins or something. "You really think this is necessary?" I asked her. "You really think I'll have to do this?"

"It's not a matter of *if.* This is just his condition right now."

I went out and bought the charcoal, and Haim's behavior over the next few days scared me half to death. In the morning, he'd be a little slow but still lucid. An hour or two later, he'd start with the slurring. An hour or two after that, he'd be drooling and completely incomprehensible. Then came the eyes rolling back in the head and the charcoal. This happened every day, without exception.

At one point, it occurred to me that he just didn't understand what he was putting people through. So, I decided to film him, at various points throughout a typical day, to show him. I wanted to put the evidence right in front of his face. The footage is devastating—by five in the afternoon, he couldn't tell me where he was, couldn't name the president of the United States. He was, to be frank, a drooling slob of a human, and I was afraid that he'd even done permanent damage.

By the time the idea for *Three's a Crowd* came about, Haim was back in Canada. I had heard he was doing better, but I needed to see for myself. I called him up, told him about the premise of the show, and gave him an ultimatum. "If you want to do this," I said, "you've got to clean yourself up. You have to lose the weight. You have to get yourself in shape."

"Don't worry, man. No problem."

"Corey, if it was that easy you would have done it already."

"Just trust me, man. Give me six months."

"Okay," I said. "But you need to understand, if after six months you show up and it's obvious that you haven't been taking care of yourself—if I even *think* you seem fucked up—I will walk. Do you understand? Right then. No hesitation."

"I got it. I really appreciate what you're doing for me. I promise, I won't let you down."

With that, we moved straight into preproduction. We had shopped the idea to a number of networks, but A&E was willing to order a full series without having to first complete a pilot. Plus, I would be one of the executive producers, which meant I would have a certain amount of control—this was essential, since I still had a bad taste in my mouth from my experience on *The Surreal Life*. I wanted to make sure that Haim and I wouldn't be manipulated. And we set up some ground rules: some things—his history of drug abuse, for one—would be off-limits, and Zen would not be in the show. I want my son to have a normal life. He can't do that if people recognize him because of me. So, Zen was not to be photographed, filmed, or in any way represented, even though he was right there with us the entire time.

We also got to work writing an outline of the entire season. *The Two Coreys* was never supposed to be a true "reality" show; it was a controlled, semiscripted sitcom. We didn't have actual dialogue—the majority of lines were ad-libbed and improvised—but every scene was planned out in advance. Episode 1, Scene 1: Haim arrives at the house; Episode 1, Scene 2: the Coreys go grocery shopping, etc. We also made the decision to shoot the show in Vancouver; because of

Haim's troublesome immigration status, it was easier if all of us came to him.

During this months-long process, Haim and I stayed in touch via the telephone, but I hadn't actually seen him. So, when it came time to film the first scene—Haim showing up at Susie's and my home (which was actually a rental; we had no desire to film in our actual house)—my reaction was a hundred percent genuine. He looked incredible. He was down more than a hundred pounds. He was lucid, totally with it. I was beyond impressed.

As a result of Haim's transformation, we did some of the best work we had ever done together. No one could make me laugh at the drop of a hat or turn my mood like Haim; he knew all my buttons. He was also one of the wittiest, smartest men I've ever known (though Haim often played dumb for the camera). There were times during filming of the first season—even during the "fight" scenes, which were scripted, totally made up for television—that the cameramen would laugh so hard their cameras would shake. There was so much potential at that point. Haim and I would look at each other and think, we're back! Then it all came crashing down.

Even before production began on *The Two Coreys*, I was approached by the folks at Warner Brothers about potentially making a *Lost Boys* sequel. There had been talk about making a sequel for years, pretty much since the original debuted and proved to be such a success. A script for *Lost Girls* was floated around Hollywood, I heard that Kiefer Sutherland had his hands on something, but nothing ever materialized. What Warner Brothers eventually sent over, however, was a cheap, schlocky script for a straight-to-DVD movie, in which I was being invited to shoot a five-minute cameo. I couldn't believe that of all the versions that had been tossed out over the years, *this* was the one they wanted to move forward with.

"Where's everyone else?" I asked one of the producers. "Where's Jamison Newlander in this? Where's Corey Haim?"

He told me the studio didn't want anything to do with Haim. At that point, he had developed too much of a reputation.

The Lost Boys had always been Haim's favorite. It was the most successful of the "Two Coreys" films, but he always thought of it as *his* movie. He was very proud of it, and he wanted to make sure that if a sequel was ever done, it was done the right way, with a solid script, a guaranteed theatrical release, and a superb director (hopefully Joel Schumacher). When I saw what Warner Brothers was proposing, I turned them down flat. There was no way I was going to appear in a *Lost Boys* remake without my brother.

Meanwhile, filming of *The Two Coreys* was well underway. In the second episode, Haim, Susie, Jamison Newlander, and myself attended a special twentieth anniversary screening of the original *Lost Boys* film. After that, Haim was on and on about writing a sequel himself, until I eventually had to tell him that a sequel was already in the works, that it was going forward without him, and that I had passed on a part. I broke the news off camera first; when I told him on camera, it was actually the second time we'd had the conversation.

It wasn't long after that when a "friend" brought Haim an enormous amount of Valium. Haim quickly returned to slurring his words. He wasn't able to get through his scenes. He would get angry, and provoke fights with Susie and I and the crew. At his worst, he became unable to differentiate between what was real and what had been scripted for the purposes of the show.

By the time we started the publicity tour in the summer of 2007, Haim's relapse hadn't been made public, but one of the *Lost Boys* producers, Mary, had seen an advance copy of the show. She attended *The Two Coreys* premiere party in Hollywood, and told me she still wanted me for the movie. The entire script had been rewritten. Not only that, but she was willing to capitulate to my demands; Haim and Jamison would both be awarded parts. I told Haim the news, again promised him that I wouldn't move forward without him. Together, we both agreed to sign on.

The problems started at the very beginning of production. Mary and another one of the producers approached me, and told me they needed me to make "the call."

"Oh, God. What happened?"

"Apparently, Haim's not coming."

"What do you mean he's not coming?"

"He doesn't like his wardrobe choices."

"You're telling me that after twenty years, and I don't know how many script rewrites, and all the shit I went through to get him in this movie, he's not coming because he doesn't like his *wardrobe choices*?"

I called Haim, and was able to talk him through his wardrobe dilemma. But the next day there was some new problem. And some new problem the day after that. He backed out of three different plane tickets, continually screwed up the shooting schedule. Finally, Haim was just fired.

I started getting calls from the network. The ratings for *The Two Coreys* were high enough that they wanted to order a second season. At that point, I didn't see how filming additional episodes would even be possible; Haim had spiraled so far, so fast. Plus, I was an executive producer—I had a contractual obligation to deliver a set number of episodes. I wasn't willing to sign myself up for certain failure. The only way to move forward, then, would be to scrap the semiscripted sitcom format and shoot a more traditional "reality" show. We'd have to film the good *and* the bad and just let it all hang out. Let the chips fall where they may.

We set about redrafting our contracts, making it very clear what we would and would not show in this new iteration. My personal requests—mainly, to keep Zen uninvolved in the production—remained the same. With regard to Haim, we would not discuss his former or current drug use, unless he visibly relapsed. If and when that happened, his struggles with sobriety would become an integral part of the show. He was fine with that arrangement. The only topic we were not to discuss, under any circumstances, was his history of abuse. "If I fuck up, I fuck up," he told me. "But you better give me your word that you never bring up those three or four names, you never talk about the fact that I was molested." I had no intention of discussing his abuse publicly, so I readily agreed.

Then, in the very first episode of the second season, he just went for it: "You let me get fucked around in my life—raped, so to speak—when I was about fourteen-and-a-half-years-old." My jaw was on the floor, and I knew the rest of the season would be a doozy.

In a matter of weeks, *Lost Boys: The Tribe* would prepare for a few days of pickups and reshoots. Despite his earlier disruptions on set, I somehow convinced the producers to let Haim try again. We would give him one more opportunity to shoot a few scenes for the movie, and incorporate the filming of those scenes into the filming of the television show.

At 7:00 A.M., I was in the makeup trailer, being fitted with a long, blond wig. (I had actually grown my hair out for principle shooting, but cut it short again before the filming of the second season.) The sun was shining, the birds were chirping, and in walked Haim—loaded out of his mind. He could barely speak, could barely string two words together, and was completely incapable of delivering his lines. We spent hours trying to nail down a single scene. I was so mad at him. I couldn't believe he had chosen this moment, surrounded by executives from Warner Brothers and A&E, to blow it so catastrophically. Ultimately, his scenes had to be cut completely from the movie.

We moved forward with the season. We shot an intervention episode. Haim and I even talked with a therapist. But I realized I wasn't helping him. When *The Two Coreys* was finally cancelled after filming wrapped on season two, I decided the best thing to do would be to walk away for a while. He had so much potential, but again, he had imploded and sold himself short.

Many people, fans of the "Two Coreys" even, seem to be under the misconception that we never spoke again, but Haim reached out to me in 2009, at the end of what proved to be the most difficult year of my life.

Marc Rocco, the director of *Dream a Little Dream,* died suddenly in May, at the age of forty-six. My grandfather, Bedford Goldstein, passed away a short time later; that was like losing a father. In June came the news of Michael Jackson's death, as shocking to me as it was to everyone else. And by the end of the year, my wife and I decided to end our marriage.

Susie and I may have had an unconventional relationship, but it worked because complete and brutal honesty was the foundation upon which the rest of our lives were built. She had been my partner and my best friend for more than seven years. But when the trust was gone, and the foundation was broken, there was no rescuing the relationship. Still, I was devastated. I felt totally alone in the world.

One day, not very long after Susie and I split up, Haim called me up out of the blue. We hadn't spoken in more than a year. He knew, of course, about the string of deaths and the divorce. But now, he told me, his mother had been diagnosed with cancer. He had cleaned himself up, had moved Judy in. And he wanted to mend things. It wasn't about our careers, it wasn't about being the "Two Coreys," it was just about being friends. I knew a thing or two about losing someone before you could repair a broken relationship. I was happy that he had called.

Haim was incredibly supportive in the months following my divorce. He spent a lot of time with Zen, and he doted on his mother. He didn't have a car, so he would walk to the store, picking out aromatherapy candles and bubble baths, trying to create for her a healing, spa-like atmosphere. He would get up early and cook her breakfast. He would take her to chemotherapy. For the first time, he was caring about someone more than he cared about himself.

Haim's career seemed poised for a turn-around, too. He had a small role in the action film *Crank: High Voltage*, starring Amy Smart and Jason Statham. He was also attached to star in a number of indie movies. Over the next few months, we grew closer than we had ever been.

In February, Haim and I went to a Super Bowl party at the Playboy Mansion; it would end up being our last public appearance. Afterward, I invited him back for an after-party at my house. He had changed. He wasn't trying to score. He wasn't interested in doing drugs. It was as if the Corey I had always known, the hyperactive kid who couldn't sit still, who was always fixated on that next thing, had maybe started to grow up.

The sun was coming up. I was sitting on the couch; Haim was sitting on the floor near my feet. He stretched out his hand, initiating the secret "Corey handshake." We had invented it years ago, when we were just kids; I think it's been incorporated into every one of our movies. He looked at me then, and smiled.

"I just wanted to thank you, man."

"For what?"

"For this weekend," he said. "For everything." He paused, looked around my living room and sighed. "I finally see the world through your eyes and it's a beautiful place."

We shook hands again and gave each other a hug and then I excused myself and went to bed. By the time I woke up the next morning, he was gone. I would never see him again.

Corey and I spoke often about going public with our respective stories. And I know that when he dropped that bomb on the show, when he admitted to being molested, it was a step—the very smallest of steps—toward admitting the root cause of all his inner demons. Still, I wanted him to come forward about the big one—the one that, even in that awkward moment in a diner in Studio City, he was still nowhere near ready to reveal. I wanted him to say the name of the man who had stolen his innocence on the set of *Lucas,* the man who walks around now, one of the most successful people in the entertainment industry, still making money hand over fist.

Even after *The Two Coreys* went off the air—after the blowup and the reconciliation—Haim was under the impression, for a while, that we were going to move forward with a third season. I had to explain to him that there would be no more seasons, that he had burned all his bridges again. I told him that his self-destructive behavior stemmed from what happened to him as a boy, that the only way he would free himself would be if he came forward with that information. If he could do that, a giant weight would be lifted from his shoulders. I told him he wouldn't find peace until then.

"Why don't you do it?" he asked me.

"Do what?"

"Why don't you tell my story?"

"I've got my own story to tell," I said. "And you've got yours. You've got to write your own story. You've got to write your own book."

At the time of his death, Haim still just wasn't ready.

When I first started batting around the idea of writing a book about my life, I had no intention of making it a "Two Coreys" story. I had no intention of discussing Corey's experiences with abuse. But in the wake of his death, I felt like I had to do the one thing he was never able to do.

After nearly forty years in the entertainment business, I have been privileged to work with some of the greatest artists and innovators of our time, and I'm honored to have made movies that people think of as classics, that they'll always remember with fondness and nostalgia. I have also lost so many, many friends to the pressures of Hollywood and the dark side of fame. I'm glad I have somehow managed to survive it all. I'm even looking forward to what the future will bring.

In 2009, I got a call from Joe Dante's office. He was teaming up with producer Roger Corman (with whom I had worked on *Rock 'n' Roll High School Forever*) to film a new project. I was more than a little surprised to hear from him—we hadn't worked together since 1989's *The 'Burbs*, days Dante had once called some of the worst of his entire career. Reteaming twenty years later felt like a chance to redeem myself. *Splatter*, a dark horror series, became the first original Web series offered from Netflix; these days, producing content exclusively for the Web is a trend that seems to be taking off.

Not long after that, I was pleased to announce the release of my second Truth Movement album. *Technology Analogy* is the album I set out all those years ago to make; I had the pleasure of recording several songs with Pink Floyd collaborators Scotty Page and Jon Carin, and was bowled over when the legendary artist Storm Thorgerson—best known for his work with the rock bands Pink Floyd, Black Sabbath, and Led Zeppelin—agreed to provide original work for the cover of the album.

In preparation for the next Truth Movement tour, I knew I wanted to try something different. Large-scale rock concerts, with their lasers and lights and amps and generators, leave in their wake a notoriously large carbon footprint. I have long been a passionate eco-activist, so I was curious about ways to make our shows more environmentally friendly. With the help of a few biodiesel generators—and the willingness of the folks at Universal CityWalk—Truth Movement was able to perform the first in a series of concerts powered entirely by an alternative energy source. It is my hope that, particularly as the technology advances, many more artists will consider moving their shows "off the grid."

As for my romantic life, I am content being single, though I am dating—and there is one woman, Courtney, who is closer to me than anyone has been in years. Maybe one day I will again love a woman completely. But my primary focus is and will always be Zen.

Zen is eight years old as I write this, and I often marvel at the fact that he has blue eyes and blond hair, despite the fact that his mother and I are both brown-eyed brunettes; it's ironic that he looks just the way my mother always thought that I should. He is, in many ways, the little boy she so desperately wanted me to be. And he never ceases to amaze. Just the other day, he sat down to do his homework: math homework. Multiplication. The skill that had been so impossible for me to master, that my parents spent hours and hours drilling—even beating—into my head. Zen, however, sat down, breezed through his homework, and got every question right. He is healthy and beautiful and brilliant, with no trace of having been a premie. Today, he's actually one of the biggest boys in his class.

Becoming a father has also, amazingly, enabled me to find peace with my own traumatic childhood. I've since forgiven my mother for the way she behaved when I was young. I know now that she was mentally unstable; I'm not sure she was capable of having done better than she did.

People are always quick to slap a label on things, perhaps especially the trajectory of a former child actor's career. And everyone experiences peaks and valleys—it's impossible to sustain a years-long string of nothing but success. But in the past few years, I've been busier than at any other point in my career. I've been hard at work on a new solo album and have been collaborating with a slew of new and talented artists, including Fred Durst of Limp Bizkit, Kaya Jones of the Pussycat Dolls, Wu-tang Klan–affiliated producer Supreme, and r1ckone, best known for his work with the Black Eyed Peas. I've reteamed with my friend and former costar Sean Astin not once, but twice: We're at work on a new *Teenage Mutant Ninja Turtles* television series for Nickelodeon; he also made a cameo in the music video for my single "Ascension Millennium," which premiered on MTV in July 2013. I've even got a new business venture in the works: Corey's Angels, an exclusive social club and management company. All that's in addition to my usual slate of one to three movies a year. (I'm especially excited to announce the upcoming release of *The M Word*, directed by Henry Jaglom, which will be my first lead role in a theatrical release in more than a decade).

Despite the highs and lows, the ups and downs, the peaks and valleys, I've never lost sight of my spirituality; I owe so much to God, and continue to put my faith in Him. I've never taken for granted the love and support of my fans; they drive me to continue creating. I've never stopped trying to be a positive voice, raising awareness for the causes that are near and dear to my heart. And I've never stopped trying to make the world a better place for our children. I've never really taken a *break*—and I have no intention of taking one now.

Really, I'm just getting started.

ACKNOWLEDGMENTS

Almighty God: I am eternally grateful that I have been blessed with this life and the opportunity to keep living it. I am grateful for the many gifts I have been given, as well as the opportunity to have my voice heard. Whenever I hear your call to defend the rights of animals, the environment, or the innocence of your children, I pray to serve thy will. I am your humble servant, and pray that this book serves your will, too.

Zen: My beautiful, amazing, brilliant, handsome, sweet, and loving son, I love you so much. Thank you for understanding when I was locked away at night, chained to my computer, consumed with telling this story. I owe you a lot of playtime! Thank you for bringing an enormous smile to my face every day. You are my driving force and the reason I get out of bed every morning. Everything I do in this world is for you. Zen, you are my everything.

My fans: I love you all so much. Thank you for never letting go, for believing in me, for sharing my dreams, and for being the reason I stay in this roller-coaster business. I hope that my art lives up to your expectations. I do, actually, love you more.

My mother, Sheila Feldman: Thank you for bringing me into this crazy world and for teaching me the most valuable lessons one can learn: patience and tolerance. Thank you, too, for instilling in me a love of animals—you showed me at an early age that animals deserve to be treated with love (sometimes even more than humans).

My father, Bob Feldman: Thank you for instilling in me a love of music, and for allowing me to spend time in all those rehearsal rooms, soaking it up. You helped me learn to hear the difference between a good note and a bad one. I definitely learned how to be a rock star from you.

My sister, Mindy: Thank you for putting up with me through those unruly times, and for all your love and support. I love you very much. I know that you have always been there for me, and I will always be there for you, no matter what. I respect you as a mother, and for holding our family together, even in the darkest hours. I am proud to call you my sister.

My brother, Devin: Thank you for always being the calm in a perfect storm. I admire your honesty and dedication to standing up for what you believe. You have always had a great concern for others, and I know you will make a great father one day. I love you.

Uncle Merv: Thank you for always being there for me as a kid. Even though *I* never got to live with you, you provided a home to my siblings and have acted as a surrogate father. For that, I am eternally grateful. I love you, Merv.

My cousin, Michael: Thank you for being my best friend in the whole world. You know more about me than probably any other person. Although we have grown apart since you moved away, you are always in my heart, and I am very grateful to have you in my life. Other family members to thank are Dara, Ari, Marci, Murray, Marianne, Mark, and Alexa, and Ashton and Dorian Wilson (my sister's kids).

Richard Donner: Dick! Thank you, my dear, dear friend. I wish I could say "I love you" often enough to explain how much I care for and respect you. You are, without question, the greatest man I have ever met in the entertainment industry. Thank you for always being there, no matter what. I could not have made it without you—that's the God's honest truth! I would also like to thank Lauren Shuller Donner and Derek and CeCe at the Donners company.

Tim Stinson: Thank you for your years of dedicated friendship. You have always been there whenever I really needed someone to talk to. There are few people in this world that I would trust with my life— and with my son's life—and you are one of them. I'm grateful to you for always having been there for me, whether I was on top or at the bottom of my career. God bless you.

Marlene Nadel: Thank you, and the entire Cri-Help staff, for saving my life. You know that I would not be alive today to write this book if it weren't for you. You are beautiful. Thank you. I would also like to thank Richard Hirsh, Jack Bernstein, John Carlson, Officer Adam Smith, Sergeant Carl, Eric Pearl, Mark Laisure, and all my old school friends who have made me laugh at my weakest moments.

Scott Carlson: Thank you for ten years of digging in the trenches with me. I am grateful for all of the projects that, through your dedication and perseverance, became realities—even those that I had given up on. This book is a perfect example.

ACKNOWLEDGMENTS

Kathy Huck: Thank you, Kathy, for believing in this project through and through. No matter how impossible it seemed at times, you never gave up hope and kept it moving forward. Thank you for helping me realize this vision, and for standing by my side as I bare my soul to the world.

Courtney Hargrave: Thank you for all the hard work on this project, and for all the late-night calls and debates. I think, for the next one, we may just have to relocate you to L.A.! Thank you for keeping me on point, and helping me convey my story in the most forgiving way possible.

St. Martin's Press: Thank you all for getting behind this and for having the courage to take on the onslaught of controversy that comes with my life. This is an important story to tell, and I couldn't have found a more respectable group of people to handle the subject matter with such class and enthusiasm. I am eternally grateful for the support of the entire company, and I hope no one will be disappointed with the outcome.

Judy Haim: Thank you for putting up with me all of these years, for being the strong woman you are, and for all that you endured with and for Corey. God bless you. Now, Corey can rest. Wake me when September ends. 222! I love you.

Brian McMullen: Thank you for your support at the times when I needed it most. You are a male angel!

Stacy Hess: Thank you for being there to help me get the truth out to the world, even when nobody wanted to listen, or when I couldn't afford to tell them.

Courtney Anne Mitchell: I love you for being a real angel in my life. Thank you for showing me so much love, even in the darkest times, and for giving me a reason to try learning how to trust again. I love you.

Hugh Hefner: Thank you, Hef, for always opening your home and your heart to me. Your free-spirited, fun-loving nature and love of art and all things beautiful has inspired me to live each moment to the fullest, and to never even consider growing old. Because of you, my goal is to live to 122. And to the rest of the Playboy family: Keith, Crystal, Morgan, Cooper and Marstin, Zach Whitlow, Sheila Moore, Ron Smith, Joel and Allison, Jimmy Van Patten, Stephen Wayda and playmates Julie McCullough, Tina Jordan, Ava Fabian, Devin DeVasquez, Cathi O'Malley, and Christi Shake.

Additionally, I would like to thank lifelong friends: Mark Marshall; Sean Astin; Joseph and Katherine Jackson and the Jackson family; Majestik Magnificent; Greg Berg; Robin Lively, Jason Lively, and the Lively family; Kristy Swanson and family; Mike and Cathy Sage; Jason Presson; Chelsea Windsor; Chuck Irwin; Rob Heskin; Pharao Barret; Mark Harris; Dr. Jeffrey Hoefflin; Mark London; Jon Carin; Scotty Page; Gary Hayes; Gavin Menzies; Keith Coogan; Dave Dunn; I love you all dearly. No matter how long between calls, no matter how long until I see you again, you are always in my heart.

And friends and inspirations: Steven Spielberg; Joe Dante; Roger Corman; Joel Schumacher; Rob Reiner; Eugenio Mira; Glen Alpert; Joel and Allison Berliner; Ciro Neili; Donald Borchers; Jeff Ballard; Henry Penzi; Susie Sprague; Vanessa Marcil; Drew Barrymore; Weird Al Yankovic; Danny Bonaduce; Peter Curzon; Miko Brando; Josh Brolin; Jeff Cohen; Ke Huy Quan; Kerri Green; Shane Black; Henry Jaglom; Tanna Fredrik; Zach Galligan; Jon Lovitz; Jerry O'Connell; Wil Wheaton; Paul Reubens; David Gilmour; Paul McCartney; Roger Waters; Ringo Starr; Jeff Chonis; Cyndi Lauper; G Tom Mac; Ron Jeremy; Ginger Lynn; Michael J. Fox; Billy Idol; Billy Siegel at Fender guitars; Richie Palmero and Richie, Jr.; Giuseppe Franco, Anna and Mike from CF.net; Kit Lenoir; The Goonies; Kiefer Sutherland; Angus Sutherland; Howard and Alan Teman; Meredith Salenger; my assistants Jake Perry and Robin Allred Zaharis, for aiding me through *The Two Coreys*' shows; Deandre Adams, for twenty-two years of security and protection; Paul Kenner; Mark Karan, Kaya Jones, Fred

ACKNOWLEDGMENTS

Durst, DJ R1ckone, Thomas Van Musser, Phil Shapiro, and Gregg Sartiano, and my band Truth Movement (Rob Heskin, Chuck Irwin, Randy Morris, Scotty Page) for all the great years of music. And finally, to all the Angels in my life, both spiritual and physical, for always protecting me.